Meeting the Needs of Diverse Learners

Paula Rutherford

Meeting the Needs of Diverse Learners

Published by Just ASK Publications & Professional Development
2214 King Street
Alexandria, Virginia 22301
Toll Free 1-800-940-5434
FAX 1-703-535-8502
email info@justaskpublications.com
www.justaskpublications.com

Printed in the United States of America
ISBN-13: 978-0-9797280-4-4
Library of Congress Control Number 2001012345
10 9 8 7 6 5 4 3

Table of Contents

CD-ROM Table of Contents

CD-ROM Table of Contents

CD-ROM Table of Contents

Dedication

This book is dedicated to the young people described in the introduction and to my grandchildren, Will, Carter, Kelly, and Quinn, who are now in our hands. While some children are more gifted than others, I believe from the top of my head to the tip of my toes, that all of our students are gifted in one way or another.

Acknowledgements

The first people to come to mind when I think about who has significantly influenced my thinking about teaching, learning, and leading are my two sons, Doug and Mike, their wives and the mothers of my grandchildren, Susan and Elizabeth, and my grandchildren, Will, Carter, Kelly, and Quinn. As I said in the introduction to **Instruction for All Students**, when it is personal, educational theory quickly becomes grounded in reality.

It takes a team to get a book from concept to press. Team members include students like those described in the introduction, the colleagues with whom I have collaborated, the teachers who have shared their classroom experiences, the administrative staff that keeps the work moving forward, the people who listen to me as I run ideas by them, those that provide technical support, and the proofreaders, researchers, reviewers, editors, and indexers. A listing of each of these people would be a book all by itself. A few, however, who must be noted individually are:

- Caitlin Cooper, research and proofreading
- Bruce Oliver, proofreading, editing, indexing, and excerpts from **Just for the ASKing!**
- Laura Pavlock-Albright, researching, editing, and organizational support
- Julie McVicker, research
- Kathi Ruh, expertise on foldables and students with special needs and cheerleading
- Shilpa Shah, cover design and layout
- Louise Thompson, examples of interest surveys and tiered assignments
- and, last but not least my husband, David, and my son, Mike, who are on the frontline putting up with the ups and downs, the writer's blocks, the frustrations with technology, and competing priorities. They demonstrate an amazingly unwavering commitment to supporting me in these writing endeavors.

Thanks to all!

Introduction

This is, of course, a non-fiction book but there is a story that must be told. So, this introduction begins with a trip down memory lane as I recall students with whom I have had the privilege to work and from whom I have learned so much.

I first used Bruner's Concept Attainment Model (See page 145.) in the 1970's with kindergartners in a lesson on homophones. First, they drew and colored pictures I had selected. When their own work was presented as positive and negative examples of "my secret idea," they formulated hypotheses about my concept. They soon reached the conclusion that some words sound alike but have different meanings. They didn't know the term "homophone" but they identified the concept from their own pictures of son and sun, mail and male, pair and pear, sent and cent, pale and pail, etc. What a powerful and fun lesson! Young children are indeed capable of abstract thinking!

One of my fondest memories of Hilda Taba's Inductive Thinking Model (See page 173.) is when I used it with 15 adolescents with learning disabilities in a 9th grade World Cultures class. When students entered the classroom on the first day of school, the ceiling line of the entire room had covers of **Newsweek** and **Time** posted like crown molding. Without pointing out those covers, I asked them to name what they thought were the top news stories of the past year. They quickly called out local, celebrity, disaster, and sporting events with a few mentions of national news and no international stories. They then grouped and labeled the groups they had created. Next, they analyzed what they had listed, sorted, and labeled and came up with a hypothesis about what constitutes a major news story. Without having read a single word, other than those they suggested and I wrote on the board, they did really high-level thinking on the first day of school. Their next task was to use their criteria for what makes a major news story to select the Top Ten News Stories. We posted those stories and located the sites of the stories on a huge map of the world. For the rest of the school year they nominated new stories for the top ten using the criteria they had established. Game on! All were competing to find major international stories since we had so few. That meant, of course, that these reluctant readers were reading newspapers on a regular basis. Once again, what a powerful and fun year-long lesson. It was ever so much more rigorous and relevant than the usual boring current event reports!

In my mind's eye I see P. J., an 11th grader in Florida, who was highly motivated to learn and succeed in school. When she took an assessment that required her to do 25 mixed-numeral problems using the same mathematical operation, she could do them with no problem. When presented with 25 problems using all four mathematical operations on mixed numerals, she was totally lost. This adolescent with learning disabilities needed scaffolding in order to be successful with that task. One small index card with models of each of the four operations and she was good to go. Thank goodness, her general education teacher understood that this accommodation was no different than a young bride using a recipe for her mother-in-law's meat loaf until she could make it without the directions.

Digging back into history, I recall my first year of teaching at National City Junior High School in Sweetwater Union School District just south of San Diego. My students there taught me a lot. The demographics of the school were approximately 40% African-American, 40% Latino, and 20% Caucasian, all lower income. Given all that I didn't know, I certainly would like "overs," but I must say that the demographics caused me to think creatively about teaching World Geography. It turned out that although most of my students could read aloud in English, many of them had no clue what they were reading. Out came the props and the realia. Out came the slides and photographs we had just taken during our military tour and travels throughout Asia. I think we did pretty well with Asia, but when one of my Latino students asked me why they needed to learn about Rhodesia, Ian Smith, and unilateral independence, I hadn't a clue. All I knew was that it was the focus story in the **Weekly Reader**. Oh, my! I had so much to learn!

Stopping once again in a kindergarten classroom in Florida, I learned that there was no need for stickers and candy rewards. While doing research for my thesis titled ***Academic versus Non-Academic Reinforcers***, these five-year-olds taught me that opportunities to engage in active, hands-on learning were just as reinforcing to them as stickers. Actually, they taught me even more. They made me decide early in my career that there was absolutely no reason to save the active, hands-on learning experiences for rewards. Why not just plan that kind of lesson in the first place? I owe much to those youngsters!

This trip down memory lane continues in Virginia. Tom, an 8th grade student, who upon notification that he was eligible for the resource program for adolescents with learning disabilities, came running back into the school at 4:00 yelling, "I made it! I made it!" This story is a treasure for multiple reasons. In our school, reviews before big math assessments were conducted in after-school focus groups. In this process, students with the same learning needs went together to review with one teacher rather than each teacher reviewing everything with all students whether they needed it or not. Tom, as a part of a focus group review, ended up in the resource room with me. He found what he saw and experienced there helpful and, while working with him, I noted some potential learning issues. It turns out that Tom was twice exceptional. He was in the program for gifted and talented students and was struggling to do the caliber of work he knew he was capable of doing. Placement in the resource program for adolescents with learning disabilities provided the support he needed to use his gifts at a high level.

In that same school I encountered Luis, a 9th grader who as a very bright second language learner was floundering despite strong school and family support. It turned out that Luis, in addition to being a second language learner, also faced the challenges of a learning disability. From Luis, I learned that not only is it difficult to diagnosis learning challenges in primary-age students, it is also extremely difficult to determine the causes of those challenges and identify the possible gifts of second language learners.

And in closing, I must mention Robert with whom I had the honor of working during his 7th and 8th grade years as a student in the resource room for adolescents with learning disabilities. The long-stem red roses I received when he graduated from The University of Virginia and was accepted into medical school tell the story of what our learners can do if we believe in them, convince them to believe in themselves, and, perhaps most importantly, believe in ourselves. We can do it!

This book is based on both research and these personal experiences. It is an effort to pull together the key concepts from multiple fields within our profession and identify not only differences but commonalities. I have attempted to avoid "educationalize" and when that was impossible, I tried to define or explain the terms that were used.

It is based on my strong belief that we all have to continuously study and use new knowledge about content, learners, and repertoire. Chapter I of this text provides a brief overview of best practice in standards-based classrooms with an emphasis on the planning process. Also included there are differentiation non-negotiables and guidance for collegial collaboration, looking at student work, and data analysis. Chapter II then focuses on the similarities and differences of our learners. It is essential that we be knowledgeable about both the content we are tasked with teaching and our learners before we can even begin to think about providing multiple pathways to learning.

Chapters III, IV, and V are designed to assist teachers in expanding and refining their repertoires so that we can provide those multiple pathways to learning. Chapter III is organized around frequently occurring scenarios and learning challenges we all encounter, Chapter IV features an extensive array of strategies and tools, and Chapter V focuses on literacy across the curriculum.

I stand in awe of all we collectively know and do but am also aware of all we have yet to do. I learned so much writing this book. I am so hopeful that you find it useful.

Teaching
and Learning in
the 21st Century

Best on the Web

Response to Intervention

http://centeroninstruction.org/index.cfm
Part of the Comprehensive Center network, the Center on Instruction is one of five content centers serving as resources for the 16 regional U.S. Department of Education Comprehensive Centers. Click on Hot Topics and then click on Response to Intervention. The Center on Instruction provides a collection of scientifically-based research and information on K-12 instruction in reading, math, science, special education, and English language learning.

Lesson Plans

www.thinkfinity.org
This site was selected by **Edutopia** magazine, a publication of the George Lucas Educational Foundation, as the top site for free lesson plans and educational materials. Associations and organizations contributing to the website are:
- American Association for the Advancement of Science
- Council for Economic Education
- International Reading Association
- National Center for Family Literacy
- National Council of Teachers of English
- National Council of Teachers of Mathematics
- National Endowment for the Humanities
- National Geographic Society
- ProLiteracy
- Smithsonian National Museum of American History
- The John F. Kennedy Center for the Performing Arts

Lesson Plans and Teaching Strategies for K-12 Social Studies

www.csun.edu/~hcedu013/plans.html
This California State University, Northridge site provides an amazing array of websites to access for planning K-12 social studies lessons.

Looking at Student Work

- www.lasw.org (lasw = looking at student work.) This website features the collaborative assessment conference and provides multiple links to related web sites.
- www.annenberginstitute.org/Products/list.php

Teaching and Learning in the 21st Century

Best Practice in Standards-Based Classrooms
Differentiation Non-Negotiables
Collegial Collaboration
Data-Driven Decisions

A variation of the next four pages appears in each of the books I have written because they communicate the foundation of our work in promoting high levels of learning for all students. Embedded in these pages are the strongly held beliefs and practices in which we must engage if we truly want to meet the needs of diverse learners. The five key points are:

- Standards guide all classroom decisions.
- The focus is always on student learning.
- Expectations for learning are the same for all students, even those who have traditionally performed at low levels.
- The final determination of the effectiveness of instructional practices is whether or not they result in higher levels of achievement for students.
- Assessment results are used to inform the teacher about the effectiveness of curricular and instructional decisions.

Following an elaboration on those five key points is a brief discussion of some component parts necessary to act on those points. This includes a look at the Standards-Based Education (SBE) Planning Process, a focus on essential understandings, big ideas, and key concepts as well as detailed information on how to task analyze the work we ask students to do.

After a brief review of the key elements of standards-based teaching and learning, the focus shifts to the role that differentiation plays in helping students achieve at the highest possible levels. Also included in this section is a brief history of **IDEA** and **Response to Intervention (RtI)**.

This chapter closes with an investigation of the ways we use data to inform our instructional practices and to frame our collegial interactions.

Teaching and Learning in the
21st Century Standards-Based Classroom

The headings in this section come from the *Facilitator's Manual for Developing a Common Ground* developed by a team of educators from Centennial BOCES, Longmont, Colorado; they were early scouts in the standards movement.

Standards guide all classroom decisions.

This statement represents where we want and need to be. Across the USA educators have access to standards developed at the state, and often at the local level, that should guide instructional decision making. The reality is that few educators can say that they are **standards-based**. What they can say so far is that they are **standards-referenced**. That is, many of us refer to the standards to see if we can justify what we had planned to teach based on teachers' manuals or on programs purchased by the district or by what they have "always" done. Teachers who are new to the profession seem to more readily engage in practices that are **standards-based** because they have no "old habits," units, lessons, or activities to give up.

Moving from Standards-Referenced to Standards-Based.

- Knowing that the standards exist.
- Knowing where to find a copy.
- Reading the standards: It is, however, possible to read the standards without really understanding the depth and breadth of the standards for a course of study. There is a danger that we will march through indicators in much the same way that we have, in the past, marched through pages in texts or workbooks.
- Posting the standards: Posting standards in "educationaleze" in a primary classroom or posting the standard, benchmark, or indicator numbers in any classroom does not meet this criteria. Posting or announcing the number as in, "Today we are working on Standard/Benchmark/Indicator II-Vb" just will not work.
- Occasionally referring to the standards during planning.
- Checking to see if what is being taught can be found in the standards. It is at this point in the journey that many of us get stuck.
- Beginning to understand the power and focus the standards provide and working to identify the essential understandings that are embedded in and that transcend the standards as they are written.
- Being able to say "I am **standards-based** because I used the standards to design assessments and instruction, and I used student work to judge whether or not the instruction was well designed for this content with these learners."

Teaching and Learning in the
21st Century Standards-Based Classroom

The first six bullets are more representative of **standards-referenced** than they are of **standards-based**. Teachers have to include the last two before they can say that they are **standards-based**. The next five headings further clarify variables that must be in place before teachers can accurately say, "**I am standards-based**."

The focus is always on student learning.

"**I have so much to cover**" continues to be the cry of many teachers. It is true that the amount of information and the number of skills we are asked to ensure that the learners master is mind-boggling. Given that, we teachers have to be thoughtful and focused about **how we spend the currency of education: time**. We need to make sure that every single learning experience students engage in is not only an interesting activity, but also the right exercise for moving their learning forward. Just because an exercise is next in the textbook, or because our teammates have been using it for years, is not sufficient reason for having our students do it. We have to ask the following questions:

- **Is this the right lesson for these students right now?**
- **Given the school-year time frame, is this learning experience worthy of the time it will cost?**
- **Is there another way to approach this learning that might work better for these learners or be more efficient in moving them along?**

Expectations for learning are the same for all students, even those who have traditionally performed at low levels.

At the same time the standards movement was sweeping across the land, IDEA made legally imperative what was already our moral responsibility. It required that all students have access to the same rich curriculum and be held to the same level of understanding as all other students. The implications are huge. The percentage of students who have been labeled as "special needs" and the percentage of English Language Learners (ELLs) is staggering.

Teaching and Learning in the
21ˢᵗ Century Standards-Based Classroom

This mandate and these students are the reason we hear so much about **differentiation of instruction**. Differentiation must start with a strongly focused curriculum based on the standards. We need strong knowledge and skillfulness with our content, a thorough understanding of how our students learn, and a deep and wide repertoire of instructional strategies for connecting the students and the content. Only then can we provide the scaffolding and extensions that provide multiple pathways to learning. The current move away from a deficit model in identifying students who need special education services increases the need for us to have that knowledge and these skills. **Response to Intervention (RtI)** provides us with an incredible opportunity to be more collaborative in our work, more purposeful in our selection of strategies, and more data driven in analyzing the effectiveness of those decisions.

The final determination of the effectiveness of instructional practices is whether or not they result in higher levels of achievement for students.

Are we making progress? We need to first gather and analyze **pre-assessment** or baseline data about what our students know and can do as they enter the learning experience. The analysis of that data leads to an instructional plan which includes the ongoing gathering and use of **formative data**. **Summative assessment data** informs us and the learners about whether or not the students are moving toward mastery of the identified standards. The question is not did they complete all the assignments and do their homework, but rather, did they learn what they were supposed to learn, did they retain it over time, and can they use it in ways that demonstrate that transfer has occurred.

Assessment results are used to inform the teacher about the effectiveness of curricular and instructional decisions.

This fifth category is different from the previous one in that it forces the issue of using not only **classroom data** but **external data** to inform our practice. The data we glean or that we are given may reveal that the pacing of instruction needs to be adjusted, that the curriculum needs to be re-examined, or that instructional practices need to be revamped to promote retention and transfer. We can look at assessment results across schools, departments, and classes so that we can examine and redesign instruction to more closely align with what is working most effectively in similar settings. We can look at the data longitudinally across the year and over several years. When we reach the point where we do this work collaboratively, we should see astonishing results in student achievement.

The Planning Process
in a Standards-Based Environment

Planning in a standards-based environment is often called "backwards" because we "begin with the end" in mind. In fact, we almost always begin with the end in mind when we plan vacations or weddings or purchase new automobiles. It is the way our colleagues in business and industry do project management/action planning. In school, teachers have always planned with "the end in mind." Often though, the end we had in mind was to work our way through the book, chapter by chapter, or through the year, project by project.

In a standards-based environment, we must be clear about "the end" we have in mind and be certain that we are working together from pre-kindergarten through twelfth grade to lead students to the achievement of commencement level standards. It is within this context that we focus on the standards, benchmarks, and indicators that have been identified as the ones students are to master during the grade or courses we teach. The end in mind cannot be a particular activity or project, chapters in a book, or completion of a packaged program. We have to be clear about how what students are doing in the classroom is tied to the outcomes we seek this year and throughout their K-12 educational experience.

Just like we have a clear picture of that perfect vacation, car, wedding, or ad campaign, we need to have a clear picture of what it looks like when our students are competent with what we want them to know and be able to do. Just as that vacation, wedding, or ad campaign will not happen without an action plan, a solid action plan is needed for each lesson we teach. Anything less means that there is a high probability that we will end up in the wrong place.

The first step in this planning process, both inside and outside the classroom, is identifying the outcome we want. The second step is creating our vision of what it looks like when we get there. Next we analyze the outcome and vision to figure out what we have to do in the third step in order to accomplish the first and second steps. It makes no sense to start the third step without **THE END** in mind.

SBE Planning Process template is on CD-ROM.

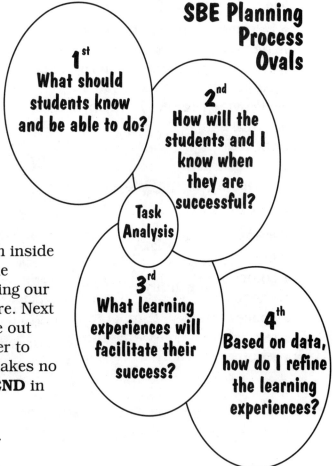

SBE Planning Process Ovals

1st What should students know and be able to do?

2nd How will the students and I know when they are successful?

Task Analysis

3rd What learning experiences will facilitate their success?

4th Based on data, how do I refine the learning experiences?

Concept-Based Instruction

Best practice in standard-based classrooms requires that we go beyond teaching facts, topics, and themes. In order to provide rigorous and relevant learning for our students we have to identify the key concepts and essential understandings on which indicators and lesson objectives are based. Facts are important but they are not enough. See the next page for an extensive list of key concepts found in many content areas. Use that list to identify the broad, timeless, universal, and abstract concepts which transcend the facts listed in the curriculum or standards you teach. You can create essential understandings (generalizations) by showing the relationship between two or more of the concepts.

Instructional Strategies to Use in the Design of Concept-Based Instruction
- Concept Attainment Model: See page 145.
- Inductive Thinking Model: See page 173.
- List-Sort-Label (First step of Taba model): See page 268.
- Advanced organizers for wall and notebooks.
- The Frayer Model: See pages 272-273.

Ways to Scaffold
- Provide graphic organizers to capture the facts, topic, concepts, and generalizations. Fill in as many components as needed for scaffolding
- Provide the data sets for the list-sort-label and/or provide the list and the sort and ask students to label
- Provide practice of the process on known concepts

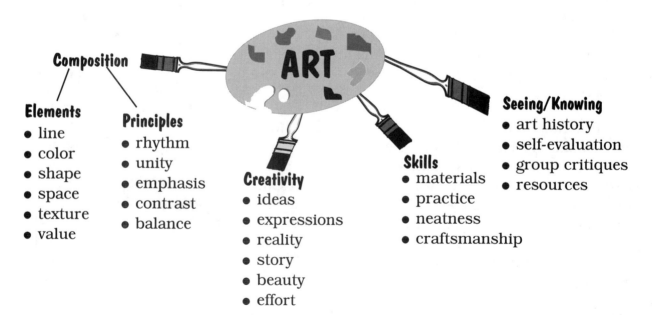

Composition

Elements
- line
- color
- shape
- space
- texture
- value

Principles
- rhythm
- unity
- emphasis
- contrast
- balance

ART

Creativity
- ideas
- expressions
- reality
- story
- beauty
- effort

Skills
- materials
- practice
- neatness
- craftsmanship

Seeing/Knowing
- art history
- self-evaluation
- group critiques
- resources

Concept-Based Instruction

A Sampling of Big Ideas and Key Concepts

Stimulus	Individual	Revolution	Organization
Belief	Balance	Renaissance	Attitude
Probability	Communication	Object	Estimation
Values	Number	Community	Message
Change	Interaction	Honor	Time
People	Variables	Challenge	Love
Celebration	Projection	Fairness	Loyalty
Production	Influence	Justice	Reaction
Needs	Relationship	Equilibrium	Survival
Space	Knowledge	Symbol	Wellness
Order	Limit	Beauty	Stamina
Force	Motion	Solution	Fitness
Complexity	Consequence	Tradition	Group
Culture	Parallel	Reciprocity	Matter
Interdependence	Tension	Stability	Sequence
Perspective	Opinion	Cohesion	History
Scale	Habitat	Disparity	Rotation
Property	Supply	Factor	Success
Behavior	Diversity	Density	Intelligence
System	Wants	Faith	Style
Adaptation	Rhythm	Fantasy	Failure
Structure	Pace	Division	Speed
Role	Conflict	Unity	Truth
Freedom	Pattern	Family	Capacity
Competition	Control	Patriotism	Power

A Sampling of Essential Understandings and Questions

- All living things need to adapt to their habitat to survive and thrive. (Grade 4 science)
- How do geographical, economic, technological, religious, and social variables affect the course of history? (K-12 social studies)
- Data that occurs in real-world situations can be examined for linear or non-linear patterns and trends. (High school math)
- There are positive and negative consequences of revolutions. (Grade 5 social studies)
- How does literature affect your life, and how does your life affect your interpretation of literature? (K-12 English language arts)

Task Analysis

Task analysis is the systematic breakdown of the tasks we ask students to complete. It allows us to identify the skills, both academic and process, that the students need in order to successfully complete the task, assignment, or project.

How To Analyze a Task

- Make sure the task is worth doing and that it is aligned with the standards of learning.
- Note and list all the components that go into accomplishing the task.
- Note and list all the skills (procedural knowledge) and bits of declarative knowledge students need to have in order to be successful with the task.
- Identify the levels of understanding they will need to complete the task.
- Use cognitive empathy to check through the task one more time. Better yet, if it is a high stakes assignment, have someone not in your class (student, teacher, or friend) read through the task and the directions to check for possible problem areas.
- Identify which students have mastered which skills. If unknown, decide how to find out or how to circumvent the need for the skill.
- Design your instruction by deciding what to do about the skills or knowledge the entire group needs, what to do about those students who lack the prerequisite skills to be successful even with the beginning components of the task, and what to do about those students who have already mastered the knowledge and skills required by the task.
- While there may be many skill sets and chunks of knowledge you include as learning experiences for the entire class, you may choose to organize mini-lessons for small groups. These mini-lessons may focus on skill remediation, extension of learning, or provide the information students will need to complete a particular part of the task. Prevention of problems, frustration, or failure, rather than intervention later, will make you and your students more successful. In the end, it will save time and energy for all involved.

The ultimate goal is for our students to task analyze independently. We should be explicit about teaching gifted and accelerated learners how to task analyze and then expect them to become skillful at task analyzing the independent studies they organize for themselves.

Task Analysis Exemplar

English 11 Standard: Students will write a multi-paragraph persuasive essay.

Assessment Task: In this RAFT students assume the role of a teenager from a specific country or the position of a teenager in the United States. After studying a selected country in detail, they write letters to the President of the United States, suggesting the role the U.S. should play in the political/economic future of that country through its foreign policy practices.

Knowledge	Skills
What must students know?	What must students be able to do?

Knowledge

What must students know?

Know (nouns):
- characteristics of argumentation/persuasion
- role of fact/opinion
- paraphrasing
- direct quotations
- summarization
- background (political/historical) information about a specific area of the world

Understand (nouns):
- U.S. foreign policy goals
- U.S. foreign policy tools
- elements of persuasion
- thesis
- the call to action

Skills

What must students be able to do?

Be able to do (verbs):
- form arguments
- create a rationale for position
- locate facts to support position
- support points with specific facts
- express thought in complete sentences
- use transitions to combine sentences into paragraphs and to connect paragraphs
- arrange paragraphs in a logical order
- frame an introduction and conclusion to serve the focus of the writing and ideas in the paragraphs
- appeal to a specific audience
- create a call to action in a multi-paragraph essay

Task Analysis

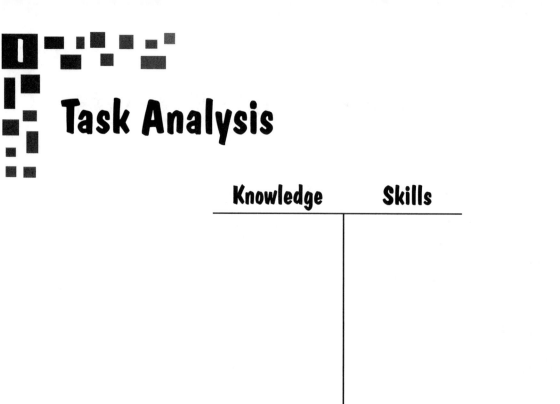

Knowledge	Skills

- Is there background knowledge or a level of understanding the entire group is lacking? How about individual students?
- Are there academic or social skills the entire group is lacking? How about the skill level of individuals?
- What shall I do in a proactive way to prevent frustrations and problems with learning?
- What shall I do with students who already know and can apply this information?

Students	Potential Problem	Possible Intervention

Task Analysis Planning templates are on CD-ROM.

Pre-Assessment

It is essential to use pre-assessment data in the process of planning instruction. Sometimes we already know who knows what and who has the needed skills to be successful with the upcoming study. At other times, we need to be purposeful about identifying learning gaps and previously mastered knowledge and skills. The good news is that pre-assessment does not have to be an arduous or time consuming task. The goal is to maximize instructional time by not repeating already learned material yet also maximizing the probability that re-teaching will not be necessary because we are better able to plan appropriate learning experiences, plan scaffolding and extensions, structure groups, and critical points where careful checking for understanding will be necessary.

Sources of Pre-Assessment Data
- Previous assignments
- Checklists
- Anecdotal records
- Journal entries
- Conversations with students
- Use of active learning strategies that also access prior knowledge and/or set purpose for learning. Examples are:
    - **Three-Column Charts**: See page 261.
    - **Anticipation/Reaction Guides**: See page 165.
    - **Signal Cards**
    - **Sort Cards**: See page 198.
    - **Frame of Reference**: See page 198.
    - **Graffiti**: See page 240.
    - **Stir the Class**: See page 198.

The ideal time to do pre-assessments is about two weeks before the beginning of a new unit of study. That way we have time to gather the resources we need to teach the unit.

©Just ASK Publications

Pre-Assessment

Pre-Assessment in Action

I used **Graffiti** as a pre-assessment to access prior knowledge of basic print resources, I made posters for each source and placed them around the library. The classes were divided into five groups and each group rotated around the room to each chart. They were given about four minutes at each chart to write down as much as they could recall about that source. There were several students with autism in the classes and this was an excellent chance for them to interact with the content and other students.

Using this strategy gave me a starting point for planning my library lessons for the next few months. I plan to use Graffiti again at the end of the lessons on these sources. I saved the first set of charts and I will post both charts so that students can see how much they learned.

Barbara Thompson, Prince William County Schools, VA

Planning Instruction Using the Top Ten Questions

The questions on the following page build on the SBE Planning Ovals. The questions associated with Ovals One and Two are addressed in the previous pages. After we are clear about what is to be learned, how we will recognize and measure success, and complete a task analysis, the questions in Oval Three, questions 3 - 10, help us make specific plans for how to structure learning experiences that will enable students to be successful demonstrating their learning.

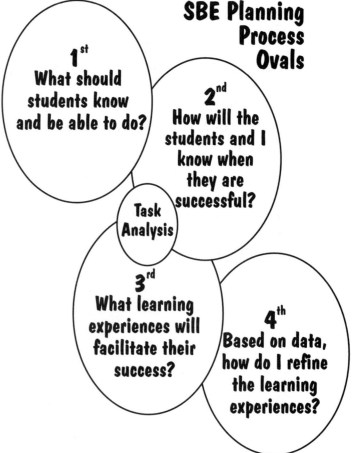

SBE Planning Process Ovals

1st What should students know and be able to do?

2nd How will the students and I know when they are successful?

Task Analysis

3rd What learning experiences will facilitate their success?

4th Based on data, how do I refine the learning experiences?

Top Ten Questions
to ask myself as I design lessons and units

Oval One

1. What should students know and be able to do as a result of this lesson? How are these objectives related to national, state, and/or district standards?

Oval Two

2. How will students demonstrate what they know and what they can do? What will be the assessment criteria and what form will it take?

Oval Three (Questions 3-10 address Oval Three)

3. How will I find out what students already know (pre-assessment), and how will I help them access what they know and have experienced both inside and outside the classroom? How will I help them build on prior experiences, deal with misconceptions, and re-frame their thinking when appropriate?

4. How will new knowledge, concepts, and skills be introduced? Given the diversity of my students and the task analysis, what are my best options for sources and presentation modes?

5. How will I facilitate student processing (meaning making) of new information or processes? What key questions, activities, and assignments (in class or homework) will promote understanding, retention, and transfer?

6. What shall I use as formative assessments or checks for understanding? How can I use the data from those assessments to inform my teaching decisions?

7. What do I need to do to scaffold and extend instruction so that the learning experiences are productive for all students? What are the multiple ways students can access information and then process and demonstrate their learning?

8. How will I Frame the Learning so that students know the objectives, the rationale for the objectives and activities, the directions and procedures, as well as the assessment criteria at the beginning of the learning process?

9. How will I build in opportunities for students to make real-world connections and to learn and use the rigorous and complex thinking skills they need to succeed in the classroom and the world beyond?

10. What adjustments need to be made in the learning environment so that we can work and learn efficiently during this study?

Top Ten Questions Worksheet template is on CD-ROM.

IDEA and Response to Intervention (RtI)
Meeting the Needs of Diverse Learners

Public Law 94-142 (Education of All Handicapped Children Act), passed in 1975, required that students with disabilities be taught in the "least restrictive environment." At that time we brought most of our students back to their home schools from outside placements. That first step toward mainstreaming led to the establishment of self-contained classrooms where core subjects were taught by special education teachers and resource rooms where special educators worked with the students in either a remedial or compensatory approach. What went on in these classrooms was usually driven by **Individualized Educational Program (IEP)** goals with little consideration of the curriculum or program followed by the rest of the students in the school.

PL 94-142, now known as Individuals with Disabilities Education Act (IDEA), as amended in 1997, requires that all students have access to the same rich curriculum as all other students and that they be held to the same level of accountability as all other students. With those requirements, there can no longer be different curricula and standards and all students must have instruction from teachers who are not only well versed in pedagogy, learning theory, and working with disabilities or language challenges (the special educators and second language specialists), but with teachers who are also knowledgeable and skillful with the content to be taught and learned (the general educators). This required that teachers collaborate in ways that had not previously been the norm.

The 2004 reauthorization of IDEA included the statement: [Schools will] "not be required to take into consideration whether a child has a severe discrepancy between achievement and intellectual ability ..." [Section 1414(b)] Instead schools can now use an approach called **Response to Intervention (RtI)** which permits the use of data about the students' response to scientific, research-based intervention to determine the type and level of support the child should have, and requires that the learner's general education teacher be a part of the team that determines whether or not the child has a specific learning disability. The important point of this change is that interventions can occur earlier and may take place in the regular classroom. That is, the student does not have to fail in school before receiving additional support; that support is to be provided in a three-tier model and may or may not include special education services. It is also important to note that students cannot be found eligible for special education services because of lack of scientifically-based reading instruction, lack of instruction in math, or limited English proficiency.

Meeting the Needs of Diverse Learners

Response to Intervention (RtI)

Response to Intervention (RtI) means "How are my students responding to the interventions/instructional strategies I implement?" Debby Mossburg, ASK Group Associate, helped clarify the intent of the law by explaining that **RtI** is a general education mandate embedded in **IDEA**, a special education law. Districts and states using the **RtI** approach provide intensive general education support for student learning prior to students exhibiting learning deficits that might lead to placement in a special education program; they expect that 80-85% of their students can be successful in the general education classroom. This means that classroom teachers need to continue to expand and refine their repertoires of instructional strategies, become more purposeful in the selection of strategies, and build expertise in using appropriate data to make instructional decisions.

It is a cause for celebration that we are now tasked with asking ourselves what is working and what is not working with given students and then planning and implementing interventions (changes) in instructional practice without waiting for a label to be placed on the child or for an outside "expert" to tell us what we should be doing. If we use our collective will and expertise in this way, we should be able to educate almost all students in general education classes and still ensure that the 5% who need special education services receive the intensive support they need.

Jon Saphier, author and founder of Research for Better Teaching, clarified my thinking about selecting interventions long before the term was used the way we are now using it. He taught me that the more closely we can identify the cause of a behavior, the better we can select an intervention. A review of multiple dictionary definitions did not yield any examples of the use of "intervention" in a classroom setting but future dictionaries no doubt will include the construct that there are classroom interventions we can use to eliminate or minimize learning problems.

See **Best on the Web** on page 2 for web-based resources on **RtI**.

Differentiation Non-Negotiables

We Must

- Be knowledgeable about and skillful with the **content** to be taught.
- Acknowledge, understand, respect, and respond to the **differences** in, and **needs** of, the learners to be taught.
- Hold and select purposefully from a deep and broad **repertoire of instructional strategies**.
- Use **multiple sources of data** to inform decisions about instruction.
- Realize that differentiation is not a set of strategies but is instead a **way of thinking** about the teaching and learning process.
- **Not differentiate who will learn what but** rather, **how we will teach** so that all students have access to, and support and guidance in, mastering the district and/or state curriculum.

Actions to Take

- Design learning experiences based on a task analysis that includes an analysis of the skills and knowledge embedded in the task plus an analysis of student readiness, background knowledge levels, interests, and information processing styles.
- Provide sources of information at various reading levels, in different languages, and in varying formats to match the needs of learners.
- Provide appropriate scaffolding and extensions.
- Provide students precise and public criteria and guidelines prior to the beginning of the learning experience or assessment; include models and exemplars with the guidelines.
- Ensure that grouping is flexible so that students are working and learning with a variety of classmates.
- Orchestrate the learning environment so that the student is given both choice and responsibility around learning.
- Collaborate with colleagues and parents.
- Ask ourselves:
  - What will we do if some students do not learn?
  - What will we do if some students already know what we want them to learn?

SBE and Multiple Pathways to Learning

Differentiation of instruction does not mean that you individualize instruction or provide something "different" from the normal lesson for struggling or advanced students. It means that you think proactively and, from the beginning, the "normal" lesson includes more than one avenue for success. It means that you think about the diversity of your learners when you are planning and don't fall into the trap of thinking that "one size fits all." Use what you know about the **SBE Planning Process** and the needs of your diverse learners to answer the following questions.

1. Identify a standard/benchmark/indicator you will be addressing in the near future.

2. What assessment opportunities might you give students to demonstrate what they have learned about the above concept?

3. Given the task analysis, what information and skills should all students experience? List a few instructional strategies and practices and/or processing activities that would facilitate that learning.

Multiple pathways to learning starts here

4. What might you do to extend and expand the thinking of students ready to and/or interested in going beyond what you've planned? Include both inside and outside of class possibilities.

5. What do you know about your struggling learners that you need to address up front? What about your ESL students? Your special education students? List specific examples of instructional strategies, adaptations, support systems that would be helpful to small groups?

6. What might you do to re-teach or help students having difficulties in understanding this concept? Include both inside and outside of class possibilities.

SBE and Multiple Pathways to Learning template is on CD-ROM.

Thinking About
Ways to Scaffold and Extend Instruction

We base our planning on the key concepts/essential understandings of our curriculum. To provide additional challenge or additional support we move from those understandings to deciding what support systems students need to master those essential understandings as well as what we will need to do to provide rigorous and challenging learning experiences for those who can easily demonstrate mastery of those understandings.

Read through the statements below, mark with an X those that you already consider in your planning, and reflect on those that you need to use to guide your thinking as you plan future instruction.

☐ I design lessons and units based on the essential understandings, key concepts, big ideas, and level of understanding required by the Common Core Standards, state standards, and district curriculum.

☐ I make abstract concepts more accessible through semi-abstract (pictures or graphs) or concrete (realia/props/exemplars) representations.

☐ I promote learning by linking new concepts and ideas to familiar concepts or experiences.

☐ I purposefully learn about my students readiness levels, interests, and learning strengths and design standards-based learning experiences that build on their current status.

☐ I increase/decrease accessibility by providing alternative resources, by giving more/less guidance, or by supplying resources.

☐ I ensure that students working at all skill levels constantly build expertise at accessing resources for increasingly independent learning.

☐ I break the task or goal into simpler parts...such as chunking the task, providing check-in points and time guidelines, or having advanced students do more independent investigations.

☐ I provide more/less structure as needed.

☐ I adjust the level of independence to ensure success without enabling.

☐ I adjust the frequency of feedback so that students can adjust their learning efforts.

☐ I adjust the time for input of new information, the meaning making, and the demonstrations of understanding as needed.

☐ I extend and enrich the learning experiences for those who are able to do complex quality work and demonstrate understanding in a short time.

Differentiation

Lilian Katz, Early Childhood Expert
When a teacher tries to teach something to the entire class at the same time, chances are, one-third of the kids already know it; one-third will get it; and the remaining third won't. So two-thirds of the children are wasting their time.

Universal Design for Learning
The CAST's formerly known as Center for Applied Special Technology, Universal Design for Learning calls for:
- Multiple means of representation so that learners can acquire information and knowledge in various ways
- Multiple means of expression so that learners can have alternatives for demonstrating what they know
- Multiple means of engagement so that we can tap into learners' interest, offer appropriate challenges, and increase motivation

Martha Larkin on Effective Scaffolding
- Identify what students know
- Begin with what students can do
- Help students achieve success quickly
- Help students to "be" like everyone else
- Know when it's time to stop
- Help students be independent when they have command of the activity

Sylvia Rimm on the Needs of Gifted Learners
The surest path to positive self-esteem is to succeed at something which one perceived would be difficult. Each time we steal a student's struggle, we steal the opportunity for them to build self-confidence. They must learn to do hard things to feel good about themselves.

Differentiation 3x3
The graphic on the next page communicates key points about how to plan instruction in a way that provides multiple pathways to learning. The purpose of the graphic is to make differentiating instruction seem less formidable. This model applies to our efforts to help students at all points on the learning spectrum. These points are elaborated on in Chapters II, IV, and V.

Differentiating Instruction 3x3

Provide a range of and choice in

1 Sources

2 Processes

3 Products

The top box matches the key principles of Universal Design for Learning listed on the previous page. As Laramie Brown, former Director of the Teacher Center in West Irondequoit, New York, so eloquently said, "We used to differentiate who would learn what. Now we work to ensure that all students learn at high levels and we differentiate everything else to make that happen."

Key points here are that differentiation is not individualized instruction but is instead a balance of whole-group, small-group, and individual instruction.

Provide a balance of instruction and learning

1 Whole-class

2 Small-group

3 Individual

In this instance, individual does not mean seat work. It means that the teacher spends individual time with students.

The box to the right displays the variables that influence our thinking about how best to plan standards-based learning experiences. They can be grouped within the three categories. They help us identify not only the best grouping configurations to use but the sources of information, the processing (meaning making) exercises and the demonstrations of learning that have the highest probability of promoting success.

Variables to consider in grouping and other instructional decisions

1 Readiness

2 Interests

3 Information Processing Styles

Collegial Collaboration
Practices that Promote School Success

Educators who collaboratively use their knowledge, skills, and energy to...

- create an inclusive culture for students and adults
- analyze standards and design instruction and assessments to match those standards
- design and prepare instructional materials together
- design and evaluate units together
- research materials, instructional strategies, content-specific methodologies, and curriculum ideas to both experiment with and to share with colleagues
- work collaboratively to design lesson plans that include scaffolding and extensions (both within and across grade levels and disciplines)
- discuss/reflect on lesson plans prior to and following the lesson
- examine student work together to check for alignment with standards and refine assignments as appropriate
- gather, analyze, and use multiple forms of data to inform practice
- agree to experiment with an idea or approach and then debrief around implementation issues, analyze the results, and make adaptations and adjustments for future instruction
- observe and be observed by other teachers
- analyze practices and their productivity
- promote the concepts of repertoire and reflection
- teach each other in informal settings and in focus groups, especially about meeting the needs of diverse learners
- use meeting time for discussions about teaching and learning rather than administrivia
- talk openly and often about what they are learning or would like to learn
- concentrate efforts and dialogue on quality and quantity of student learning, rather than on how many chapters have been covered in the text

greatly increase the probability of higher student achievement.

Collegial Collaboration

Working with Instructional Coaches

Instructional coaches may be called literacy coaches, math coaches, Title I coaches, inclusion coaches, induction coaches, or many other titles. The commonality in their job descriptions is that they are charged with providing classroom teachers support in the design and delivery of successful learning experiences for students. The formats in which that support is delivered includes:

- Planning instruction
- Classroom observations with feedback
- Problem-solving sessions with individual teachers or groups of teachers
- Analysis of student work
- Demonstration teaching/modeling a lesson
- Co-teaching of a lesson or unit
- Professional development

Co-Teaching

Co-teaching situations are most often collaborative efforts of general education and special education teachers or general education and teachers of second language learners. In either collaboration there are several approaches to working together in the classroom. They include:

One Instructor, One Observer: One teacher has primary instructional responsibility, while the other observes and gathers data on students, their performance, their interactions, and their behavior in general; each teacher can assume either role.

One Instructor, One "Floater:" One teacher has primary instructional responsibility, while the other assists students with their work, monitors behavior, corrects assignments, etc. Each teacher can assume either role.

Station Teaching: Teachers divide instructional content into two parts (e.g., vocabulary and content, or new concepts and review). Each teacher instructs half the class in one area. Both groups of students rotate through instruction with each teacher.

Parallel Teaching: Each teacher instructs half the student group; the same content is taught simultaneously to all students though instructional methods may vary.

Remedial Teaching: One teacher instructs students who have mastered the material to be learned, while the other works with students who have not mastered the key concepts or skills.

Supplemental Teaching: One teacher presents the lesson in standard format. The other works with students who have difficulty mastering the material, simplifying, and otherwise adapting instruction to meet their needs, or works with students who have already mastered the material to provide enrichment and extension. This option is often used when special education teachers and regular education teachers first work together.

Team Teaching: In this model, the most sophisticated form of co-teaching, the teachers collaborate to present the lesson to all students. In fully developed team teaching situations, the teachers are so comfortable with their roles, the content, and the students that they are able to pick up on nuances and read each other's signals so well that they essentially teach as one.

What Works in Inclusive Classrooms

This list of suggestions was developed by teachers working in inclusive classrooms in Honeoye Falls-Lima School District, New York.

- Establish common goals.
- Discuss roles and methods before school begins...and then revisit your decisions and adjust as necessary.
- Be flexible! Be focused but not limiting!
- Communicate constantly. Be specific. Be positive.
- Keep your sense of humor.
- Demystify special education.
- Accept responsibility! Always do at least your share and a little more.
- Think our kids, not yours and mine.
- Remember one size doesn't fit all!
- Differentiate learning and enrich the environment with 3x3 tactics.
- Become familiar with all learning styles and alter teaching styles to suit.
- Incorporate activities that reach the different intelligences.
- Allow for divergent thinking by students and teachers.
- Practice wait time in the classroom and with each other.
- Do informal task analyses.
- Don't make assumptions.
- Incorporate active learning into the fabric of the classroom life.
- Don't differentiate between special needs students and others in public.
- Demonstrate utmost respect for all colleagues, students, and parents.
- Have special education teachers work with all students.
- Tap into students' interests.
- Take the risk to give up or set aside the tried-and-true and try something new.
- Schedule time together throughout the year to work on goals and skills.
- Seek out professional development opportunities.

Fundamentals of Co-Teaching

Successful co-teaching relies on effective communication. Simple matters, if not clarified, can lead to misunderstandings that interfere with the co-teaching success. Before you co-teach, and throughout the process, be sure to discuss these and any other fundamental issues you identify.

Instruction and Assessment

What should students know and be able to do, and how will they demonstrate their learning? When you are working together in a standards-based classroom there must be a clear understanding of what standard(s) is the focus of the instruction. Adaptations around assessment for special needs students may require much discussion. Will rubrics or performance task lists be used? What flexibility is built in and what might be areas of contention?

Planning

Who is going to take responsibility for which parts of the planning? When does planning get done? Does it happen one year, one month, one week, or one day in advance? Who designs the tasks, the assessment, and the criteria for demonstrating competency?

Instructional Format

How will the lesson be delivered and who will deliver it? What will be acceptable additions or clarifications? Which option for co-teaching will you use? How will a wide array of resources be assembled and organized? Who will take the lead for which tasks?

Teacher Status

How will it be clear to you and the students that you hold **equal status**? For example, think about how to do introductions to students, parents, and others, titles to be used, which names are on the report cards, who calls parents, and classroom allocation of adult space (such as desks and chairs).

Noise

How will the sound level in the classroom be monitored and adapted? Noise includes teacher voices, instructional activities, noise of machines or equipment, student voices, movement, and environmental sounds.

Fundamentals of Co-Teaching

Classroom Routines

What expectations does each teacher have for how classes should operate? This includes everything from headings on student papers to permission to use the pencil sharpener or restroom. **Equal status** means that each teacher has input into such decisions.

Discipline

What are the acceptable standards for student classroom behavior? What is absolutely intolerable for each teacher and what is okay some of the time in some situations? What are the systems for rewards and consequences for behavior?

Feedback

When will you meet to assess how the co-teaching arrangement is operating and how you will discuss both successes and problems? Identify timelines for feedback and the format of the feedback in advance.

Grading

What will be the basis for grades and who will assign them? A discussion of the effect of instructional/assessment modifications on grades is an important topic.

Data Gathering and Analysis

What data will you need to gather to make future instructional decisions? How will this data about the effectiveness of instructional decisions and about student learning be gathered and analyzed?

Teaching Chores

Who scores assignments and tests? Who duplicates materials, reserves technology resources, contacts speakers, arranges field trips, corrects papers, records grades, and so on?

Pet Peeves

What other aspects of classroom life are critical to you? The issue for you could be the extent of organization of materials, the ways students address teachers, or the fact that it really bothers you when someone opens your desk drawer without asking. Try to identify as many as possible in advance.

3-D Teams
Data-Driven Decision Teams

Groups of teachers meet once or twice a month to review and analyze student work in an effort to use data to make solid instructional decisions. The analysis, reflection, and collegial collaboration provides a framework for decision making about future instruction. This practice is a particularly useful tool for teachers who are striving for consistency across classrooms in a standards-based learning and assessment environment.

The group members bring samples of student work to the meeting. Hanson, Silver and Strong, in descriptions of their Authentic Achievement Teams, suggest that each teacher bring six pieces of students' work to the meeting; they further recommend that the samples represent different achievement levels or different levels of success on this particular assignment. For example, two might be from the top third of a class, two from the middle, and two from the bottom. An alternative approach would be to analyze the work of "regular" students and that of ESL, advanced, or inclusion students. It is also helpful to bring copies of any directions given to the students.

If the group members have not planned together, ten to fifteen minutes are spent looking through the student work samples and any teacher artifacts so that all participants get a good idea of what kind of work they will be discussing and analyzing.

The participants can agree to analyze all the work of their students around the same set of criteria, or each teacher can indicate the questions, concerns, or criteria to be considered for that set of student work. In either case, the outcomes of the discussion might be directed toward:
- checking for **validation** about the appropriateness of the work for the developmental stage of the students
- checking to ensure that the task is **congruent** with the stated mastery objective and/or state or district standards
- checking for **consistency** of opinion about the assessment and evaluation of the work
- possible **adjustments** in teacher directions and **support** for all/some of the students

Cause/Effect Analysis

Cause/Effect Analysis and Revision Planner for Family Unit

Standard: History 6 - Students know that religious and philosophical ideas have been powerful forces throughout history.

Benchmark: 6.1 Students know the historical development of religions and philosophies.

Indicator: Student can recognize and describe family customs, traditions, and beliefs.

Desired Effect - What were the **desired** group and/or individual assessment results? Given 100% **Not Proficient** on narrative pre-assessment the desired effects are at least 75% of students will score **Proficient**, or **Above Proficient** and none will score **Not Proficient** on overall assessments.

Effect - What were the **actual** group and/or individual assessment results? 88% scored **Proficient or Above Proficient** and 0% **Not Proficient**. On the narrative post-assessment 28% scored **Proficient** or **Above Proficient** and 33% scored **Not Proficient**.

Cause: Methods

Methods used this time:
- Literature
- Class discussions
- Guest speaker
- Individual family inquiry
- Modeling/scaffolding

Potential changes for next time:
- Concentrate on origin and describing practice
- More modeling
- More peer sharing

Cause: Materials

Materials used this time:
- Paper and pencil
- Computer with KidPix program

Potential changes for next time:
- Better organizer for outlining presentation
- More fine-tuned naming and saving process
- Organization matrix to report responses on pre- and post-assessments

---

Cause: People

People involved this time:
- Teacher
- Peer
- Family

Potential changes for next time:
- Have students interview family about specific family customs, traditions, or beliefs including origins
- Oral sharing with peers before post

Cause: Time

Time used this time:
- 5 days planning
- 9 days designing
- One session

Potential changes for next time:
- Use timeline for how long to work on each page to help with time management
- Possibly more than one session

Cause/Effect Analysis template is on CD-ROM. **29**

1st Grade Third Trimester Action Plan

School Goal: 70-75% of students will be reading at or above grade level

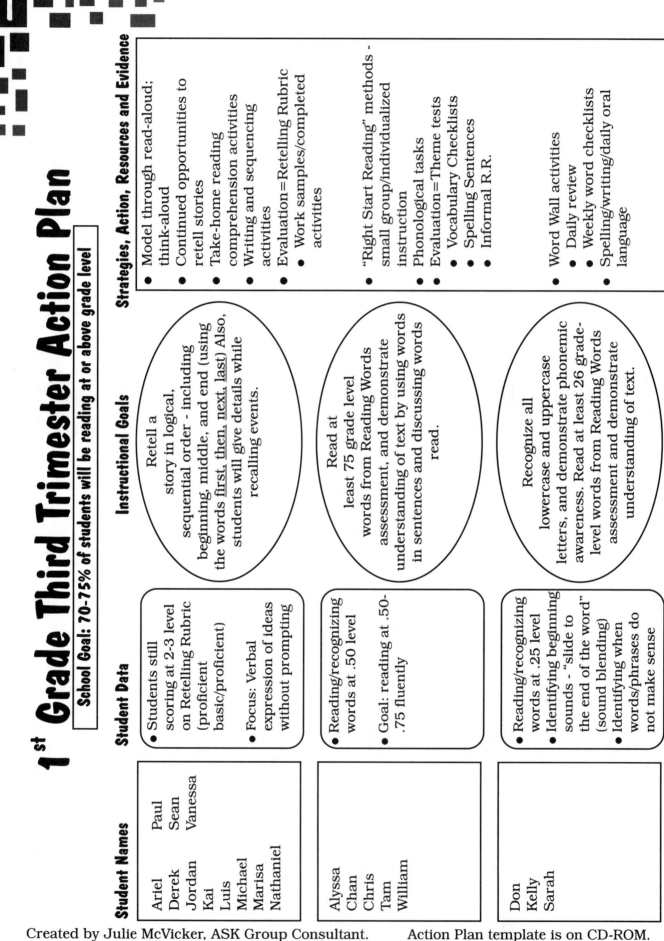

Student Names	Student Data	Instructional Goals	Strategies, Action, Resources and Evidence
Ariel Paul Derek Sean Jordan Vanessa Kai Luis Michael Marisa Nathaniel	• Students still scoring at 2-3 level on Retelling Rubric (proficient basic/proficient) • Focus: Verbal expression of ideas without prompting	Retell a story in logical, sequential order - including beginning, middle, and end (using the words first, then, next, last) Also, students will give details while recalling events.	• Model through read-aloud; think-aloud • Continued opportunities to retell stories • Take-home reading comprehension activities • Writing and sequencing activities • Evaluation=Retelling Rubric • Work samples/completed activities

Alyssa
Chan
Chris
Tam
William
	• Reading/recognizing words at .50 level
	• Goal: reading at .50-.75 fluently
		Read at least 75 grade level words from Reading Words assessment, and demonstrate understanding of text by using words in sentences and discussing words read.	• "Right Start Reading" methods - small group/individualized instruction
			• Phonological tasks
			• Evaluation=Theme tests
			  • Vocabulary Checklists
			  • Spelling Sentences
			  • Informal R.R.

Don Kelly Sarah	• Reading/recognizing words at .25 level • Identifying beginning sounds - "slide to the end of the word" (sound blending) • Identifying when words/phrases do not make sense	Recognize all lowercase and uppercase letters, and demonstrate phonemic awareness. Read at least 26 grade-level words from Reading Words assessment and demonstrate understanding of text.	• Word Wall activities • Daily review • Weekly word checklists • Spelling/writing/daily oral language

Created by Julie McVicker, ASK Group Consultant.

Action Plan template is on CD-ROM.

Student Achievement Data

Data Analysis for Instructional Decision Making

- Identify and analyze general trends or patterns observed.
- Identify percentage or number of advanced proficient, proficient, and not proficient.
- Disaggregate data by **demographics** such as gender, ethnicity, time in district, English language proficiency, students on IEPs, and free and reduced lunch (required by No Child Left Behind Act of 2001).
- Compare current data to **data from past assessments** at this grade level.
- Complete a **longitudinal** comparison of the work of individuals or groups of students over time.
- **Analyze data by subsets** such as specific standards, benchmarks, or indicators.
- **Cause and effect analysis**
  - Analyze how and when the assessed concepts, facts, and processes were taught.
  - Consider which strategies were used.
  - Consider what materials were used.
  - Consider how much time was allocated.
  - Consider the level of thinking the students/student groups now use and the level required by the assessment.
  - Review the alignment of the learning experiences with the knowledge, skills, and level of thinking required by the assessment task.
  - Ask what changes need to be made the next time these points are taught or to whom they should be retaught.
- **Compare classroom assessment data and external assessment data**.
- **Do an item analysis**
  - Which items were missed by most students?
  - Which items were missed by highest performing students?
  - Which items were missed by almost proficient students?
  - Which items were missed by students with special needs?
  - Which items were missed by English Language Learners?
- **Create tables that show the data by students, by subgroup, by item, or broader categories such as benchmarks or standards**.

Following the data analysis, identify the baseline data for which targets will be set. Identify targets and then make action plans based on what was learned from the data analysis.

Data Review Teams

Data Review Teams meet on a regular basis to review progress based on the Data Review Questions. During the review team members engage in an honest conversation about student learning.

Why Data Reviews Are Important

The regular review of student performance data helps us:

- Understand what students know and need to know
- Evaluate progress of school toward important initiatives; grade levels toward team goals; classrooms toward benchmarks by group, gender, and individual
- Communicate with greater accuracy to parents
- Design and assign interventions now, before it is too late
- Look at the impact instruction is or is not having
- Provide data for student goal setting
- Look for patterns and trends in learning
- Regroup students for performance
- Reallocate school resources (money, people, and time)

Keep in Mind

Student learning is the goal. Control and compliance is not the goal. Seat time is not the goal. It is student learning for which we hold ourselves accountable. Data reviews are one way to use the body of evidence we collect to change the way we teach.

Analyzing the data is not optional and is not enough. It is the data-driven adjustment we make in our professional practice that must make a difference. We must, therefore, not be defensive about data and use it to inform our practice. It is the decision we make and the action we take as a result of the data analysis for which we are accountable.

> It is not acceptable for us to know a child is failing and not do something about it. Further, conflict avoidance in the face of poor performance is an act of moral neglect.
>
> Michael Fullan, *The Moral Imperative of School Leadership*

Data Review Questions

General

- What do we know from looking at this data?
- Do we know which students are learning and not learning?
- What patterns can we observe?
- What concerns are raised by a review of the data?
- What other data sources would clarify and inform our teaching practice?
- How do the programs we have in place connect with the concerns identified?
- What can we do about what the data reveal?
- What additional data should we collect?

Specific

- How well, overall, are our students doing on each benchmark?
- Do all of the items on each benchmark have a high percentage of correct answers?
- If not, which items under each benchmark have a high percentage of incorrect answers?
- On the incorrect test items, is there an incorrect answer that was picked by a high percentage of students?
- What kind of mistake is represented by this choice?
- What items do we need to disaggregate to find out if there is a pattern of students not doing well (boys/girls, free lunch, ESL, LD, etc.)?
- Write statements describing your findings using the template below:

    It seems that ......because......

> Marcia Baldanza developed this data review process while she was a principal in Alexandria City Public Schools, Virginia. She used the questions as the supervisor of the Superintendent's Schools in Broward County Public Schools, Ft. Lauderdale, Florida, and is using them now as the Lead Restructuring Administrator for the School District of Palm Beach, Florida.

Data Review Questions template is on CD-ROM.

Who Are Our Learners?

Best on the Web

The Council for Exceptional Children (CEC)

CEC's mission is to improve the educational success of individuals with disabilities and/or gifts and talents. This website is a vast storehouse of definitive information on identification, instruction, and assessment of students of all exceptionalities. Access the website at www.cec.sped.org.

Gifted Education

These four websites provide extensive information about the identification and education of gifted and talented students. Multiple websites are listed because there is not universal consensus about the definition of gifted and talented.
- Center for Gifted Education at The College of William and Mary: http://cfge.wm.edu
- Neag Center for Gifted Education and Talent Development is a collaborative effort of the University of Connecticut, City University of New York, Stanford University, and The University of Virginia: www.gifted.uconn.edu
- Georgia Department of Education - Gifted Education: www.doe.k12.ga.us/ci_iap_gifted.aspx
- PA Association for Gifted Education: www.penngifted.org

National Clearinghouse for English Language Acquisition (NCELA)

NCELA collects and publishes a broad range of research and resources in support of an inclusive approach to high quality education for English Language Learners (ELL). Access the NCELA website at www.ncela.gwu.edu.

The Education Alliance at Brown University

The Education Alliance website provides extensive information on culturally responsive teaching. Access it at www.alliance.brown.edu/tdl/tl-strategies/crt-principles.shtml.

North Central Regional Educational Laboratory (NCREL)

NCREL's website presents comprehensive information about at-risk students and also includes multiple links to a wide range of experts who provide further information from a variety of perspectives. Access the website at www.ncrel.org/sdrs/areas/issues/students/atrisk/at600.htm

Who Are Our Learners?

Our Diverse Learners
Gifted and Talented or Advanced
At Risk (At Promise)
Resistant and Reluctant
Struggling
Culturally Diverse
English Language Learners
Students with Learning Disabilities
Students Diagnosed with ADHD
Students on the Autism Spectrum
Students with Other Exceptionalities

This chapter provides an overview of the wide range of student similarities and differences represented in our schools. Some of our students have traveled abroad, some have lived abroad, and others were born abroad. Some have not yet traveled beyond state borders or city limits. Some were born into affluent families and others into families with far fewer financial means. Some speak English with everyone they know and others speak two or more languages on a daily basis and English may or may not be their first language. In both groups there are some who cannot read or write proficiently in any language while others read well beyond grade level not only in English but other languages as well. Some of our students are born with special needs and all are born with interesting and possibly challenging quirks. Certainly all process information and learn in different ways.

In reality, our students are more alike than they are different. William Glasser was right on the mark when he wrote that beyond survival needs, our basic needs are to belong, to gain power, to be free, and to have fun. If we pay attention to those needs we are off to a good start with most of our students. Unfortunately, some of our students come to the classroom without their basic needs for safety and security being met. For those students, the focus is on survival. The challenge for us is to know our children well and to accept them as they are with respect.

It is essential for us to believe in our capacity to teach the children who enter the schoolhouse doors, to believe in their capacity to learn given the right conditions, and to act on those beliefs each and every day.

Our Diverse Learners

Diversity Is in the Eyes of the Beholder

- Those who have always lived "back East" think that folks "out West" are diverse... and vice versa.
- Those who live in a university town know that there are at least two diverse groups... "town" and "gown."
- Those who are "military juniors" think that it is normal to move every two years or so and expect to live abroad at least part of the time. You can recognize them because they call the U. S. "The States."
- Those who have grown up surrounded by people who speak the same language tend to view those who speak another language as diverse.
- Those who grew up in a high-rise apartment in the Bronx are not considered diverse in the Bronx but certainly are when they move to Montana.
- Those who pursue high levels of athletic success do not think they are diverse when they are on the ice rink four or five hours a day, but others clearly might.
- Those who have always had a solid roof over their heads cannot imagine what it is like to live on the streets or in a car.
- Those who have siblings cannot imagine what it is like to be an only child.
- The three young men who won a Tony for their lead role in *Billy Elliot* were no doubt considered diverse when they were the only boys enrolled in the local dance classes just as a female on the football team is considered diverse.
- Those who did not grow up in small town America have no idea what it is like for everyone to know who you are, where you are supposed to be, what you are supposed to be doing, and will inform your parents if you are even one step out of line.
- Those who have always been in the ethnic and racial majority have difficulty understanding what it is like to be the lone member of a minority group.
- And, try as we might to change it, any high school has among its diverse student body those known as the brains, the jocks, the rah-rahs, the bandos, the goody-two-shoes, the geeks, and those who defy description and classification.

General Similarities and Differences

The many ways we see, hear, speak, move, read, write, attend, organize, socialize, engage, and remember transcend language, gender, ethnicity, culture, family size, birth order, socio-economic status, religion, and geography. While the verbs in the previous sentence may well be influenced by the nouns that follow, the number of possible configurations is mind-boggling. This chapter explores some of the variables most likely to impact teaching and learning.

Our Diverse Learners

An Array of Linguistic Proficiency

- English is the only language of student and family. (There is a wide range of proficiency in this one possibility.)
- English is the first language of student and family and other languages are used proficiently by student and family.
- A language other than English is the first language of student and family; English is spoken in the home.
- Student is proficient in English but parents are not proficient in English; another language is spoken in the home.
- Student is proficient in speaking/listening/reading/writing in both English and first language.
- Student is proficient in speaking/listening/writing in first language other than English but not with English.
- Student is proficient in speaking/listening in first language other than English but not proficient with reading or writing in first language.
- Student is proficient with social language use in speaking/listening in English but not with academic language use.

Social and Cultural Influencers

- Age
- Gender
- Developmental stage
- Family size and structure
- Geographic location
- Educational experiences of student and family members
- Life experiences
- Travel opportunities
- Student interactions with teachers and other adults
- Family's role in education of children
- Economic factors
  - Poverty: generational or situational
  - Parental job loss
  - An allusive "middle class" status
  - Relative affluence

Our Diverse Learners

Physical Factors
- Wellness
- Nutrition
- Vision
- Hearing
- Muscular
- Coordination

Information Processing/Learning Styles, and Multiple Intelligences
Four of the most widely used indicators of information processing preferences, learning styles, and intelligences strengths and websites dedicated to them are:
- McCarthy's 4MAT (www.aboutlearning.com)
- Myers-Briggs Type Indicator (www.myersbriggs.org)
- Tony Gregoric's Mind Styles (http://gregorc.com)
- Howard Gardner's Multiple Intelligences Theory (www.infed.org/thinkers/gardner.htm)

Modalities (Receptive and Expressive)
- Visual
- Auditory
- Kinesthetic

Student Readiness for a Given Task
- Reading
- Writing
- Speaking
- Mathematics
- Academic background knowledge
- Organization
- Social Skills
- Attention
- Persistence
- Sense of self-efficacy

Our Diverse Learners

Exceptionalities

> More than 50% of the students receiving special education services in the United States are identified as learning disabled. Some educators estimate that between 5% and 10% of children between ages 6 and 17 have a learning disability.
>
> ERIC Clearinghouse on Disabilities and Gifted Education

In an attempt to be as accurate as possible, the following information and brief descriptions are paraphrased or quoted from the Council for Exceptional Children (CEC) website: www.cec.sped.org. CEC is the preeminent authority on exceptionalities and the website provides extensive information about each of the exceptionalities and useful and research-based instructional strategies for each. Given the availability of this rich resource, it is not the intent of this book to provide in-depth information about exceptionalities but instead to provide an array of instructional strategies educators can use to support a wide range of students in their learning journey.

- **Autism Spectrum Disorder/Asperger's Syndrome:** This developmental disability that impacts social interaction and communication skills typically appears during the first three years of life. It is estimated that one in 150 children have autism, and it affects boys at a four to one ratio over girls.
- **Attention Deficit Hyperactivity Disorder (ADHD):** ADHD is a syndrome characterized by serious and persistent difficulties in attention span, impulse control, and hyperactivity. It is estimated that three to five percent of the school-age population is affected by ADHD.
- **Behavior Disorders/Emotional Disturbance:** Achenbach suggests two discrete patterns that he calls "externalizers" who are aggressive, disruptive, and act out and "internalizers" who are withdrawn, anxious, and depressed. (ERIC Clearinghouse on Disabilities and Gifted Education)
- **Blindness/Visual Impairments**
- **Communicative Disorders:** This includes language, speech, and hearing impairment.
- **Developmental Disabilities**
- **Gifts and Talents:** The categories of giftedness and talents are:
  - Intellectual
  - Creativity
  - Artistic
  - Leadership capacity

Our Diverse Learners

- **Learning Disabilities (LD):** Individuals with LD generally have average or above average intelligence, yet they often do not achieve at the same academic level as their peers. Weaker academic achievement, particularly in reading, written language, and math, is perhaps the most fundamental characteristic of LD. Significant deficits often exist in memory, metacognition, and social skills as well. (CEC)
  - Auditory discrimination: sounds
  - Auditory memory
  - Visual discrimination
  - Visual memory
  - Visual perception: what is seen
  - Dyspraxia: motor
  - Dysgraphia: writing and spelling
  - Dyslexia: language
  - Dyssemia: social cues and signals
- **Intellectual Disability:** These students with limitations in intelligence or in adaptive behavior are provided access to the general education curriculum and the opportunity to interact with and learn from general education classmates. At the elementary level the focus is on helping these students develop functional academic skills such as reading and mathematics skills that are used frequently in everyday life (e.g., reading signs or instructions, counting change, or taking measurements.) At the secondary level, the curriculum for these students is focused on career preparation and life skills.
- **Other Health Impaired:** This includes Tourette Syndrome, diabetes, intrauterine growth restriction, Fetal Alcohol Spectrum Syndrome, and cancer.
- **Physical Disabilities**
- **Traumatic Brain Injury:** Such injuries are head injuries that can cause changes in one or more functions such as: thinking and reasoning, understanding words, remembering things, paying attention, solving problems, thinking abstractly, talking, behaving, walking, and other physical activities. (CEC)
- **Twice Exceptional:** Students who are both gifted and disabled.

Who Are Our Successful Learners?

As stated on the first page of this chapter, it is essential for us to believe in our capacity to teach the children who enter the schoolhouse doors and to believe in their capacity to learn given the right conditions. It is our responsibility to act on those beliefs and create those learning conditions each and every day.

Listed below are some descriptors of successful learners. As you read the rest of this chapter that describes a wide range of learners, consider how you can help each of those students be successful learners as they move forward in their learning journeys. Many years ago Bruce Joyce posed a question that is a fitting one to frame our work. That questions is: How will these learners be different as a result of having spent this time with me?

Our Most Successful Learners

- have had many successful learning experiences in the past
- set learning goals
- think about what they know
- take responsibility for their own learning
- anticipate what they are to learn
- participate actively in their classes
- assimilate, consolidate, and integrate new knowledge
- are organized and try to manage their time well
- are persistent and are effective problem solvers
- seek comprehension and meaning
- monitor their own learning
- construct meaning
- have strong reading skills and extensive vocabularies

Learning More about
Student Learning Preferences

Our own life experiences combined with our tendencies to process information in certain ways, greatly influence our teaching decisions. It is important to remember that others, both students and colleagues, may well view the world and process information, and even authority, in very different ways. Knowing yourself well is a prerequisite to knowing and accepting your students as they are. It is natural tendency to struggle at times with understanding and working with people who view the world through the lens opposite our own.

Use the questions below first to focus on your own preferences and then use them to determine how your students view the world. Do not think for one minute that you have the correct view and they have the wrong one. It is a waste of time and energy to try to convince others to see the world through your lens. The way you interact with students and the ways that you structure learning experiences must take into account the entire spectrum of possibilities.

Are you an introverted or extraverted thinker? Do you prefer to respond to new information immediately, doing your thinking aloud, or do you prefer information in advance so that you have time to think about the issues before you have to respond? Data from the Myers-Briggs Type Indicator reveal that 75% of us are extraverted thinkers who think best when we can discuss our thinking aloud. When we tell an extraverted student to stop talking, we are in effect telling him to stop thinking. On the other hand, introverted thinkers need time to process silently before being asked to respond. A quick-paced, whole-class discussion can leave these learners out of the learning community.

Do you process information and tasks globally or analytically? Do you prefer to have the big picture as the scaffolding on which to hang details or do you prefer to see bits and pieces and then put them into the whole? Analytical learners tend to be sequential and logical in their approach to tasks and information. They look for differences, are time-oriented (Do I need to know this information right now?), and have little patience with ambiguity. On the other hand, global thinkers look for similarities, are spatially oriented, and are more spontaneous and random in their approach.

Are you more interested in the concrete or the abstract? Are the facts and clear expectations what interest you most or do you prefer to focus on theory or possibilities? Do you prefer to deal with what you can see, hear, and touch or do you tend to go with gut instincts? These contrasting lenses can cause grave communication problems because those who prefer concrete and specific information tend to tune out when the focus is theoretical and those with a more abstract preference often tend to ignore or forget the details that make the world right for their concrete teachers.

Learning More about
Student Learning Preferences

Are you decisive or open-ended? Do you tend to make quick decisions and stand by them or do you prefer to continue to gather information and have several options? Either approach can be helpful or detrimental for teachers and learners. Overly decisive people jump to conclusions and often have trouble seeing alternatives. Those who are too open-ended may never reach closure on tasks or projects. Helping students learn to move deliberately while considering multiple perspectives and possibilities is a herculean task.

Do you rely more on logic or intuition? Do you prefer to measure and quantify things or are you comfortable knowing without knowing how you know? There are those among us who do not wish to be confused with logic and others who prefer a logical explanation for everything. 75% of us rely more on logic while the other 25% of us are content "just knowing." Both approaches are correct but the differences in lens has the potential to cause conflict in the classroom.

Do you tend to ask why or how? Which question is the first to come to your mind when someone presents information, "Why is that a good idea?" or "How would that look?" or "How do you want me to do it?" Teachers generally prefer the "how" question, especially elementary teachers who reportedly favor the "how" queries four to one. According to Bernice McCarthy, the developer of 4MAT, about 25% of our students have "how" as their primary question and 25% favor "why." The latter students do not give up easily and certainly will not respond positively to "because I said so!"

Do you plan ahead or wait until the last minute? Do you finish projects well in advance and put them away until needed or are you inclined to fill all available time no matter when you start? No amount of nagging will change those of us who prefer to wait until the last minute or "fill all available time." In fact, the last minute folks are amazed that a project can be done ahead of time and then not revisited to see if there is not some way to improve it.

After you have considered your preferences, use these questions to analyze your interactions with students. Chances are that those students with whom you have the strongest relationships view the world through a lens much like your own and that those students who seem to get under your skin view the world through a lens not aligned with yours. The challenge, as stated before, is to resist the temptation to make others see the world as you do, and instead figure out how to appreciate and teach them as they are.

Learning More about Our
Gifted and Talented Students

The following characteristics, gathered from the resources listed on the next page, are often noted in children who are identified as gifted and talented. These characteristics are notable when children are being compared with peers of the same chronological age. No gifted child will have all of these traits but it is likely that she will have many of them. These students may:

- Learn new information quickly.
- Find pleasure in intellectually challenging games and conversations.
- Enjoy playing with words.
- Like to create, invent, investigate, and conceptualize.
- Have a vivid imagination.
- Be a voracious reader.
- Learn easily and readily.
- Rebel against irrelevant learning requirements.
- Have a wide range of interests.
- See humor with an adult-like lens.
- Display intellectual curiosity and ask lots of questions.
- Explore wide-ranging and special interests often at great depth.
- See connections that others do not see.
- Frequently ask "what if" questions related to issues big and small.
- Use vocabulary which is superior in both quantity and quality.
- Memorize and retrieve from memory easily and quickly.
- Make good grades most of the time, but resist tasks seen as irrelevant or non-challenging.
- Prefer reading or learning about a topic of interest rather than doing an assigned reading.
- Follow complex directions easily.
- Seek out intellectual challenge.
- Spend time beyond assignments on project of interest.
- Be bored with memorization and recitation and worksheet-type assignments.
- Ask provocative questions that challenge parents and teachers.
- Generate many ideas and multiple solutions to problems.
- Have unusual sensitivity to the feelings and expectations of others.
- Be concerned with justice and fairness.
- Have high expectations of self and others.

- Respond and relate to older children and adults and often prefer them to chronological peers.
- Evidence friendliness and outgoingness in desire for social acceptance.
- Display leadership qualities.
- Have keen insight into thinking, abilities, and motivations of others.
- Have a highly developed sense of social and moral responsibility.

Resources

- Talent Identification Program at Duke University: www.tip.duke.edu/resources/parents_students/characteristics.html
- The Queensland Association for Gifted and Talented Children, Inc.- Traits Common to Gifted Children: www.qagtc.org.au/traits-common-gifted-children
- Tulsa Public Schools, Tulsa Oklahoma: Checklist of Characteristics of Gifted Children: www.tulsaschools.org/depts/specialed/pdf/gifted checklist - revised 1-06.pdf
- Georgia Department of Education *Resource Manual for Gifted Education Services*: www.doe.k12.ga.us/ci_iap_gifted.aspx. Click on Resource Manual and go to page 91 for Appendix D - Characteristics of Gifted Learners.
- *Understanding and Challenging the Gifted:* www.penngifted.org/page-psea-booklet.pdf - go to page 8.
- How to Spot a Gifted Student: www.teachersfirst.com/gifted/spot.html

Learning More about Our
At-Risk Students

The term at-risk is used to describe students who are likely to struggle or fail in school because of social circumstances. Poverty is often a major factor. Conditions of poverty that contribute to an at-risk status often include:

- lack of resources
- homelessness
- high mobility
- parents who work multiple jobs or perhaps struggle to stay employed because of competing responsibilities
- parents who themselves struggled in or dropped out of school

Robert Slavin recommends that we view these students as "at-promise" rather than "at-risk." His use of that term captures the potential these students have. One person who exemplifies that potential is Donna Beegle who holds a Doctorate in Educational Leadership from Portland State University. She grew up in generational migrant poverty, was homeless, dropped out of high school, and married at 15. Her story is a powerful way to learn more about at-risk students, their life experiences, and view of the world. Access an interview with her at http://educationnorthwest.org/webfm_send/782

Students who live in poverty experience trouble in school if teachers incorrectly assume that they have had middle-class experiences. Such assumptions can lead to inappropriate placement in special education programs. The frequent moves these at-risk students often make can lead to a delay or inconsistency in transfer of student records. That means that students who have correctly been identified as special needs and have an IEP may not receive appropriate services in their next school or end up being tested over and over.

At-risk students may
- be focused on survival
- have difficulty making friends or even withdraw socially
- experience a delay in language development or reading
- lack resilience and skillfulness when dealing with obstacles and conflict
- lack at-home resources needed to complete assignments
- attend school irregularly

See **What Do You Do When... Learners Are Struggling** on pages 98-103 for a categorized list of interventions that can support the learning of these students.

> There is no such thing as a culture of poverty. Differences in values and behaviors among poor people are just as great as those between poor and wealthy people.
>
> Paul Gorski

Learning More about Our
Resistant and Reluctant Learners

Why are they struggling? Is it a lack of will or lack of skill?

Identifying the causes of the behaviors of resistant, reluctant, and struggling students is a real challenge. While we have "definitions" or at least widely accepted explanations for other students who struggle in the classroom, determining the causes here is problematic. The more closely we can identify the cause of a behavior, the better we can plan the intervention. It is, therefore, essential that we get to know our students well enough to determine the underlying causes of low levels of learning.

While this list of problematic behaviors appears overwhelming, there are definitive actions we can take to break the cycle of failure these students are experiencing. See **Chapter III: What Do You Do When...?** And **Chapter IV: Scaffolding and Extension Tools** for hundreds of suggestions for your consideration.

Students who are not achieving academic success often exhibit one or more of the following behaviors:
- Focus on survival
- Poor reading skills
- Short attention span
- Poor work habits
- Poorly developed language and communication skills
- Lack of confidence
- Apparent lack of curiosity
- Lack of creativity
- Problematic retention and memory
- Anxiety
- Fear of failure
- Poor self-concept
- Poor organizational skills
- Retention appears limited
- Continued difficulty with basic skills
- Concrete thinking
- Easily distracted
- Appear to be social isolates
- Lack of analysis of the effectiveness of their efforts
- Do not appear to see cause and effect relationships
- Do not seem to learn from previous mistakes or errors in judgment
- Avoid failure by avoiding tasks
- Appear to avoid responsibility and independence
- Make external attributions
- Lack of skill in dealing with stress and anger

Learning More about Our
Culturally Diverse Students

Get to Know All Your Students as Individuals

We need to know information about all our students' background and family. We want to, without being perceived as nosy, know all our students in the same personal way that people who have lived their entire lives in a small town already know their students. When you or your students are new to the school useful information to note includes learning:

- How long the student has been in this city, state, and country and where they have previously lived
- Family members and their roles
- Responsibilities students have at home
- What parents believe their children should learn
- What parents see as their appropriate role when they interact with school staff
- Previous school experiences, successes, and struggles
- Cultural norms around:
  - collaborative group work or individual achievement
  - interaction between males and females
  - expression of emotions and feelings
- Restrictions (religious, social, financial, etc.) concerning topics that should not be discussed in school
- Events, people, and accomplishments that are sources of pride for the student
- Holidays and celebrations appropriate for recognizing or observing in school.

Points to Ponder

- There are many comprehensive lists of characteristics and norms of various ethnic, racial, and cultural groups. They must be used with care because it is dangerous to over generalize. We know that all students who speak English do not share the same life experiences. We need to be vigilant in not thinking that students who share another language, live on farms, live in the city, are from wealthy families, or financially poor families share the same life experiences, beliefs, or values.
- Each student, whether or not he is fluent in English, lives in a rural area or in the city, etc. has a unique set of characteristics that impact his learning. While there are similarities in learning profiles, teachers cannot expect all members of any ethnic or linguistic group to benefit from the same instruction or learn in the same way.
- A lack of assessments that factor in the life experiences and linguistic differences has, in some instances, led to culturally diverse learners being inappropriately placed in special education programs. We need to be extremely cautious when making such recommendations.

Learning More about Our
English Language Learners

Factors that Influence English Language Acquisition

- Age of learner
- The skillfulness of the student in reading, writing, listening, and speaking his/her first language
- The similarities and differences in the structure of the student's primary language and English. The structure of Asian languages are very dissimilar from English while there are many structural and cognate similarities between English and most European languages.
- The primary language the family speaks at home and in the community
- The family's level of education
- The family's country of origin and the life experiences of the family in that country of origin
- Learning style of learner
- Quality of instruction

Learning More about Our
English Language Learners

Challenges in the Social Studies Classroom

- Little background knowledge of U.S. history, government, and geography
- Limited skills in determining what is important in text, lectures, and discussions
- Extraordinary amount of content covered in each course

Challenges in the Science Classroom

- A huge vocabulary to be learned, the mastery of which is complicated by the fact that many words are used differently in the scientific context
- Many ELLs have no experience with the inquiry method of learning so making predictions may be totally new to them
- Multi-step directions
- Students come to science classrooms with naive understandings and misconceptions. The Annenberg video clip, A Private Universe, demonstrates that even Harvard graduates have long-held misconceptions about topics like the causes of the seasons and the phases of the moon which are taught at the elementary level. Access the streaming video at www.learner.org/resources/series28.html

Challenges in the Math Classroom

- Possible lack of experience with the standard measuring system (The U.S. is the only country to not use the metric system.)
- May use entirely different algorithms from those customarily used in U.S. classrooms

Challenges in the English Language Arts Classroom

- Idioms and figurative language
- Pronouns and their antecedents
- Word order and sentence structure

Visit the National Clearinghouse for English Language Acquisition website at www.ncela.gwu.edu to access specific strategies to use in secondary math, social studies, and science classrooms.

Students with Learning Disabilities

Students with learning disabilities have average or above average intelligence as measured on currently used measures of intelligence. The legal definition (IDEA) of learning disabilities (LD) is:

- A disorder in one or more of the basic psychological processes involved in understanding or using language.
- May manifest itself in an imperfect ability to: listen, think, speak, read, write, spell, or do math.
- Does not include learning problems that are the result of other disabilities or environmental, cultural, or economic disadvantages.

Receptive (Input) Challenges

These receptive challenges can be caused by issues with auditory perception, visual perception, or both.

- Auditory challenges may include:
  - discrimination between slight differences in sound (such as between Jenny and Ginny or pen and pin).
  - a limited or lack of ability to focus on appropriate auditory input because of distraction by environmental or background noises.
- Visual challenges may include:
  - difficulty discriminating between slight differences in letters (d and b or P and R).
  - rotation or reversal of such letters.
  - tracking lines of print across the page.
  - judging depth and distance, or visual motor problems which make it difficult to catch a ball, play tennis, or line up correctly for a putt on the golf course.

Processing and Memory Challenges

- Copying or writing may be painful or slow.
- Listening and writing at the same time can be a real challenge making note taking next to impossible.
- Math challenges
  - Sequencing
  - May not see patterns
  - Difficulty reading word problems
- Memory challenges can be manifested as problems with auditory memory, visual memory, or both.

Learning More about Our
Students with Learning Disabilities

- Working memory: Remembering in the moment the words in a sentence, the sentences in a paragraph, or the steps in directions. A primary example is a student who is slow or frustrated with copying from the board because she cannot hold in her working memory the letters, numbers, or words long enough to get them onto her paper.
- Short term memory: Storing and retrieving information over a short period of time
- Long term memory: Storing of information or long-term retention and retrieval

Expressive (Output) Challenges

These expressive challenges can manifest as auditory or motor challenges.

- Auditory expressive challenges can take the form of word retrieval issues or problems with organizing thoughts when attempting to answer a question.
- Small motor challenges may lead to problems writing or cutting and gross (large muscle) motor challenges that may cause awkwardness in running or even moving across the room in a straight line.
- Writing problems may include:
  - printed and cursive writing that may be illegible or hard to read.
  - inconsistent spacing between words, mix of print and cursive writing or upper and lower case letters and unfinished or omitted words.

Learning More about Our
Students on the Autism Spectrum

The construct of "spectrum" or "continuum" is used to describe students who are autistic. The severity of the condition ranges from one in which individuals need special care throughout adulthood to the other end of the spectrum where we find students who are best placed in general education classes. That makes describing these learners extremely difficult because of the wide variation in the degree of the symptoms. On the high functioning end of the spectrum students are often identified as having Asperger Syndrome.

We know that each child is different, but in the case of learners on the autism spectrum we must be especially careful to not think of all of them as clones of one another. It is essential that teachers get to know each child well so that they can anticipate what might trigger disruptive behavior. Having said that, behaviors or characteristics that are often associated with students on the autism spectrum include:

- Rigidity of thought and behavior
- Limited imagination or imaginative play
- Limited verbal and non-verbal communication
- Difficulty with social relationships
- Focus on minor details
- Unable to pick up on the emotions of others
- Sometimes unable to understand own thought processes
- Literal interpretations and understanding
- Preference for routines
- Confusion by and avoidance of change
- Poor to relatively strong expressive language

Learning More about
Our Students with Other Exceptionalities

Students Identified as ADHD

ADHD is a medical diagnosis rather than an educational diagnosis. According to the University of West Virginia website: http://eberly.wvu.edu and others, the characteristics displayed by a student with ADHD may include several of the following:

- Fidgets, squirms, is restless
- Has difficulty sitting still
- Is easily distracted
- Has difficulty waiting for his turn
- Blurts out answers
- Has difficulty following instructions
- Is disorganized: Teachers often mistakenly think that these problems with organization and planning are the result of a lack of planning and motivation.
- Has difficulty sustaining attention
- Shifts from one uncompleted task to another
- Has difficulty playing quietly
- Talks excessively
- Interrupts or is rude to others
- Does not appear to listen
- Often loses things necessary for tasks: These students may actually finish an assignment or homework but neglect to turn it in.
- May not ask for help

Students with Behavioral Disorders

- Initiate aggressive behavior and react aggressively toward others
- Display bullying, threatening, or intimidating behavior
- Are physically abusive of others
- Deliberately destruct other's property
- Show little empathy and concern for the feelings, wishes, and well-being of others
- Show callous behavior toward others and lack of feelings of guilt or remorse
- Tend to blame others for their own misdeeds

Our Students with Other Exceptionalities

Students with Oppositional Defiant Disorder (ODD)

These students exhibit an ongoing pattern of uncooperative, defiant, and hostile behavior toward authority figures that seriously interferes with school. Symptoms of ODD may include:

- Frequent temper tantrums
- Excessive arguing with adults
- Often questioning rules
- Active defiance and refusal to comply with adult requests and rules
- Deliberate attempts to annoy or upset people
- Blaming others for mistakes or misbehavior
- Often being touchy or easily annoyed by others
- Frequent anger and resentment
- Mean and hateful talking when upset
- Spiteful attitude and revenge seeking

What
Do You Do
When... ?

Best on the Web

Inclusion in Science Education for Students with Disabilities

www.as.wvu.edu/~scidis

This website, established by the West Virginia Department of Education, contains lengthy lists of suggestions of strategies to use with students with disabilities in science classrooms. Exceptionalities addressed include ADHD, Learning Disabilities, Behavioral Disorders, Intellectual Disorders, Communication Disorders, Motor/Orthopedic, Hearing Impairments, and Visual Impairments. It also links to related sites: Inclusion in Math Education for Students with Disabilities and Equity in Science Education.

National Clearinghouse for English Language Acquisition (NCELA)

www.ncela.gwu.edu

NCELA collects and publishes a broad range of research and resources in support of an inclusive approach to high quality education for ELLs.

Multiple Intelligences Survey

http://surfaquarium.com/MI/inventory.htm

Gifted Education

- Center for Gifted Education at The College of William and Mary: http://cfge.wm.edu
- Neag Center for Gifted Education and Talent Development is a collaborative effort of the University of Connecticut, City University of New York, Stanford University, and The University of Virginia: www.gifted.uconn.edu
- Georgia Department of Education - Gifted Education: www.doe.k12.ga.us/ci_iap_gifted.aspx
- PA Association for Gifted Education: www.penngifted.org

Students with Exceptionalities

Council for Exceptional Children: www.cec.sped.org
LD OnLine: www.ldonline.org

What Do You Do When...

Students Do Not Meet Your Expectations
Or
When Your Students Are:
Divergent in their Learning Profiles and Interests
Gifted and Talented
Struggling
Culturally Diverse
English Language Learners
At Risk
Learners with Special Needs
Or... All of the Above?

This chapter addresses many of the classroom scenarios that we encounter on a regular basis. Always be suspicious of any source that says that if you take this action, then all will be well. There is no one intervention or action that will work all of the time. Given that, the suggestions included here are intended to provide the reader with a multitude of options from which to choose.

We need to be sure that we connect with all students in ways that cause them to see us as trustworthy and invested in their success. We need to, in word and deed, send the messages that:

- We understand that there is no one correct way to process information or be organized. We want to send the message that we believe students can learn to self-assess the effectiveness of their efforts, and then self-adjust accordingly.
- We are comfortable with having students who may know more about the subject than we do and are pleased to not be the smartest person in the room.
- We understand that learning is a journey and that errors and false starts are a natural part of the journey. We do that by providing second chances and by encouraging risk taking and question asking.
- We do not equate not being able to read, write, and speak well with not being able to think and learn.
- We do not equate not speaking English with not being able to think and learn.
- For us, all means all, even if some students do not look or dress like us.
- We believe that we have not taught if students have not learned.

What Do You Do When...
You are committed to the achievement of high standards by all students?

Recognition of the amazing number of differences in learners' needs allows you to plan proactively to provide multiple pathways to learning. Additionally, thinking about alternative approaches and potential problem situations in advance keeps you from being so surprised or frustrated when your enthusiasm and excitement about teaching and learning doesn't transfer to one or more of your students. Rather than being reactive, you can be proactive because you have already thought about your options before the situation occurs.

This chapter focuses on some of the more common life experiences, approaches to learning, and learning challenges students bring into our classrooms as well as on recurring scenarios that are likely to occur in almost every classroom. These challenges include:

- Students learn in many different ways
- Students do not meet expectations
- Students do not participate or answer
- Students do not do their homework
- Students are off task during class
- Students do not demonstrate mastery on an assessment
- Students do not contribute to group work
- Students do not like to work with others
- Students do not get along with others
- Students give up and blame others for their failure
- Students rush through their work and do not seem to learn from feedback
- Students are disorganized
- Students are dealing with anxiety, frustration, or anger
- Students are at risk because of social situations such as poverty
- Students constantly seek attention
- Students have exceptionalities that interfere with their learning
- Students are struggling with reading and writing
- Students have language challenges
- Students have already mastered what is to be learned
- Students constantly seek attention
- Students who have emotional problems
- Students who do not seem motivated
- Students who can't or won't read
- Students who are frequently absent

What Do You Do When You Want to Address
Visual, Auditory, and Tactile Learning?

To Emphasize Visual Learning

- Write directions on the board, as well as giving them verbally. Provide a copy of assignments in written or electronic form on a weekly or daily basis.
- Use flash cards printed in bold colors.
- Supplement lectures with colorful visuals. Also use models, charts, graphs, and other visual aids.
- Allow students to read assignments rather than depend on oral presentations.
- Use and teach students to use graphic organizers.
- Have students take notes on important words, concepts, or ideas.
- Provide a desk copy of board work if student has difficulty copying.

To Emphasize Auditory Learning

- Record assignment directions on tape or in podcasts so that students can replay them as needed.
- Give verbal as well as written directions.
- Tape textbook materials for students to listen to while reading. Tape only the most important information and simplify or explain the vocabulary.
- Give an oral rather than written test or allow tests to be administered by the special education teacher in the resource room.
- If practice is needed, have students tape record or prepare a podcast and then play it back. Students can also practice aloud with other students.
- Substitute oral reports or other written projects for written assignments.

To Emphasize Kinesthetic or Tactile Learning

- Use frequent classroom demonstration and participatory modeling.
- Allow students to build models, draw pictures, make displays or videos, do experiments, or give dramatizations.
- Use role plays and simulations.
- Provide a lecture outline for students and give note-taking instructions.
- Build in movement.
- Use manipulative objects, especially when teaching abstract concepts, such as fractional parts, measurement, and geometry.

What You Do When You Want to Address
Analytical and Global Learning Preferences?

Analytical Thinkers	Global Thinkers
• process through intellectual lens	• process intuitively
• structured/planned	• spontaneous
• control feelings	• let feelings go
• sequential	• creative/responsive
• logical	• more abstract
• remember names	• remember faces
• rational	• more likely to act on emotions
• solve problems by breaking them apart	• solve problems by looking at whole
• time-oriented	• spatially oriented
• auditory/visual learner	• kinesthetic learners
• prefer to write and talk	• prefer to draw and handle objects
• follow spoken directions	• follow written or demonstrated directions
• prefer T/F, multiple choice, matching	• talk to think and learn
• take fewer risks	• "picture" things to think and learn
• look for differences	• prefer essay tests
• think mathematically	• take more risks
• think of one thing at a time	• look for similar qualities
• judge objectively	• think simultaneously
	• judge emotionally

Three Key Points

- Provide learners with opportunities to work in their "comfort zone" and opportunities to stretch their thinking and develop skills at working in ways that are not as natural for them.
- Be aware of which students are comfortable/uncomfortable with the tasks they are doing and help them maximize their efforts.
- We have a tendency to ask students to work and think in ways that are comfortable or productive for us so it requires careful planning to include learning experiences for all learning preferences.

What Do You Do When You Want to Address
The Multiple Intelligences?

The purposeful use of Multiple Intelligences (MI) Theory in the design of assignments we ask students to complete minimizes the need to differentiate instruction. When students spend a significant part of their day working in a comfortable learning environment, they are better able to work at other times during the day in situations that are less comfortable for them.

Use these questions to plan lessons and units:

- How might I have the students process information by reading, writing, speaking, and listening? How might I ensure that students use a balance of these four communication skills?
- How might I teach students to process information and demonstrate learning through the use of numbers, calculations, logic, classifications, and patterns?
- How might I use color, art, and graphs to explain key concepts? How might I have students process information or demonstrate learning through visualization, graphs, color, art, manipulatives, or metaphors?
- How might I have students process information through rhythms, patterns of sound, and mnemonics? How can I incorporate music or environmental sounds to create a mood or make a point?
- How might I have students process information and demonstrate learning through movement and dramatics? What "hands-on" experiences might I include?
- How might I help students learn to use effective collaboration and communication skills in learning and working situations? How might I have students demonstrate and assess their learning and the effectiveness of their efforts in collaborative situations?
- How might I promote reflection and metacognition? How might I include multiple opportunities for goal setting and self-assessment?
- How might I bring the outdoors and nature into the learning environment?

Purposeful Use of Multiple Intelligences Theory

- Puts an emphasis on learning rather than teaching
- Promotes a positive mental model of all students as capable learners
- Calls for wider use of performance assessment
- Promotes an enhanced sense of self-efficacy for learners
- Leads to lessons that promote relevance and enhance real-world connections

Strategies for the Multiple Intelligences

Intrapersonal

How can I evoke personal feelings or memories or give students choices?

- journals/diaries
- personal reactions to topic
- independent projects
- self evaluation
- visualization
- self discovery
- create own classwork schedule and environment
- relate topic to real life
- reflection periods
- goal setting

Bodily/Kinesthetic

How can I involve the whole body or use hands-on experience?

- models
- skits or plays
- puzzles
- scavenger hunts
- dances or movement sequences
- labs
- projects
- manipulatives
- board or floor games
- learning centers
- sports/games
- simulations
- field trips
- role playing
- environmental studies

Naturalist

How might I bring the outdoors and nature into the learning environment?

- scrapbooks, logs, and journals
- collections
- pattern recognition
- similarities and differences
- cultural artifacts
- drawings, pictures, photographs or specimens
- categorizations and data about objects or species found in the natural world
- outdoor lessons

Interpersonal

How can I engage students in peer sharing, cooperative learning, or large group simulations?

- cooperative work
- diverse points of view
- interviews
- peer feedback
- teaching others
- outside resources
- plays and simulations
- field trips
- co-curricular activities
- group projects and presentations

Strategies for the Multiple Intelligences

Verbal/Linguistic

How can I use the spoken or written word?

- letters, poems stories
- oral discussions
- interviews
- creation of story problems
- lectures
- audiotapes
- storytelling
- brainstorming
- journal writing
- mnemonics
- reading, reading, and more reading

Logical/Mathematical

How can I bring in numbers, calculations, logic, classifications, or critical thinking skills?

- lists of facts
- logic problems
- data analysis
- story problems
- puzzles
- experiments
- hypothesizing
- graphic organizers
- classifications
- categories
- timelines
- outlines

Musical/Rhythmic

How can I build in music or environmental sounds, or set key points in a rhythmic or melodic framework?

- musical vocabulary as metaphors
- song titles that explain content
- melodies that capture a mood or concept
- music associated with content or time period
- choral readings
- new lyrics to old song
- mnemonics

Visual/Spatial

How can I use visual aids, visualization, color, art, or metaphor?

- charts, posters, graphs, diagrams
- videotapes
- collages
- use of color and shapes
- demonstration
- map making
- visualization
- picture metaphors
- idea sketching
- graphic symbols
- manipulatives
- illustration
- drawing

Multiple Intelligences Unit Plan template is on CD-ROM.

What Do You Do When You Want to Know Your Students' Learning Preferences and Interests?

You can interview students, use interest inventories, read journal entries, and just listen in and observe to gather data about students' background, interests and best conditions for learning. Knowing students as individuals allows you to give them a voice in how they access, process, and demonstrate learning. Such choice appeals to students' ever changing interests and to their need for independence. When these decisions are entirely teacher-centered and the same for all students, the learning journey is a rocky one and students are deprived of the opportunity to learn to independently select productive learning experiences for themselves.

Massachusetts teachers in our **Meeting the Needs of Diverse Learners** workshops created the learning preferences and interest surveys found on the following pages. Use those surveys as written or a combination of items from several along with your own items to quickly find out important information about your students.

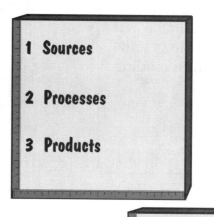

1 Sources

2 Processes

3 Products

As you select or design your own learning styles and interest surveys, consider the Differentiation 3x3 model shown to the right in planning your questions and prompts.

1 Whole-class

2 Small-group

3 Individual

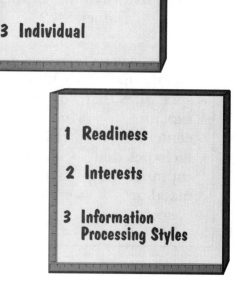

1 Readiness

2 Interests

3 Information Processing Styles

Learning Preferences Survey

Directions

Knowing your learning preferences is helpful to me. Please read each statement and identify the answers that describe how you think you learn best. You can select more than one answer, but please star (*) the best choice for your learning.

1. **When reading in Language Arts or History, do you prefer to...**
   - ☐ Read independently
   - ☐ Read as a whole group
   - ☐ Read with a partner
   - ☐ Be read to by the teacher

2. **What helps you to best process (understand and remember) new information?**
   - ☐ Reading summary notes about the topic
   - ☐ Writing about the topic
   - ☐ Discussing what you learned with others
   - ☐ Drawing your understanding

3. **When you have a unit project do you prefer to...**
   - ☐ Work independently
   - ☐ Work with a partner
   - ☐ Work with a small group

4. **What types of projects or activities do you prefer if you are asked to create a product that showcases your understanding about a topic?**
   - ☐ Models, dioramas, salt maps, etc.
   - ☐ Writing a report or a creative writing piece that demonstrates your understanding
   - ☐ Writing and acting in a play or puppet show
   - ☐ Creating a game
   - ☐ Creating a PowerPoint or Publisher presentation
   - ☐ Creating a tri-fold display or a collage
   - ☐ Teaching others about what you know

Learning Preferences Survey template is on CD-ROM.

High School
Learning Preferences Survey

Check the boxes in the survey that best describe your learning preferences.

- ☐ I am curious about how things work and like to investigate new things.
- ☐ I can react quickly if there is an emergency situation.
- ☐ I do well in math activities.
- ☐ I like word-based humor and puns.
- ☐ I prefer individual sports and games, including swimming, fitness machines and bowling.
- ☐ I like to study about a subject or topic completely, knowing all of the details.
- ☐ I prefer knowing the routine of my day.
- ☐ I enjoy animals and animal care.
- ☐ I like participating in community service and volunteering.
- ☐ I like to do artistic work.
- ☐ I like to investigate new places or activities.
- ☐ I prefer to make decisions based on a set of rules.
- ☐ I prefer team sports and games, including soccer, baseball, or basketball.
- ☐ I prefer days that are not routine and are full of unexpected events.
- ☐ I prefer to make decisions based only on my own experiences.
- ☐ I enjoy listening or singing to music.
- ☐ I enjoy dancing and movement activities.
- ☐ I like most computer activities.
- ☐ I like being in places where there are lots of people and excitement.
- ☐ I like to perform in front of others.

High School Learning Preferences Survey template is on CD-ROM.
Beth Taylor, Newburyport Public Schools, MA

Learning Preferences Survey

Please complete the following survey by identifying the answer that best describes you.

1. **I learn better by (choose as many as apply to you)**
   - ☐ Using my body, hands-on activities
   - ☐ Using numbers, logic, or critical thinking
   - ☐ Using visual aids, color, or art
   - ☐ Relating information to my own self, individual activities
   - ☐ Relating information to music or rhythm
   - ☐ Writing or speaking
   - ☐ Peer sharing or cooperative learning
   - ☐ Relating information to the outdoors or nature

2. **When in class, I prefer to sit**
   - ☐ At a table with other students
   - ☐ At a desk in rows
   - ☐ At a desk in a large circle

3. **I test better**
   - ☐ Orally
   - ☐ Written
   - ☐ Other (name it) _____

4. **I remember information better if I get it by using**
   - ☐ Graphic organizers (ways to take notes using maps or pictures)
   - ☐ Note taking
   - ☐ Reading information and answering questions individually
   - ☐ Reading information and answering questions (discussions) in a small group
   - ☐ Reading information and answering questions (discussions) in a large group

5. Name your favorite class in school._____

6. Name your favorite interest outside of school._____

7. Name one success you have encountered in or out of school._____

8. Name something you have struggled with in or out of school._____

9. Aside from academics, name an interest that is school related._____

10. Name any areas of expertise you might have._____

11. Name a topic related to this class about which you would like to learn more._____

Learning Preferences Survey template is on CD-ROM.

My Spanish Survey

In order to help me prepare my lessons to better suit your style of learning, I would appreciate your thoughtful response to each of the following questions.

1. How long have you been studying Spanish?

2. What are your **three top reasons** for continuing to study Spanish?
   A.

   B.

   C.

3. What type of activities have you **enjoyed the most** in learning Spanish?
   A.

   B.

4. What type of activities have you **enjoyed the least** in learning Spanish?

   A.

   B.

5. How do you **learn new vocabulary**? Do you make lists? Do you make flash cards? Do you repeat out loud? Any other method used?

6. How do you learn conjugations of irregular verbs? Do you repeat in your mind? Do you write them out several times? Do you make flash cards and study from them? Any other method used?

7. Do you understand the teacher when she uses only Spanish in class to communicate? What do you do when you do not understand?

8. Two suggestions that you would like me to implement to help you learn Spanish.

   A.

   B.

My Language Survey template is on CD-ROM.
Beatriz DesLoges, Lexington Public Schools, MA

Interest/Learning Profile Survey

Use the scale 1-5 to rate your interest and talent.
1=not much, 5=a lot

1. I enjoy drawing	1	2	3	4	5
2. I enjoy singing	1	2	3	4	5
3. I enjoy dancing	1	2	3	4	5
4. I enjoy reading	1	2	3	4	5
5. I enjoy math challenges	1	2	3	4	5
6. I enjoy writing stories	1	2	3	4	5
7. I enjoy working with others	1	2	3	4	5
8. I know myself	1	2	3	4	5
9. I write to remember	1	2	3	4	5
10. I use pictures/visuals to remember	1	2	3	4	5
11. I enjoy doing scientific experiments	1	2	3	4	5

Please complete the following statements.

1. When I read I like to read stories about

2. When I have free time I like to

3. One thing I am really good at is

4. One thing I would like to be better at is

5. One thing I do to help me understand something new is

6. One more thing I would like to tell you about myself is

Interest/Learning Profile Survey template is on CD-ROM.
Debbie Ireland, Waltham Public Schools, MA

Literacy Interest Inventory

Interests at School
- Favorite academic subject:
- Favorite special subject:

Other Interests
- Favorite hobbies:
- Sports:
- T.V. show you like:
- Movies:
- Favorite singing groups:
- Songs you like:
- What types of activities do you do after school:
- Do you write or receive letters or e-mail from anyone?_____
  With whom do you correspond? _____
- About how much time do you spend on homework?_____
- Do you study with the radio, television, MP3, or CD playing?_____

Reading Preferences
- Newspapers: Which sections do you read?
- Magazines: Which ones?
- Hobby or craft books?
- Comics: Which ones?
- Novels:
- Other:
- When you read stories or watch movies, which types do you enjoy most - sports, humor, romance, mysteries, adventures, animal stories, nonfiction, science fiction? (Write in your choices and add any others)

_____

_____

_____

Literacy Interest Inventory

- Finish this sentence: I wish there were more books (movies) like:

  _____

  _____

Reading/Study Skills

- Do you learn better if you read silently or out loud?_____
- Do you often have problems just reading the words?_____
- Is it hard for you to understand what you read? _____
- Is it hard for you to remember what you read? _____
- Does your mind wander a lot when you read? _____
- Do you feel that you read too slowly?_____Too quickly?_____
- Do you sometimes skip a line as you read down the page?_____

Miscellaneous

- Do you sometimes/often doodle pictures on your papers while the teacher is teaching?_____
- Would you rather talk instead of listen in class? _____
- What distracts you in class? _____
- Which teacher was your favorite? _____
- Why was that teacher your favorite? _____

  _____
- What would help you do better in school? _____

Literacy Interest Inventory template is on CD-ROM.
Created by a teacher in Louise Thompson's **Meeting the Needs** workshop series.

My Reading and Library Survey

Name:_____ **Date:** _____

Part One
Put a check before the sentences below that describe you:
- ☐ I like to read books.
- ☐ I think I'm a good reader.
- ☐ I read before I go to sleep.
- ☐ My mother or father reads to me before I go to sleep.
- ☐ I enjoy listening to stories read aloud.
- ☐ I like books about real things (nonfiction).
- ☐ I like chapter books.
- ☐ I tell my friends about books I like.
- ☐ I have a library card for the public library.

Part Two
1. What kind of books do you like to choose most when your class comes for book selection? _____

   _____

2. What is your favorite part of the library? _____

3. What kind of books do you think we need more of?_____

   _____

4. Do you know how to look up books on the computer? _____

5. Do you sometimes help your friends look for books?_____

6. What is your all time favorite book and why? _____

   _____

7. What kind of projects do you like to do best in the library?

   _____

8. Do you like to get more books before it's time for your class's weekly book selection time?_____

9. How many books do you think students should be allowed to check out each time?_____

My Reading and Library Survey template is on CD-ROM.
Alice Pedersen, Waltham Public Schools, MA

Students Do Not Meet Expectations?

Don't

- Focus on finding fault. Instead, catch students being right.

- Use rewards for good behavior. Students begin to work for the reward rather than because the work is interesting or the behavior is the right thing to do.

- Ask students to make promises. They often promise anything to get us off their backs.

- Nag, scold, and threaten. These may lead to immediate compliance, but there is high potential for resentment and frustration.

- Chastise in public. Names on the board is not acceptable practice.

- Blame the parents. We do not teach the parents. We have the next generation of parents in our classes today. If we miss the chance to influence difficult students, they may become even greater problems in our society later, as parents and citizens.

- Be overly concerned about your own authority base. Real authority comes from knowing what you are talking about and modeling respectful behavior.

- Use double standards. The same standards should apply for students and teachers.

Do

- Identify causes of inattentive or disruptive behavior and match your response to the perceived cause.

- Clearly communicate your expectations for work and behavior. Focus on future behavior rather than on past behavior.

- Establish a relationship based on trust and mutual respect with each child.

- Wait to hold discussions about inattentive or disruptive behavior, or unmet expectations, until both of you are calm.

- Use logical consequences directly related to the behavior. Logical consequences are designed to get students back to work.

> Some teachers tend to focus on what is happening rather than on what is being learned. They may wish simply to stop the incident rather than consider which of many possible interventions is most likely to stimulate long-term development and learning.
>
> Lilian Katz

What Do You Do When...
Students Do Not Meet Expectations?

Do

- Teach that fairness has to do with equity rather than equality. That is, you get what you need when you need it rather than everyone getting the same thing at the same time.

- Distinguish between the behavior and the person exhibiting the behavior. Build self-efficacy by focusing on what effort is needed.

- Admit your own mistakes.

- Work for responsibility, motivation, and respect...not obedience, compliance, and fear.

- Remember that responsibility is taught by giving responsibility. Include students in developing procedures for handling inappropriate behavior or unmet expectations.

When the Going Gets Rough

- Stay calm, move slowly, get close, be quiet, and relax.

- Make eye contact.

- If you must talk, lower your voice rather than raising it.

- Try to keep the situation in perspective. Don't overreact and escalate minor incidents into major confrontations.

- Avoid public confrontation. An audience for a confrontation escalates any differences.

- Avoid threats you can't or don't want to carry out.

- Keep both feet on the ground emotionally! It is easy to get knocked over if you try to balance on one foot!

> Responsibility, motivation, and respect are not the same as obedience, compliance, and fear.
>
> Alfie Kohn

Students Do Not Meet Expectations?

Stop the Stoplight!

Do not even think about putting student's names on the board! Do not consider placing student's names on red construction paper hearts and moving them in and out of an outline of your heart! Save stoplights for traffic control in the streets! Lee Canter, author of **Assertive Discipline**, stated over twenty years ago that he was mistaken when he had in the past advocated such practice. Just imagine how we would feel if the principal or workshop leader wrote our names on the board when we arrived late, forgot our materials, had a side conversation, or some other infraction. If that response would make us feel bad, it has to be true for children as well. Yes, we should communicate clear expectations and have attitude adjustment chats with students, but we should have them privately. Nagging and public humiliation does not work in international relations and it does not work in the classroom. We want to provide students growth-producing feedback on both academic and behavioral issues and then provide scaffolding so that they can be successful.

Stop the Pop Quizzes!

We should not use assessment as a management tool. The purpose of assessment is to help the students and teacher know what is being learned and to provide feedback on the effectiveness of the instructional program.

Design a Strong Instructional Program!

Rather than focusing time and energy developing and implementing an elaborate control and compliance system, spend your time and energy on designing a strong instructional program. Humans, young and old, tend to act out when they are frustrated or bored. Given clear and realistic expectations along with engaging and relevant learning exercises, learners will almost always join in the learning process with enthusiasm.

So, what do you do when clearly communicated and realistic expectations are not met? See pages 77-78 for alternatives to public humiliation and the gotcha' game of pop quizzes.

The best management program is a strong instructional program!

What I Did When...
Students Did Not Meet Expectations

We had been having trouble getting organized in the morning. The children come into the classroom at 8:20; the bell rings at 8:30. A couple of mornings a week we have a special class at 8:35 or 8:45. We weren't ready to go. I was feeling frazzled. The kids weren't responding by moving more quickly. The end of the day was the same. They got very chatty as we began preparing for departure. Kids were missing things I wanted them to take home.

When the children came back from art (the 8:35 class for which we were late), I said "I have a problem that I'm trying to work out in my head. I'm just not enjoying the beginning and the end of the day. It's like having a great sandwich and the bread keeps falling off. The pieces of bread that hold our day together are the beginning and the end." Then I talked through the possibilities that maybe I was expecting them to do too much before art, maybe we need to do some of these things after art, maybe we should have no talking until everybody's settled in, maybe at the end of the day I need to allow more time...

I asked them if they had ever heard of Dear Abby. Most had. I said I thought I needed to write a Dear Abby letter. I wrote "Dear Abby" on chart paper, stated my problem, and signed it "Frustrated Teacher." Then I asked them if they'd please be Abby and write back. Every child did. Then I had them meet in groups of four to share their solutions and make a list of what the group thought were the best choices. One person recorded for the group. We then came back together, shared the ideas and wrote them on chart paper with no comment until all were recorded. After all the solutions were shared, we discussed them. Eventually we agreed on the ones we would try.

Both the group sharing process and the solutions were impressive! They suggested that we should have the people with "Morning Jobs" come in five minutes early to get their backpacks and other materials put away, get their desks organized, and get set up for their jobs. It's made all the difference in the world and I didn't think of it!

Kay Nelson, West Irondequoit Central School District, Rochester, NY

What Do You Do When...
Students Do Not Participate?

It is unacceptable for students not to participate, so we need a multitude of strategies for helping them become active members of the learning community. The better we can identify the cause for the lack of participation, the better we can select our intervention. No one of these options is guaranteed to work all the time, but teacher commitment to having all students participate is the first step.

- Use wait time. That is three to five seconds, not three minutes!
- Give choices. "Is it A or B?"
- Ask opinion questions. "If you had to decide which action to take, what would you do/recommend?"
- Repeat question using simpler language.
- Use positive non-verbal encouragement such as nods, smiles, eye contact.
- Have students call on another student by naming that student and repeating the question for that student.
- Use limited number of "I Pass On This One" cards.
- Use slates or signal cards as a means of non-verbal responses.
- Have students work in pairs and report their partner's answer.
- Listen in during small group discussions/work to see if the student is responding/participating in that setting. If so, either you or a student in the group can paraphrase what the student said.
- Interact with the student during small group discussions.
- Conventional wisdom is that questions should be "beamed" to the entire class. With students who tend not to participate, call the name before asking the question as in, "Jose, how did...?" To hold the rest of the class accountable, you can call on another student with a follow-up question such as, "Maria, what variable did he have to analyze to...?"
- Hold private conferences for building relationships, identifying causes of lack of participation, and pinpointing areas of interest or concern of student.
- Following private personal interaction, meet the student at the door and privately use one of the following statements as appropriate to the situation:

  a. "Here is the answer to #10. I'll call on you to answer it."

  b. "We're going to review Exercise 2B and I am going to ask you to answer #5. Be ready."

  c. "We're going to be doing exercise 2B. Look through it and signal me which one you'll be ready to answer."

What Do You Do When...
Students Do Not Complete/Turn in Homework?

First, do a check on the kind of homework you are assigning and then a check on who is doing what homework with what degree of success.

A review of Lee and Pruitt's homework classification system makes it clear that most of the homework we assign falls in the practice and preparation categories. Common sense and our own experiences as learners tell us that extension and creative homework assignments are much more likely to engage students in the learning and minimize the ever-present problems of incomplete or copied homework.

Practice homework helps students master skills and reinforce in-class learning; it can be boring and repetitive. Unless we differentiate homework assignments, it is guaranteed that some students are wasting time practicing something they have already mastered and that some are trying to practice something they have not yet learned. Practice homework should be given only when it is clear that the learner can work with the skill independently. Avoid repetitiveness of practice homework by giving students the five most difficult problems to do. If they can successfully complete those, they do not need to do the easier problems. Better yet, let students identify the practice exercises they need to do; both teacher and student track the effectiveness of that practice and adjust as necessary. Examples are:
- most questions at the end of chapters
- vocabulary drill
- memorization of facts
- calculations

Preparation homework prepares students for the upcoming lesson or unit. Reading a chapter on material to be covered in class is not good preparation homework. Reading research clearly indicates that comprehension is low if the students have no prior experiences with and/or discussions about the topic. The reading of chapters is best assigned following class work.

Extension homework helps students take what they learn and connect it with real life. This type of homework often gives students the option to choose their method of gathering data, processing learning, and demonstrating learning. Examples are:
- RAFT assignments: See page 205.
- higher levels of Bloom's Taxonomy: See page 201.
- Williams' Taxonomy assignments: See page 97.
- daily journal writing from thought-provoking stems: See page 248.
- interactive notebooks: See page 193.
- real-world applications of the knowledge and skills: See pages 205-206.

Creative homework helps students integrate multiple concepts (possibly from more than one curricular area); often presented in the form of long-term projects. Students should be asked to react to rather than report on what they are learning. This promotes development of critical thinking and problem-solving skills. Projects, especially those involving student choice and interdisciplinary links, and performance assessment tasks are examples of creative homework.

When Many Students Are Not Doing Homework

- Check for unplanned or irrelevant homework. Perhaps there is a homework policy and you feel compelled to assign something even when it isn't appropriate.
- Be sure that assignments are not given at the very end of class with no time for clarifying purposes or explanations of confusing directions.
- Consider whether the assignments may seem like busy work to students and/or parents because they are not moving students closer to competency with the standard on which they are working. They may already know how to do what they are being asked to do, this type of activity has not been productive in the past, or it is overly repetitive.
- Ensure that the assignments do not call for knowledge and skills not currently in the students' repertoire and there is, therefore, little chance for success.
- Have students complete a limited number of questions/problems. Then have them create several problems or questions using the same content or skills.

When Students Are Doing Homework But Not Turning It In

After you have determined that the dog really did not eat it, try to identify where the problem is occurring. Check to see if the breakdown is because it was left at home or on the bus, lost in the bottom of the book bag, or stuffed in some forgotten place. In such cases, lack of organization skills rather than skill or willingness to do the work could be the issue.

Resources

There are miniature templates for two tools on the next page. The first, **Homework Planning Sheet** provides teachers with a format to use in planning homework across the four categories. The second, **Incomplete Assignment Log**, is a document students submit when homework is not completed. The latter is placed by the student in his notebook until the assignment is completed or mastery of the identified outcomes has been accomplished in another way.

Homework Tools

Homework Planning Sheet

As you plan a unit of study, use the homework categories below to thoughtfully design homework that will help your students move toward mastery of the standards on which the unit is based and will also give you good formative assessment data.

📖 Practice

💻 Preparation

☎ Extension

🖼 Creative

What language could you use to communicate the homework assignments in a way that students know what to do, know why they are doing it, and know when they are successful?

Incomplete Assignment Log

Title of Assignment:

Name:

Date:

Period:

I did not complete this assignment because:

My plan for meeting the requirement is:

Homework Planning Sheet and Incomplete Assignment Log templates are on CD-ROM.

Students Give Up and Blame Others?

Failure Syndrome Students

According to Jere Brophy, there are Failure Syndrome Students who exhibit what psychologists call learning helplessness. They approach school work with little belief that they can be successful and give up at the slightest sign of difficulty. They are so sure that they will not be successful that they spend their time and energy preserving their own sense of self-esteem and appearing to not care about school success. Brophy says that attribution retraining, efficacy training, and strategy training are three approaches we can use to move these students forward on the learning journey.

Attribution Retraining

See the next page for an overview of **Attribution Theory** and some basic guidelines on how to help students move from making external attributions to believing that they have control over their own destiny.

Efficacy Training

Jeff Howard's efficacy training is based on the slogan that "Smart is not something you are. Smart is something you get." The efficacy paradigm is that confidence leads to effort which leads to development.

Strategy Training

The purpose of strategy training is to equip students to not only be successful in school but in life as well. Students might be taught:
- Problem identification and solving skills
- Self-assessment and self-adjustment based on error analysis
- Knowing how they learn best
- Reflection on and analysis of what learning strategies worked when and why
- Reading strategies used by successful readers
- Social skills for small group work and personal interactions

> A lack of motivation and a dislike of school as well as truancy and dropping out are often associated with the slow learner. These are not innate behaviors, but a defense against repeated failure and the constant pressure to keep pace. Despite the odds, many slow learners are persistent and motivated, and they may eventually succeed in school with substantial support.
>
> Kimberly Kaznowski

What Do You Do When...
Students Give Up and Blame Others?

Development of the intrapersonal intelligence causes one to examine the effectiveness of one's effort. Teaching students to assess what works and what doesn't work for them in the learning process may be the most important thing we teach them. Younger children believe ability and hard work combine to promote success. As students get closer to adolescence, they tend to believe that those who succeed are smart or are just plain lucky. One thing they "know for sure" is they do not want to be caught trying, because if they fail, everyone will know they are dumb! This perception is a reality for them that greatly impacts their willingness to expend effort. **Attribution retraining** can make a huge difference in the lives of our students.

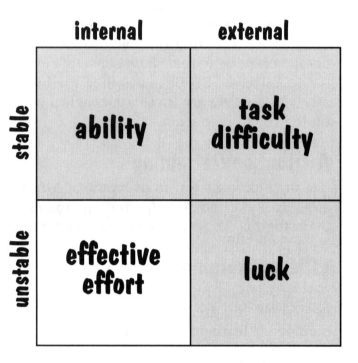

Attribution Theory

	internal	external
stable	ability	task difficulty
unstable	effective effort	luck

Weiner, 1970

A learning environment where students learn how to learn includes opportunities for students to reflect on their efforts and to learn from their errors. Successful adults know that it is the effectiveness and efficiency of effort that determines how well we reach the goals we set for ourselves. Our tendency is to tell students this "fact of life" rather than systematically teaching them through our modeling and by insisting that they analyze their own work.

The single most effective way to respond to students who say the task was too hard, or they were unlucky, or that they are just too dumb is to say, "Given that you believe/think/feel that, what might you do about it?" The least effective response is to try to confuse them with logic by pointing out how unclearly they are thinking; they will not buy it. Allow them to see the world as they see it and create conditions that cause them to consider how they might do something to improve the results in the future. For example, catch them being right and point out that effort must have played a part, mention that you work hard to prepare interesting and challenging lessons, and include recognition of effective effort in your verbal and written praise.

What We Did When...
Students Were Off Task

Because many of the students in our co-taught English class are receiving special education services, there is a wide variety of learning differences. We are finding that even with two teachers in the room, we are sometimes outnumbered by the growing demands of student needs. I sometimes leave class feeling unsatisfied because we were not able to get through the planned lesson. I found myself being interrupted by the need for constant verbal or physical cueing to the many students who consistently fall off task.

I came up with a strategy that has turned into a very successful tool. Instead of interrupting the speaker or myself to cue a student, I have started "passing notes." I often walk around the room as I am teaching anyway, but now I walk around the room discreetly putting post-it notes on kids' desks. I was able to find a stack of gray colored post-it notes that are not very obvious so as not to embarrass a student. As I am teaching, or talking, or walking, I can write "Please take your book out" or "We're on page 15" and the point is well taken. I have also been making an effort to put some positive comments down as well.

I have noticed that the students respond to this type of cueing much better. They do not have to be singled out or reprimanded verbally, but can still recognize the urgency or tone through the note. Also, for kids with ADD, the note is a constant reminder on their desks to keep focused. Some kids do not want to be singled out even when they are doing something positive. By discreetly showing them that you are noticing their behavior, kids seem to respond more positively. I am very pleased with the way this has been working out so far and wish to continue and share this with other teachers who feel their lessons are constantly being disrupted.

Suzanne Kisielica, New Trier Township High School District 203, IL

What I Did When...
Students Returned from Absences

Did you do anything while I was gone? This question makes me crazy!

One of my biggest frustrations has always been how to deal with students returning from absences. I have tried "Study Buddies," but have not felt that they were particularly successful. I have tried writing out what we did, but that proved to be too time-consuming. A colleague mentioned the idea of having a student take notes on what goes on during the class period, placing these notes in a notebook, and then when the absent students return, they can go directly to the notebook and read what they have missed. I thought it was worth a try. I developed a one- page form which is filled out by two students in each class. My reason for having two students do it is to assure that all the information has been noted on the sheets.

I have been very pleased with how this has worked, so pleased that I wonder why it took me 20 years to figure out how to do this. The sheets are kept in a folder in the back of the room. Students are pretty well schooled by now to know that if it is their day to be the scribe, they must pick up a sheet, fill it out, and place it in the notebook. I quickly read over their notes, making any corrections or additions, which I seldom have had to do, and place any handouts in the notebook. Students also know that they need to look in the notebook if they have been absent. Only if I forget to put the handouts in the notebook, or if they are really confused, do I need to take time to talk to them when they first return.

In addition to really reducing the stress on me of keeping absentees informed, this system has proven to be a valuable piece of feedback for me. By that I mean, when I read over the scribe sheets, I can tell if the students have "gotten" from that day's lessons what I had intended that they should get. It has also increased the attentiveness of at least two students in each class each day and provided practice in note taking for those students. It has also placed the responsibility of finding out what work was missed directly on those who have been absent.

Gail Rainey, St. Vrain Valley School District, CO

Daily Log for _____

Name of Class

Name of Scribe

Standards and Essential Understandings

Summary of Activities (include page references and handouts)

Papers Collected

Work Assigned   **Due Dates**

Questions Asked/Discussed

Reminders Given

Other Important Information

Daily Log template is on CD-ROM.

What Do You Do When...
Students Do Not Demonstrate Mastery?

It is important to remember that the emphasis should be on learning and not just grading. When students have been unsuccessful in demonstrating their mastery of content it is vital that we take the time to analyze the assessment results and to determine the next steps. We should routinely make data-driven decisions by asking ourselves:

- Which students need additional support?
- Which students require some tutoring, re-teaching, or one-on-one assistance?
- Which students need an additional opportunity to reach mastery on the current content?

After the Assessment

- Allow students to re-take assessments to correct errors or mistakes. Students often miss questions because they read them too quickly or make careless errors.
- Make it a regular practice to give students multiple opportunities on assessments to reach mastery level learning (e.g., 80% or above).
- Break down the skills or content on the assessment to determine where misunderstanding occurred after an assessment and use the data to provide follow-up support.
- Change roles. Ask the student to teach the content to you (in his or her own words) to determine where the breakdown in comprehension occurred.
- Make a copy of the student's test. Have the student make corrections in a different color (for emphasis). Review the student's work and give the student credit for the corrected work.
- Return the assessment to the student. Have the student re-write missed questions in his or her own words, then answer the questions, and resubmit the test for credit.
- Complete an error analysis after the students finish an assessment to ensure that questions were clearly stated.
- Re-teach the incorrect or misunderstood content to students in one-on-one sessions and allow re-testing.
- Reflect on the unit just completed in order to determine what worked well and what may need revision in instructional delivery in upcoming unit(s).
- Have students write out their improvement plans in preparation for future units for both in-class behaviors as well as ways to improve study habits. (Written plans are more likely to be followed than simply "thinking" about how to improve.)
- Build on mistakes or answers that are partially correct instead of emphasizing what the student(s) did wrong.

What Do You Do When...
Students Do Not Demonstrate Mastery?

Before the Next Assessment

- Provide extra help to selected students during available times such as before school, during lunch, or after school.
- End instruction 10-15 minutes early. Allow students who understand the lesson to do extension work and then you can work individually or in small groups with students who are struggling.
- Offer materials at lower skill levels to match a student's beginning point. As the student makes progress, increase the level of the instructional materials.
- Have students establish specific learning/improvement goals prior to the next unit of study.
- Give students the opportunity to choose a different way to show what they have learned.
- Use formative assessment data to make instructional decisions so that you are able to clarify content and correct misunderstandings prior to administering the assessment.
- Pre-assess student knowledge and skills prior to teaching a unit to determine which students may be lacking in basic skills or have gaps in their prior knowledge.
- Check for student understanding on a regular basis during instruction using a variety of approaches (e.g., direct questions, white boards, summarizing techniques, etc.). Use the data from these checks to determine which students can work on enrichment while you provide more direct instruction for students who may need additional time to learn.
- Encourage students to self-assess their comprehension of the content as new learning is presented.
- Tell students with specificity how to use their time to study for or prepare for the upcoming assessment.
- Vary the types of assessments that are administered to students (e.g., short answer, essay, performance tasks, etc.) in order to give students a variety of ways to show what they have learned.
- Provide specific and detailed feedback about what each student is doing right rather than what they are doing wrong.
- Establish peer tutoring sessions prior to testing to help students prepare for the upcoming test.
- Build student confidence by pointing out where they have shown growth in specific skills and knowledge.

Adapted from the May 2009 *Just for the ASKing!* by Bruce Oliver ©Just ASK Publications. All rights reserved.

Adapted from the May 2009 *Just for the ASKing!* by Bruce Oliver ©Just ASK Publications. All rights reserved.

Adapted from the May 2009 *Just for the ASKing!* by Bruce Oliver ©Just ASK Publications. All rights reserved.

Meeting the Needs of Diverse Learners

How is teaching advanced and struggling learners alike and different? In reality, all our students are more alike than they are different. While the strategies and pacing we use may vary, the same principles of respect and instruction apply to both. Compare and contrast your instructional approach with these learners.

Teaching Advanced Learners

Do you...

1. Discover and acknowledge what they already know?

2. Provide a balance of skill-building and meaning-making activities?

3. Plan and guide them in planning projects that capitalize on their interests?

4. Allow them some flexibility in the way they use their time?

5. Allow them to learn at a different pace than their peers?

6. Plan a variety of relevant learning experiences; both teacher and students monitor the effectiveness?

7. Help them to be aware of and use productive learning strategies?

8. Teach them to be self-sufficient; only do for them as much as you need to do?

9. Encourage them to demonstrate mastery in a wide variety of ways?

Teaching Struggling Learners

Do you...

1. Discover and acknowledge what they already know?

2. Provide a balance of skill-building and meaning-making activities?

3. Plan and guide them in planning projects that capitalize on their interests?

4. Allow them some flexibility in the way they use their time?

5. Allow them to learn at a different pace than their peers?

6. Plan a variety of relevant learning experiences; both teacher and students monitor the effectiveness?

7. Help them to be aware of and use productive learning strategies?

8. Teach them to be self-sufficient; only do for them as much as you need to do?

9. Encourage them to demonstrate mastery in a wide variety of ways?

III

What Do You Do When...
Learners Are Gifted and Talented?

Students who are gifted and talented or students who already know what they are supposed to learn could provide a real challenge for classroom teachers. There is a natural tendency to give them more work to do which they, quite correctly, see as patently unfair. There are many ways to plan learning experiences for these learners, ensure that their school experiences are rich and engaging, and still have time to have a life. The reality is that many times they are more than able to help you figure out what they might do next. (N.B. This grandmother/author is delighted to know that her gifted grandchildren know far more about Panama, Fantasy Football, rock climbing, Peru, crafting, computers, and our national park system than she does.) As you work with these students to plan their learning experiences, consider the following suggestions.

- Use task analysis and pre-assessment to determine mastery of the regular curriculum.
- Based on the indicated mastery, compact the curriculum and design learning experiences that allow these students to explore the content in depth or engage in study of related content of interest to them. See page 152.
- Use flexible grouping so that they are frequently allowed to work together.
- Base and teach students to base their study on essential understandings, big ideas, and key concepts, and then develop essential questions to investigate.
- Use an inductive rather than deductive approach. See Bruner's Concept Attainment Model on page 145 and Taba's Inductive Thinking Model on page 173.
- Use analogies and teach students to use analogies and metaphorical thinking. See pages 132-133.
- Set up and help students set up situations where they can explore information and ideas from multiple perspectives, investigate alternative ways of completing tasks, and solve problems.
- Do not require gifted/accelerated students to do more work; ask them to do different work that keeps them engaged and moving forward in their learning.
- Structure the learning environment so that students are required to use multiple kinds of thinking and analyze their thinking as to its effectiveness and transferability to other situations.
- Purposefully set up situations where learners are challenged and need to develop skills at working through challenges without undue frustration.
- Set up opportunities for the use of research skills used by professionals, both traditional and 21st century.
- Focus their work on real-world applications.
- Eliminate or at least reduce the amount of direct instruction, lecture, worksheets, drill, and practice.
- Create opportunities for students to present their learning and products to real audiences.

What Do You Do When...
Learners Are Gifted and Talented?

- Give students the opportunity to engage in independent study. See page 172.
- Teach students to establish criteria by which their independent study projects will be assessed and to use that criteria to evaluate their own and each other's work.
- Provide students a list of alternative responses to their reading and let them select formats that match their interests. See pages 296-300.
- Have students focus on Tier Three vocabulary words and have students identify their own vocabulary lists. See pages 264 and 267.
- Focus math instruction on themes such as architecture, astronomy, and statistics so that the learning is focused on concepts, problem solving, and application of mathematics in real-world concrete situations.

Renzulli's Triad Enrichment Model

The triad enrichment model includes three types of learning experiences.

- Exploratory opportunities that allow students to investigate a variety of interests and then select a topic, issue, or problem to study in depth. Karen Sterbling, GT Specialist in Fairfax County Public Schools, Virginia, issues her elementary students a **Learner's License** that gives them permission to be in charge of their own learning and investigate topics of interest to them. Kelly, upon the receipt of her license, first decided to investigate how every product we use comes from the earth's natural resources. Upon reflection, and with guidance, she decided to narrow her study to an investigation of how soccer balls are made.
- Learning experiences during which students develop skills and thinking processes needed to investigate their selected research topics. In the above mentioned program, students are explicitly taught Bloom's Taxonomy.
- Investigative activities in which students explore their topic or solve their problem through individual or small group work. Students then develop an end product that reflects their learning. Kelly's research into how soccer balls are made led her to a sophisticated discovery.

How Soccer Balls Are Made

A soccer ball is made to kick fast and straight. Soccer balls are usually made in China, India, or Pakistan. Soccer balls are synthetic materials. Synthetic materials are made from oil. A lot of soccer balls we use are made from kids that are forced to make them. Some Indian kids instead of going to school or playing are payed 5 cents an hour to sew the balls including the ones that say "Child-labor free." See http://laborrights.org/stop-child-labor.

Kelly Rutherford, 3rd Grade

Good for All But Especially for Gifted and Accelerated Students
Rigor and Relevance Framework

The International Center for Leadership in Education created the Rigor/Relevance Framework for use in designing tasks, projects, and assessments that go far beyond what we usually ask of our students. In this framework, Willard Daggett and his colleagues at the Center have combined Bloom's Taxonomy with an Application Model. When we design tasks that ask students to apply knowledge to real-world, unpredictable situations as required in Quadrant D, we are providing them the opportunity to develop the skills that the Partnership for 21st Century Skills has identified as essential for the future.

Access a PowerPoint presentation on the Rigor/Relevance Framework at: leadered.com/PP/Rigorrelevance.ppt

Learn about the skills identified by the Partnership for 21st Century Skills at www.p21.org/documents/P21_Framework.pdf or www.p21.org/documents/P21_Framework_Definitions.pdf

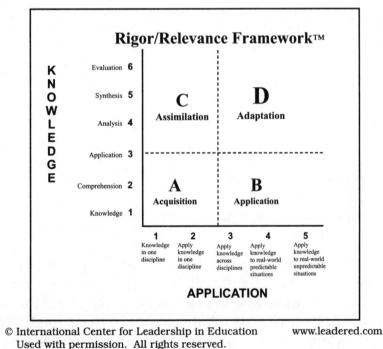

© International Center for Leadership in Education   www.leadered.com
Used with permission. All rights reserved.

The Application Model moves from knowledge in one discipline, to application of knowledge in one discipline, to application of knowledge across disciplines, to application of knowledge in real-world predictable situations, and ultimately to application of knowledge in real-world unpredictable situations.

Good for All But Especially for Gifted and Accelerated Students
Habits of Mind (Costa and Kallick)

According to Costa and Kallick, "A Habit of Mind is knowing how to behave intelligently when you don't know the answer. A Habit of Mind means having a disposition toward behaving intelligently when confronted with problems, the answers to which are not immediately known: dichotomies, dilemmas, enigmas, and uncertainties."

They go on to say that the "focus is on performance under challenging conditions that demand strategic reasoning, insightfulness, perseverance, creativity, and craftsmanship. The critical attribute of intelligent human beings is not only having information, but also knowing how to act on it. Employing Habits of Mind requires drawing forth patterns of intellectual behavior that produce powerful results. They are a composite of many skills, attitudes and proclivities."

The 16 Habits of Mind identified by Costa and Kallick are:
- Persisting
- Thinking and communicating with clarity and precision
- Managing impulsivity
- Gathering data through all senses
- Listening with understanding and empathy
- Creating, imagining, innovating
- Thinking flexibly
- Responding with wonderment and awe
- Thinking about thinking (metacognition)
- Taking responsible risks
- Striving for accuracy
- Finding humor
- Questioning and posing problems
- Thinking interdependently
- Applying past knowledge to new situations
- Remaining open to continuous learning

To help students develop an understanding of what these habits look and sound like you might have them create Graffiti charts or poster-size T-Charts for selected habits over time. The task would be to have students represent what one would be doing or would see and hear if a given habit was well-developed. These charts could then be used as rubric-like tools for peer and self-assessment.

Learn more about Habits of Mind at
- www.habits-of-mind.net, www.habitsofmind.org
- www.mindfulbydesign.com
- www.artcostacentre.com/html/habits.htm

Good for All But Especially for Gifted and Accelerated Students
Williams' Taxonomy
of Creative Thinking

Williams' Taxonomy provides a framework for designing or having students design learning experiences that are well matched to the learning needs of gifted, talented, and accelerated learners.

Fluency
is a thinking skill that allows a learner to generate many ideas.

Flexibility
is a thinking skill that allows the learner to adapt everyday objects to fit a variety of categories by taking detours and varying size, shape, quantities, time limits, etc.

Originality
is a thinking skill that allows the learner to seek a unique or twist by suggesting unexpected changes.

Elaboration
is a thinking skill that allows the learner to expand, add on, enlarge, enrich, or embellish a list of ideas in order to build on previous thoughts.

Risk Taking
is a state of mind and skill that allows the learner to explore the unknown by taking chances, experimenting with new ideas, or trying new challenges.

Complexity
is a competency or skill that allows the learner to be "multi-tasked," to deal with intricacies, competing priorities or events, and to create structure in an unstructured setting or bring logical order to chaos.

Curiosity
is a way of thinking that allows the learner to follow a hunch, to inquire, question alternatives, ponder outcomes, and wonder about options.

Imagination
is the capacity to fantasize possibilities, build images in one's mind, picture new objects, or reach beyond the limits of the practical.

Williams Taxonomy Planning template is on CD-ROM.

What Do You Do When...
Students Are Culturally Diverse

The Bottom Lines

- Learn which name each student wants to be called and learn how to pronounce those names correctly.
- Monitor use of student names in examples to ensure that each student hears her name in a positive way on a regular basis.
- No matter what the content area, use examples and stories that reflect positively on multiple cultural, social, economic, and ethnic perspectives.
- Let students know when you are expressing an opinion rather than an established fact or principle by saying, "From my perspective," or "Based on what I think I know." Ask them for their perspectives.
- Let the students get to know you as an individual.
- Hold and act on high expectations for all students by providing appropriate scaffolding and extensions.

Students in our classrooms have their own life experiences and these experiences may not match the life experiences students are generally assumed to have had. Textbook publishers are working to minimize that problem, but it is inevitable that gaps in background knowledge and experience will occur. Teacher-selected stories and examples must also be monitored for such assumptions.

Do not assume that because students speak the same language, live in the same conditions, or are from the same racial or ethnic group that they share the same life experiences, beliefs, or values. It certainly is not true of students for whom English is their first language and the same holds true across all people.

Use a wide range of racial, ethnic, cultural and language perspectives when
- Selecting examples and stories
- Using names in positive examples
- Describing historical, social, and political events

What Do You Do When...
Learners Are Struggling?

All learners have unique learning profiles, but some learners have greater needs than others. Our goal is to have as many students as possible participate in regular classroom instruction. The **Response to Intervention (RtI)** model is a strength-based rather than a deficit-based model that requires that we try multiple interventions to help students be successful in a general education setting. One important tenet of this model is that when students are provided appropriate scaffolding they should be able to achieve in our classrooms; only a few should need special education placement.

When we are committed to educating all students in the least restrictive environment, we have to identify the ways in which the learning problem is manifesting itself and then have a repertoire of strategies to consider in planning our interventions and teaching approach with that student. The list below provides an extensive array of interventions to consider.

If Reading Is an Issue
- Use paired reading or **Think-Pair-Share** to allow students who have difficulty decoding words the opportunity to work with a partner. See page 202.
- Provide a variety of books at different reading levels for students to select and read independently.
- Use books on tape, when available, or engage parent volunteers to read with students.
- Provide books at the student's instructional level with pictures and/or diagrams to aid in comprehension of the text.
- Teach students to use supports built into most textbooks:
  - Headings, sub-headings, and captions
  - Increased font size, bolded text, and italicized words
  - Pictures, maps, charts, graphs, and other visuals
- Use peer tutoring.
- Ask students to quietly read aloud.
- Teach self-questioning.
- Paraphrase and summarize key points and have students do the same.
- Use and teach students to use graphic organizers.
- Sequence key points as a reading guide for students.
- Identify main ideas, especially if they are not stated in the first sentence of the paragraph.
- Identify 5 Ws: who, what, when, where, and why.
- Encourage highlighting of text passages, key words, or concepts. Use inexpensive transparencies to lay over the page so text is not permanently marked up.

What Do You Do When...
Learners Are Struggling?

- Use removable sticker dots to highlight main ideas, key vocabulary words, or other points of interest.
- Use and teach students to use mental imagery.
- Place wide Wite-Out® tape in the margin for students' notes "in the text."
- Use pre-reading and post-reading activities such as **Anticipation/Reaction Guides** and **Three-Column Charts** to pre-teach or reinforce main ideas. See pages 165 and 261.
- Explain idioms that appear in reading passages.
- Teach text structure, the signal words for each structure, and the graphic organizer to use with each text structure.
- Use **Reciprocal Teaching**. See page 259.
- Scaffold text by
  - Highlighting key points or vocabulary words with highlighter or erasable crayon.
  - Using removable sticker dots to highlight main ideas, key vocabulary words, or other points of interest.
  - Making a copy of the text pages and highlighting key vocabulary words
  - Covering margin with wide Wite-Out® tape and writing focus questions or key vocabulary words in the taped margin.
  - Creating a study guide for the text.

If Writing Is an Issue

- Provide computers or Alpha Smart word processors for students who have difficulty with paper and pencil tasks.
- Provide a tape recorder so students can first dictate and record information, then listen to the recorded information, and write it at their own pace.
- Supply students with models and checklists for revisions and editing when given a writing assignment.
- Engage parent volunteers to act as scribes for youngsters with fine motor problems that significantly affect writing output.
- Use oral quizzes or tests in place of written examination.
- Have students dictate ideas to peers.
- Require lists instead of sentences.
- Use sticky notes for organization.
- Provide note takers.
- Provide students with frequent writing conferences and assistance opportunities with teachers, peers, and parents.
- Provide students computer time for composing and/or assistance by scripting their writing.

What Do You Do When...
Learners Are Struggling?

If Attention Is an Issue

- Help the student set and monitor personal goals.
- Set up a space that restricts visual distraction and noises so students can concentrate on their work.
- Break up the task to be completed, and give the student a time frame in which to complete each part of the task.
- Pair the student with another student who is task oriented to help the student stay on task.
- Create novel assignments and activities that will grab the student's interest so that he/she will be motivated to complete the task.
- Use proximity to reinforce on-task behavior.
- Build in movement within a lesson.
- Teach self-monitoring strategies. Provide opportunities to change tasks or activities more frequently.
- Provide reminder cues or prompts.
- Use private signals to cue appropriate behavior.
- Prepare the learner for changes in routine.
- Use graphic organizers.
- Connect previous learning to new information.
- Use flow charts.
- Use active learning.
- Give students some choice of working contexts: individual, whole class, small group, partners, etc.
- Provide frequent feedback.
- Give forced choices such as, "Do A or B."
- Recognize effective effort.

If Persistence and Completion Are Issues

- Identify the cause of the lack of persistence and plan intervention accordingly. Consider whether or not it is an attention issue, an organization issue, a lack or skills or knowledge issue, or ...? Set up a schedule of frequent checkpoints.
- Use a timer or stopwatch to orchestrate short work periods with frequent breaks; gradually increase length of work periods.
- Set reasonable goals and celebrate both the completion of the task and steps along the way.
- Point out to students what they have already done correctly and how what they have done so far can assist them in doing the unfinished components.
- Provide exemplars of the completed product and have students compare and self-assess their work against the exemplar.

What Do You Do When...
Learners Are Struggling?

If Organization Is an Issue

- Provide organizers such as color-coded pocket folders for each assignment to help the student keep track of the paper work.
- Offer students an organization system; for example, try a folder with several pockets used only for this task/assessment and help them develop a strategy for using it.
- Pair students with organized peers who will encourage them to keep their work orderly.
- Provide a materials checklist of the materials necessary to complete a task. Assign a checklist buddy to make sure the student has all the items on the list before beginning the task.
- Teach time management skills so the student knows how much time should be allotted to each task.
- Break up the task to be completed and give the student a time frame in which to complete each part of the task.
- Use a calendar for long-term assignments. List all the assignments to be completed, then schedule the time needed to accomplish each task in order to meet the deadline.
- In an elementary setting
  - Introduce a system for students to keep track of completed and uncompleted work.
  - Develop a color-coded system in which each subject is associated with a certain color; that is, the notebook or folder, posted schedule, and words on the word wall related to a given topic are all the same color.

If Speaking Is an Issue

- Use Wait Time and Think-Pair-Share. See page 202.
  - The student may be one of the 25% of our students who is an introverted thinker and need wait time before answering.
  - Word retrieval may be a processing problem and the additional time is needed to vocalize the answer.
  - Translation time for English Language Learners can slow down their response.
- Have student use a slate, think pad, or whiteboard to respond.
- Ask student to interact with you privately.
- Have student point to answer.
- Have student nod when you point to correct answer.
- See page 81 for more suggestions.

What Do You Do When...
Learners Are Struggling?

If Self-Confidence Is an Issue

- Have students give oral reports to you after school and then transition to small group presentations before requiring large group presentations.
- Provide frequent reassurance and encouragement.
- Provide advance notice that you are going to call on them.
- Use attribution retraining. See page 86.

If Social Skills Are an Issue

- Supervise closely during transitions.
- Provide guidance and rehearsals.
- Identify essential social skills and focus on teaching and reinforcing those skills, one at a time. See pages 210-211.
- Recognize small steps forward.
- Do mini-lessons in small groups as needed.
- Complete **See and Hear T-Charts** to quantify social skills in action. See page 213.

If Anxiety, Frustration, and Anger Are Issues

- Be patient and understand that what appears to be lack of motivation as well as withdrawal, inappropriate laughter, talking out, and avoidance of school tasks are learned behaviors; they are caused by anxiety, frustration, or anger.
- Provide "two-minute warnings" of upcoming transitions and changes in activity.
- Establish a signal to let students know you have noticed and support them as they struggle to gain control of their emotions.
- Set students up for success by foreshadowing what the next events will look like and help students get a mental and emotional set about how to function in the new, and possibly unfamiliar, situations.
- Teach students to visualize themselves being successful in the new or fear-producing activity or environment.
- Help students learn to recognize the beginning stages of anxiety, frustration, and anger and have them learn to give themselves space in a "time-out" way.
- Provide appropriate forums for expressing these feelings. Use preferred learning styles when possible.
- Avoid public criticism, sarcasm, and discipline at all times.
- Do not suggest that students should not have these feelings.
- Acknowledge the feelings as real and suggest a cool down or relaxation period.

What Do You Do When...
Your Students Are English Language Learners?

General Guidelines for Instructional Decisions

To determine the best approaches to use with an individual student consider:
- The student's background knowledge and life experiences
- The student's previous educational experiences
- The level of student's receptive (listening and reading) and expressive language (speaking and writing) in his first language
- The language(s) used in the home
- The command of the language used at home by the student's family members
- The student's information processing style or preference
- The student's strongest modalities
- The role of the family in the education of this student
- Cultural norms that might impact student behavior in the classroom

Speech

- Ask all students to speak in complete sentences. Such an expectation provides frequent and positive models of correct speech, reinforces correct grammar, and promotes meaning-making because sentences represent complete thoughts.
- Use active rather than passive voice.
- Speak slowly.
- Enunciate clearly.
- Use wait time. Wait time gives students time to translate an oral question or comment or written word into their first language, formulate a response in their first language, and then translate that response into English.
- Use nonverbal language such as facial expressions, gestures, and dramatization.
- Read students' body language.
- Do not interrupt or correct grammar errors when ELLs are speaking. Interrupting is rude in almost all situations. When one of the speakers is using a second language, it not only breaks the speaker's chain of thought, it slows down translation and English word retrieval. Most importantly, it reduces the willingness of the speaker to continue or try again. Do model the correct use in your response.

Use Sheltered Language

- Simplify the language of instruction, not the concept being taught.
- Shelter (control or guard) academic vocabulary embedded in the directions or explanations. Be mindful that academic use of words may not match how they are used in social settings.

- Personally avoid the use of idioms, slang, clichés, and colloquialisms and monitor their use by students, texts, and digital sources. Many teachers have found it useful to use bulletin board space for idiom translations. A humorous way to help English Language speakers in your classroom recognize the comprehension problems idioms and words with multiple meanings cause ELLs, read the class Fred Gwynne's *The Chocolate Moose*.

- Be aware of the language you use. If you have a large number of Latino students there are many words that they will be able to readily translate because they are cognates such as describe to describo, comprehend to comprehendo, analyze to analizar. Other words can throw them for a frustrating or, at the very least, a distracting loop. For instance, media in English means a method of communication while medias in Spanish means stockings or hose. As appropriate, point out cognates that sound and look similar to the English word. Many Spanish words are similar to their English equivalents so Latino students, with guidance, can connect the English word with the Spanish word and place it in their memory. There are, however, few cognates in Asian languages.

- Repeat rather than paraphrase previous statements. A paraphrased sentence is a new sentence to second language learners and they tend to start the translation process all over when they hear a paraphrased sentence.

- Use fewer pronouns. It is difficult to track antecedents in a second language.

- Use simple language structures. When you use, hear others use, or note compound or complex sentences in a text, translate those sentences into two simple sentences.

- Use realia, props, visual clues, movement, and manipulatives to support oral language.

Vocabulary Development
- See pages 263-275.
- Identify the stage of vocabulary development.
- Limit the number of new terms.
- Define and provide descriptive and visual clues for words with double meanings or synonyms.
- Have students create and use a bilingual vocabulary chart in the classroom and in their own notebooks. The chart would include the word and definition in English and the student's first language. Have them add pictures and symbols to increase comprehension.
- Identify and explicitly teach content specific vocabulary. Mole, pitch, borrow, and mass are examples of words that have social or generic meanings and also

What Do You Do When...
Your Students Are English Language Learners?

have multiple content specific meanings. Other words are used in only one specific content area and are seldom heard beyond academic discussions. Examples include photosynthesis, genre, circumference, and peninsula.

Reading

See **Chapter V: Literacy Across the Curriculum**.

- Record, or have student service groups or volunteers record, reading passages to facilitate comprehension and to ensure that correct pronunciation and inflections are heard frequently.
- Establish a classroom library of alternative and supplementary materials written in easy-to-read English.

Student Work Support

- Provide outlines/graphic organizers that communicate the big ideas and concepts from the lesson no matter what the source of the information.
- Task analyze to identify potential obstacles that might block students' understanding; prepare or find realia and visuals to support the learning.
- Provide written or pictorial instructions to be taped to the desk or placed in a notebook so that students can check back for steps in the process which they may miss in the original delivery of directions.
- Use consistent vocabulary for directions.
- Use multiple modalities to communicate important information.
- Provide models and exemplars.
- Clearly signal transitions in areas of focus and between activities. While all students benefit from clearly-articulated transitions, ELLs benefit even more when they are given notice that a transition is about to take place and information about what is going to happen next.
- Tape record lessons and presentations of material so that students can listen to the information as many times as they need to do so.
- Use think-alouds to model thinking processes. See pages 231-232.
- Use demonstrations to model processes.
- When students are new to American schools, teach learning strategies that may have been taught in earlier grades.
- Provide dictionaries with pronunciation keys, simple explanations, contextual clues, and, when possible, visuals.
- Display models of lower case and upper case alphabet letters in print and cursive with pictures of objects beginning with that letter.
- Create and use a library of content-related materials such as magazines, catalogs, postcards, charts, and other heavily illustrated documents.
- Label items in the classroom.

Student Interaction

- Provide frequent opportunities for students to use English to communicate their thinking and to ask questions. Use partner discussions, learning buddies, and table discussions rather than relying on whole-group discussions. **Think-Pair-Share** is the perfect strategy to use multiple times in any class period.
- Use heterogeneous cooperative groups.
- To ensure opportunity and responsibility, assign roles in cooperative groups. See pages 170 and 211-212.
- Do social skills training. See pages 210-213.
- Structure student interaction with **Talking Tokens**, **Paired Verbal Fluency**, etc. See pages 211-212 and 281.
- Use **Reciprocal Teaching**. See page 259.

Formative Assessment

- Check for understanding frequently.
- Elicit requests for clarification.
- Pose questions of varying levels of complexity so that parts of the answers to more complex questions are shared earlier.
- Use checklists/anecdotal records.

Points to Ponder

- There are four kinds of fluency: reading, listening, speaking, and writing.
- When students are working in a second language, homework can take two to three times longer to complete.
- Comprehension precedes production so ELLs may tend to observe from the sidelines rather than participate in classroom discussions.
- Do not confuse social and academic language proficiency. Social language develops much more quickly than academic language. Fluency in social interactions in no way indicates student proficiency in decoding and comprehending school work.

What Do You Do When...
Your Students Are At Risk (or At Promise)?

> We can, whenever and wherever we choose, successfully teach all children whose schooling is of interest to us. We already know more than we need to do that. Whether we do it or not must finally depend on how we feel about the fact that we haven't so far.
>
> Ron Edmonds

Building on the classic Edmonds quote above, Pellino writes in **The Effects of Poverty on Teaching and Learning**, "Poverty should not be an excuse for us to expect less from our students. They indeed come to us with numerous issues and challenges that interfere with their learning. We need to focus on their learning, find ways to help them overcome these challenges and gain the most they can from their education. Their education is likely their one chance to break the poverty cycle and escape. Just because they are poor doesn't mean they cannot succeed."

To educate students regardless of their socioeconomic status or family background:

- Hold and act on high expectations.
- Activate prior knowledge.
- Promote the transfer of new levels of understanding into long-term memory.
- Use heterogeneous grouping.
- Use graphic organizers and other nonlinguistic representations to help students organize information.
- Avoid any inclination to focus only on basic skills. Provide interesting and engaging learning opportunities where students access and use basic skills in meaningful ways.
- Provide opportunities for rehearsal and practice.
- Use multiple modalities to present and have the student process new information.
- Scaffold instruction so that these learners can build confidence in their capacity to learn that which they are asked to learn.
- Include frequent opportunities for students to make connections to their lives and the lives of others beyond the classroom.
- Check with other school authorities to ensure that, as appropriate, these students have access to nutritious breakfasts and lunches.

What Do You Do When...
Learners Have IEPs?

- Focus on individuals first and exceptionality second. Always say, "student with learning disabilities" not "a learning disabled student."
- Ensure that inclusive education includes inclusive language and professional practice.
- Consult with the special education specialist to gain an understanding of the specific nature of the learning challenges of individual students and to access the expertise that specialist can offer you.
- Establish an ongoing communication system with the special education specialist that is productive without being time intensive.
- Work collaboratively with all adults involved with the students (parents, psychologist, counselor, paraprofessionals, and special educators).
- Read and use the information in the Individual Education Program (IEP).
- Make data-driven decisions about instructional strategies or interventions to use with students.

Accommodations Request

Student:

Teacher:

Monitor Teacher:

Writing/Note-Taking Accommodations
☐ Use a tape recorder in the classroom
☐ Use another student's notes
☐ Use teacher's notes
☐ Have a scribe in the class
☐ Use a computer

Test-Taking Accommodations
☐ Have extended time on tests or quizzes
☐ Take test in a quiet area
☐ Have test read orally
☐ Take test orally
☐ Dictate answers to a test or quiz

Additional Accommodations
☐ Use digital recordings of textbooks
☐ Have an extra set of books for home (physical accommodation)
☐ Restroom use (medical accommodation)
☐ Use a calculator in class
☐ Use a calculator on tests or quizzes
☐ Use a dictionary in class
☐ Use an electronic speller
☐ Have seating in front of the class
☐ Have a class outline with due dates for assignments and tests
☐ Have extended time on nonstandard tests such as: PSAT, SAT, and ACT
☐ _____
☐ _____

Accommodations Request template is on CD-ROM.
Adapted from J.E.B. Stuart High School, Fairfax County Public Schools, VA

Accommodations Questionnaire

Student: **Subject:**

Teacher: **Monitor Teacher:**

1. **When you need extra help in class, which of these are most likely to help you?**

   ☐ Taped lectures   ☐ Using a computer
   ☐ Extra time on assignments   ☐ Alternative tests/assignments
   ☐ Class notes   ☐ Asking questions during a lecture
   ☐ Taped textbooks   ☐ Joining a study group

2. **When preparing for a test or exam, which of these accommodations would be most helpful to you?**

   ☐ Asking for extra time on the test   ☐ Asking for writing assistance
   ☐ Asking to take the test in another   ☐ Asking to read your answers into a
     room   tape recorder
   ☐ Asking to have the test read to you

3. **If you have reading difficulties, which of these are most likely to help you?**

   ☐ Asking to have textbooks taped   ☐ Asking for study guides
   ☐ Asking for someone to read to you ☐ Enrolling in a reading skills class

4. **If you have writing difficulties, which of these are most likely to help you?**

   ☐ Using a computer   ☐ Asking to give oral reports
   ☐ Asking for proofreading help   ☐ Asking for a scribe
   ☐ Dictating written work to someone ☐ Tape recording lectures

5. **If you have math difficulties, which of these are most likely to help you?**

   ☐ Asking for extra explanations   ☐ Using a calculator
   ☐ Listing steps of a process in your ☐ Setting up time to work alone with
     notes   the teacher
   ☐ Using graph paper

6. **If you have trouble with organization, which of these are most likely to help you?**

   ☐ Asking for a syllabus/course   ☐ Keeping a calendar of assignments
     schedule   ☐ Breaking large assignments into
   ☐ Getting assignments ahead of time   parts

Accommodations Questionnaire template is on CD-ROM.
Adapted from R. E. Lee High School, Fairfax County Public Schools, VA

Assessment Accommodations Planner

Changes in Setting

☐ Use preferential seating to place student closer to source of oral instructions and/or demonstration equipment.

☐ Assess small group of students in a separate location.

☐ Assess student individually in a separate location.

☐ Provide special lighting.

☐ Provide adaptive or special furniture.

☐ Assess student in study carrel or room with minimal distractions.

Changes in Timing/Scheduling

☐ Allow more time to complete assessment.

☐ Allow student to take assessment at his best time of day and during periods when emotional agitation is relatively low.

☐ Provide opportunity for additional breaks between subsections of the assessment.

☐ Provide opportunity to move around during the assessment.

☐ Allow student to extend assessment across several sessions/days.

Changes in Presentation

☐ Repeat and clarify the directions

☐ Allow student to record answers in test booklet rather than separate answer sheet.

☐ Allow student to underline key words and to write notes in margins of test booklet.

☐ Encourage the student to complete the task.

☐ Increase spacing between items and place fewer items per page.

☐ Break up the assessment into smaller sections or fewer steps at a time.

☐ Provide organizational aids such as templates, graphic organizers, or graph paper.

☐ Read only the directions orally.

☐ Read the directions and assessment items orally.

☐ Computer reads assessment to student.

☐ Provide audiotape version of assessment.

☐ Translate orally only the directions in the student's native language.

☐ Translate orally the directions and assessment items in the student's native language.

☐ Sign only the directions to the student.

☐ Sign the directions and assessment items.

Assessment Accommodations Planner

☐ Provide large-type version of assessment.
☐ Provide written translation of assessment in student's native language.
☐ Provide Braille version of assessment.
☐ Permit the use of whatever augmentative or assistive technology the student uses on a daily basis (e.g., magnifying equipment, noise buffers).
☐ Provide scoring guides which value content and ideas rather than form and neatness.
☐ Provide more complex, open-ended items which allow gifted and talented students to fully demonstrate the depth and range of their understanding and creativity.
☐ Provide scoring guides which reward sophistication, complexity, and originality at advanced level.

Changes in Student Response

☐ Permit use of augmentative or assistive technology on a daily basis (e.g., word processor, Braille, calculator).
☐ Permit responses in student's native language.
☐ Use scribe to record student's oral responses.
☐ Use signing to communicate responses.
☐ Use pointer to communicate responses.
☐ Allow student to use another modality (e.g., an oral presentation or an illustration rather than an essay).

Assessment Accommodations Planner template is on CD-ROM.

What Do You Do When...
Learners Have Learning Disabilities?

First Steps to Take

- See **Learning More about Your Students with Learning Disabilities** on pages 53-54.
- Consult with the special education specialist to gain an understanding of the specific nature of the learning disability of individual students and to access the expertise that specialist can offer you.
- Establish an ongoing communication system with the special education specialist that is productive without being time intensive.
- Accept, acknowledge, and accommodate the reality that student learning challenges may occur in the reception of information, the processing of information, the production of information, or all three. See pages 112-113 for accommodation planners.
- Empower not enable. Do not do for students what they can do for themselves. At the same time, do not neglect to provide appropriate supports.
- Encourage students to let you know when they did not understand what you said or what they read. Do so privately and often. Make yourself available. Realize that students may not follow through and that you will most likely have to work on this the entire year. Remember, too, that they may not know what they do not know.
- Have students paraphrase the directions and expectations to a neighbor to ensure that they know how to proceed.
- Recognize that some students may have difficulty copying material from a distance (boards, Smartboards, PowerPoint presentations, etc.) and, therefore may need important information placed on their desks.

Empowering Students

- Explicitly teach students a repertoire of compensatory strategies.
- As students with learning challenges get older they need to learn what strategies work best for them, build expertise in making good decisions about how they can adapt the learning environment so that they can do their best work, and to advocate for themselves. The Onion Mountain Technology website at www.onionmountaintech.com/files/PersonalChoices.pdf provides an excellent 16-page pamphlet titled Personal Choices for students to use in determining what they need to do to maximize their learning.
- Teach students to advocate for themselves.

Learners Have Learning Disabilities?

Organizing the Classroom for Learning

- Give a signal when you are about to give directions or an assignment. Follow the five steps laid out on page 157 to increase the likelihood that the student can productively start to work.
- Read aloud what you write on the board.
- Eliminate classroom distractions such as excessive noise, flickering lights, etc.
- Provide checklists that identify the steps in an experiment or other assignments. Have student check off each step as it is completed. Set up teacher check-in points appropriate to the skill level of the student.
- Establish a routine for student recording of assignments, materials needed, and directions for completion of task. Be prepared to try different methods when the first one does not work.
- Model outlining, use of graphic organizers, and other methods of note taking on the board or an overhead transparency during classroom presentations.
- Give assignments in writing and orally.
- Ask students to underline, circle, or otherwise highlight key words or directions. Use removable sticker dots or highlighting tape in texts.
- Teach mnemonic strategies.
- Address all modalities by presenting key concepts using more than one modality.
- When sequence matters, use 1st, 2nd, and 3rd rather than 1, 2, and 3.
- Write/type legibly and use large print/type on the board and on handouts. See page 242 for guidelines on the creation of text on visuals such as PowerPoint or Keynote slides.
- Carefully erase/clean boards so that what is written there is easily read.
- Provide tip sheets or cue cards identifying the steps of a process or procedure. Place each step on a separate card and fasten the cards together with a ring.
- When introducing new concepts, start with concrete, move to the semi-abstract such as pictures, pictographs, charts and graphs, and then to the abstract word.
- Structure the learning of new concepts by providing examples, stories, and analogies, and ask students to make connections by creating and sharing their own examples and stories.
- Review and discuss with the student the steps involved in any extended assignment. Think about which step(s) may be difficult for the student's specific learning challenges.

What Do You Do When...
Learners Have Learning Disabilities?

- Note and point out correct and/or improved work.
- Provide growth-producing feedback. See pages 159-160.
- Use color to emphasize key words or information. This includes colored chalk, colored markers, and brightly-colored text for selected points on PowerPoint and Keynote slides.

Reading

- Create an information-rich classroom with materials that support the learning standards students are to master. Collect children's books, magazines, journals, pictures, newspaper articles, work of past students or students from other classes, information from the Internet, etc. Garage sales are great sources of such materials or you can organize a class contest to bring in contributions. Be purposeful in providing a variety of reading levels and sources even in advanced classes.
- Use role playing and simulations to make abstract content more concrete.
- Use audio books or have student organizations record texts as a community service project.
- Read aloud to provide models of good reading and aid in student comprehension.
- Build background knowledge.
- Ensure that students access their own prior knowledge and deal with naive understandings and misconceptions.
- Model previewing of text and then have students practice doing the same. See page 262 for description of **SQ3R**.
- Provide reading panes like EZC Readers.
- Encourage students to practice using content specific words in discussions with classmates. Create a silent cheer to be used when the use of such words is heard.

Math

- Provide students with a multiplication table.
- Teach students to create their own multiplication table.
- Provide models of problems on posters and tip sheets that students can keep at their desks. (For example, create four posters each with a model of how to use one of the four operations on mixed numerals.)
- Put steps of problems on strips of paper and have students put the steps in the proper sequence.
- Have students turn paper sideways so that the lines on the paper can help keep columns of numbers aligned.

Learners Have Learning Disabilities?

- Teach students to use calculators.
- Draw or have students draw pictures of word problems.
- Use rhythm, music and mnemonics. See pages 184-185 and 187.
- Provide manipulatives for student use.
- Teach students to do error analyses. See pages 227-228.

Oral Expression

- See **What to Do When Students Do Not Participate** on page 81 for a menu of approaches to increase student oral participation in class.
- Have students work with you one-on-one, then slowly increase the number of students in the conversation.
- Use **Think-Pair-Share**. See page 202.

Resources

- Assessment: See pages 112-113 for an extensive list of possible assessment accommodations. Select from that list the accommodations that would be most appropriate for a given student.
- Learners struggling with reading, writing, organization, and social skills problems: See pages 99-103.
- Scaffolding Tools: See **Chapter IV**.

Students Who Are Twice Exceptional

Many students are both learning disabled and gifted. It is sometimes difficult to understand the learning and behavior of such students because one exceptionality hides the other. At the elementary level a student's giftedness may mask the learning disabilities but at the secondary level teachers often begin to notice students who have previously excelled are now no longer working up to their previously-identified potential. When that is the case, the best course of action is to investigate possible causes. Start by interviewing the student and the parents to get their historical and current perspective on the matter. Another tactic would be to review some common characteristics of students with learning disabilities and then consider some of the instructional scaffolding suggested for supporting their learning.

2e Twice-Exceptional, a bi-monthly newsletter, is an excellent resource and is available at http://2enewsletter.com.

What Do You Do When...
Learners Are Diagnosed as ADHD?

- Allow frequent breaks.
- Build in movement.
- Provide squish balls or other small quiet toys for students to manipulate.
- Break tasks into components creating multiple beginnings and endings.
- When possible, schedule the most rigorous tasks early in the day.
- Establish routines and notify the child well ahead of time if there are to be changes in the daily routine. Assist the student in learning to self-monitor and to react accordingly.
- Use earphones to provide white noise or quiet instrumental music.
- Have a quiet decompression/refocusing corner and teach students to remove themselves from distracting and possibly problematic situations (This alternative to a "time-out" situation empowers the students to begin self-monitoring and self-adjusting.)
- Plan lessons that provide students with frequent opportunities to interact with the content and each other. Possibilities include signal cards, slates, choral responses, **Learning Buddies**, **Think-Pair-Share**, manipulatives, small group work with assigned roles and social skills training, role plays, and simulations.
- Play music to signal a change in task. Consistently use the same music for a given task.
- If necessary, establish a token economy. While internal motivation is the preferred way of being, in some situations it may be necessary to set up an external system in which a student collects "tokens" for attending during previously-identified short periods of time. What happens with the tokens? That is up to you and the student. You can collaborate with the parents and the special education specialist to identify appropriate recognition or perks the student receives as a result of having earned tokens. There is no reason these perks cannot be academically related. There is no need for stickers or candy. The goal is, with reasonable expectations, to gradually increase the time and eventually eliminate the token system.

Vivienne Coleman, Prince William County Schools, Virginia, reports that her 5th grade special education students all have some form of ADHD. She found **Ticket to Leave** is easy to adapt and translate to almost any subject area. This strategy can easily be related to answering essential questions. All that is required are bright, colorful sticky notes and markers. Her students feel empowered and are attracted to the bright colors. It engages them and it sparks discussion and interest in the subject matter. The students look forward to completing a **Ticket to Leave** at the end of class and it makes the perfect closure to a lesson or even at transitions. As a result, it is the perfect assessment tool especially where time is of the essence.

Learners Are on the Autism Spectrum?

- Create a sense of calmness and consistency.
- Establish and practice predictable procedures and routines.
- Prepare students ahead of time when there are going to be changes in the daily schedule or routines.
- Have quiet cool-down area in classroom.
- Provide student with personal desk copy of routines and schedule.
- Increase wait time.
- Minimize environmental distractions (both auditory and visual).
- Avoid idioms, slang, colloquialisms, and tongue-in-cheek humor because the language can be confusing.
- Address student individually because she may not recognize that she is included in "group" directions.
- Teach social skills including turn-taking and personal space.
- Use visuals and manipulatives.
- Build movement and exercise into the schedule.
- Provide the student with quiet toys to manipulate.
- Give quiet, honest recognition of good effort and accomplishments.
- Provide opportunities for repetition and revisiting of important information and processes.

©Just ASK Publications

What Do You Do When...
Learners Have Behavior Disorders?

Behavior management techniques, such as positive reinforcement, token economies, contracting, and time-out are often used with these students. Ask past teachers what strategies worked well with a given student in previous years.

- Focus on the behavior not on the person.
- Identify patterns of classroom conditions that seem to lead to inappropriate behavior and play proactive interventions.
- Use modeling and role play to identify appropriate and inappropriate behaviors.
- As appropriate, check on medication schedule and become aware of timeline and changes in behavior related to that timeline or missed administration.
- Sometimes students act out as a way of obtaining attention. Provide reinforcement and recognition on an appropriately frequent basis to minimize the need for the student to seek negative attention.
- Consult with specialists such as a special education teacher, social worker, guidance counselor, and school psychologist.
- Back-talk self extinguishes. Fred Jones says that it takes two to turn back-talk into a conversation. Do not take the bait.
- Recognize and celebrate effective effort on the part of the student.
- Organize the classroom so that it is structured yet flexible enough to meet the needs of all students.
- Use "I Messages" rather than arguing with or confronting students. ("When you throw an object across the room, it endangers other students, and makes all of us lose our concentration.")
- Clearly articulate in advance consequences for given inappropriate behaviors. If possible, design the consequences in collaboration with the student.
- Teach students to self-assess and recognize the fact that they are getting ready to act inappropriately and then take action to avoid that behavior. Ideally, they learn to put themselves in self-imposed time-outs or cool-down situations.
- Keep both feet on the ground. Be calm, consistent, and controlled.
- Do not expect immediate improvement in student behavior.

What Do You Do When...
Learners Have Other Exceptionalities?

Learners Who Are Visually Impaired

- Ask the student what you can do to best help them learn.
- Enlist the class in supporting the student.
- Prepare handouts in large print and, in collaboration with the special education specialist, supplement these materials with audiotape or computer disk, and when possible in Braille.
- Use white paper with black ink and 16-18 point font. If handouts are prepared in a standard 12 point font, set the copy machine for 170 to 200% enlargement. Print on 11 x 17 paper.
- Most computer software allows students to enlarge text for greater ease of reading. You can scan in materials, save as PDF, and then student can enlarge to read.
- Remind the student to use the voice input commands with computers.
- Clearly describe what is occurring in the classroom as well as any information posted on the board.
- Have back-up magnifiers on hand.
- Announce speakers and have them speak so that students can associate voice with speaker.
- Try to keep materials and supplies in the same place.
- Establish emergency procedures.
- Access more suggestions at www.as.wvu.edu/~scidis/vision.html

Learners Who Are Hearing Impaired

- Ask the student what you can do to best help them learn.
- Enlist the class in supporting the student.
- Face the student when talking.
- Be aware of the lighting so that your mouth is not in the shadows.
- Write all assignments, instructions, due dates, and changes in routines.
- Monitor background and environmental noises. The presence of a student with hearing impairment provides yet another reason for students to not hold side conversations. Turn off equipment when it is not being used.
- Be sure you have the attention of the student before giving directions or providing information.
- When possible, provide outlines in advance of presentations.
- Use active voice rather than passive voice.
- Access more suggestions at www.as.wvu.edu/~scidis/hearing.html

off

121

©Just ASK Publications

What Do You Do When...
Learners Have Other Exceptionalities?

- Use caption feature on DVDs and other electronic presentations.
- Keep mustache trimmed.
- Repeat questions asked by other students, mentioning name of person who asked question, so that the learner who is hearing impaired knows exactly what is happening. If an interpreter is present, speak directly to the student, not to the interpreter.

What Do You Do When...
You Are Not Getting the Results You Want?

Bruce Oliver wrote in the June 2007 issue of *Just for the ASKing!* titled **"Stop!... In the Name of Learning"** that too often we operate on automatic pilot and rely on past practices without truly thinking about why we are doing what we do. He concluded that we need to take a second look at some of those practices and consider alternative practices that might lead to greater student engagement and learning. He suggested the following changes.

Stop... planning one-size-fits-all lessons and units. When teachers plan lessons and units that require all students to do the same thing at the same time using the same materials, it should not come as a surprise that some students struggle or are completely lost and unsuccessful, while others complete the lesson quickly and then appear to be bored or disengaged.

Start... making differentiation of instruction a regular part of planning lessons and units. Begin by gathering pre-assessment data to learn what students already know about future content. Using pre-assessment data, complete a task analysis to determine what prerequisite knowledge and/or skills are necessary for students to be successful in the upcoming unit. The task analysis enables teachers to determine how best to meet the needs of the entire class or sub-groups within the class. The data obtained from the pre-assessment helps the teacher know which individuals will require one-on-one instruction using varied materials and teaching approaches and which have already mastered the content.

Stop... sending students who do not bring books or supplies out of class. Students are often seen sitting outside a room or in the main office with nothing to do. When asked why they are there, they offer a variety of excuses including that they forgot their homework, they did not have a pencil, or they left their book in their locker. When a student is excluded from the classroom, one thing is for sure: No learning is occurring!

Start... providing the students the necessary materials. Some students forget materials on purpose because it will let them opt out of the day's learning activities. Teachers sometimes argue that when we provide materials for students, we are not teaching them to be responsible. On the other hand, when we send students out of class, they are "getting off easy" because they do not have to complete the same work as the other students.

Stop... having students read without a purpose. When teachers give students a reading assignment without setting a purpose for the reading, very little is occurring cognitively and the content of the reading is not registering with the student. Often students simply stare at the page to while away the time. They rarely remember what they have read and are not prepared to discuss the content of the reading with any depth of understanding or personal connections.

What Do You Do When...
You Are Not Getting the Results You Want?

Start... making sure that students are reading with a specific purpose in mind. Strong teachers preview the reading for the students and point out specific areas of the reading that are the most important. Teachers should employ techniques such as an Anticipation/Reaction Guide or a Word Splash as described in Paula Rutherford's book, ***Why Didn't I Learn This in College?*** that help the students read more purposefully. Providing relevant questions that accompany reading assignments helps students make connections to their own lives.

Stop... requiring students to copy notes. Time is the most important currency teachers have with their students. When time is spent having students copy from a slide or copy notes into a notebook, it is not a good use of time. When students doing such an assignment are asked what they are writing they often do not know. They were simply transcribing words from a source to a piece of paper.

Start... providing a template for the students to fill in as they are processing information. Provide students notes on which they can write their own ideas or summaries at various points during the presentation. Space should be provided on the notes for students to fill in their own thoughts and make their own connections to the content under study.

Stop... limiting checks for understanding to fact-based questions or recitations. When teachers conduct class discussions or include checks for understandings in their lessons, the types of questions they pose to students are generally ones which have a right or wrong answer. These questions require students to recall lesson content but may not require rigorous thinking.

Start... carefully crafting questions which require students to demonstrate their understanding of the lesson content at varying degrees of complexity. Questions should not be limited to one or two word answers but instead should require students to infer, interpret, analyze, or evaluate lesson content. In short, a teacher should challenge students at all levels on Bloom's Taxonomy and not limit checks for understanding exclusively to the recall and comprehension levels.

Stop... summarizing the lesson content for students. Some educators wrap up lessons by saying something like, "Okay, let me summarize what we have learned today." In the minds of students, this means that a transition is going to take place and they begin to prepare mentally and physically for the end of class. While the teacher is pulling together the lesson content, students are not paying attention and thus, the teacher's summary is not accomplishing the necessary purpose.

Start... developing a repertoire of summarizing techniques that require the students to summarize their own learning. When students grapple with lesson content and determine what they do or do not understand, they are able to self-assess their own learning. Also provide multiple opportunities for students to process and summarize learning during lessons.

Stop... assigning complex at-home projects. Teachers can be very creative in the design of projects. Even when at-home projects are clever, creative, and support the essential understandings of the unit, teachers need to be sure that all students have the necessary language skills, the necessary home support to complete such a project, and the funds to purchase the materials required for the assignment.

Start... asking whether or not the project is a worthwhile use of student time, if the project reinforces the learning that represents the essential understandings of the unit, and if all students have access to success. A second question to ask is: If the project is worth doing, can it be done in class so all students have a "level playing field?" Some students thrive on projects because they have the skills, materials, and creativity to produce outstanding work plus they can rely on help from parents or other adults in their lives. Others may not have access to the same support.

Stop... giving students only one opportunity to demonstrate their learning. Many educators prepare summative assessments at the end of a unit, administer the assessment to students, determine and record individual student grades, and then move on to the next unit.

Start... providing students feedback on their first efforts, giving them opportunities to use the feedback to take corrective actions, and then the opportunity to be assessed a second time. If more teaching is required, the teacher can use data from the first round of assessments to adjust instruction.

Scaffolding and Extension Tools

IV

Best on the Web

Assistive Technology

www.fcps.edu/ss/its/websites/websites.htm
The Fairfax County Public Schools, Virginia, assistive technology department website provides links to an extensive array of sites that provide both content-specific resources and assistive technology information that support the learning of students with special needs.

Research-Based Strategies

www.netc.org/focus
Thirty classroom examples highlight the use of research-based strategies supported by technology. The examples are composites, drawn from observations in hundreds of classrooms. Each example showcases the power of the individual teacher to improve learning results, while also acknowledging the common challenges that teachers face every day.

Regents Exam Prep Center

www.regentsprep.org
This website presents content-specific teaching strategies, study tips, sample test questions, and interactive learning experiences designed by Oswego City School District, New York. The algebra and geometry pages are especially useful.

Read, Write, and Think

www.readwritethink.org/index.asp
This website, sponsored by the International Reading Association (IRA), the National Council of Teachers of English (NCTE), and the Verizon Foundation provides lessons, student materials, and web resources. From the website: ReadWriteThink offers a wide array of standards-based lesson plans that meaningfully integrate Internet content into the teaching and/or learning experience. Lessons can be selected according to grade band (K–2, 3–5, 6–8, 9–12) and area of literacy practice. Each lesson is research-based, and includes a detailed instructional plan. The lessons are written for the teacher but include student-ready materials such as worksheets, interactives, and reviewed Web resources.

Scaffolding and Extension Tools

Scaffolding Theory was first introduced in the 1950s by Jerome Bruner, a cognitive psychologist. It is important to realize that differentiation is not a set of strategies but is instead a way of thinking about the teaching and learning process. That thinking includes providing whatever modeling and support is necessary in the presentation, processing, and production stages of learning and the withdrawal of that support as the learner moves toward independence.

Curriculum compacting was introduced by Joseph Renzulli and Linda Smith in 1978 as a way to provide students in general education classrooms enriched and accelerated learning opportunities. An important point to note is that more work or more difficult work is not the goal; instead, the goal is to provide students who already know what we planned to teach alternative learning opportunities matched to their knowledge, skills, and interests.

Requirements for Scaffolding and Extending Learning

Knowledge of Content: Chapter I of this text provides an overview of Teaching and Learning in the 21st Century. It is impossible for teachers to scaffold or extend learning without solid knowledge about the content to be taught.

Knowledge of Students: Chapter II focuses on the similarities and differences our learners bring into the classroom. One can know content but cannot be skillful with it if she cannot organize it in ways that make it accessible to all learners.

Knowledge of Learning Theory: Chapter III looks at what approaches might work best with students exhibiting certain characteristics. It is clear that the better we can determine the cause of learner success or lack thereof, the better we can plan our interventions.

Repertoire of Strategies and Tools: This chapter and Chapter V explore research-based tools and strategies that we can use to scaffold and extend the learning of our students.

Chapter IV begins with a two-page menu of over 60 tools. Following that listing are one- to six-page user-friendly descriptions and examples of those tools. In many instances there are website addresses where more user-friendly information and practitioner examples of how they use these tools in their classrooms can be found.

> What the child is able to do in collaboration today he will be able to do independently tomorrow.
>
> Vygotsky

Menu of
Scaffolding and Extension Tools

Just as scaffolding is used to support buildings during the construction process, educational scaffolding provides support systems for students during the learning process. And, just as extension ladders allow us to reach higher levels than we might if we stood on the ground, educational extensions promote new heights (depths) and breadths of learning. Each of the research-based scaffolding and extension tools discussed in this chapter can be used with all students or used to differentiate instruction.

In addition to the scaffolding and extension possibilities explored in this chapter, there are more suggestions throughout the text especially in **Chapter III: What Do You Do When...?** and **Chapter V: Literacy Across the Curriculum**.

When a template can be found on the CD-ROM it will be noted at the bottom of the page. The CD-ROM is located on the inside back cover of the book. Scaffolding and extension tools discussed in this chapter include:

- Analogies, Metaphors, and Synectics (Gordon)
- Anchoring Activities
- Assistive Technology
- Bookmarks and Highlighting
- Charts, Tables, and Maps: See Visuals.
- Concept Attainment Model (Bruner)
- Cooperative Learning
- Cubing and Think Dots
- Curriculum Compacting (Renzulli and Smith)
- Cyber Guides: See technology integration.
- Digital Recordings
- Directions, Giving
- Effort and Error Analysis with Goal Setting: See Student Self-Assessment.
- Essential Understandings/Generalizations, Big Ideas and Key Concepts: See **Chapter I: Teaching and Learning in the 21st Century**.
- Feedback, Growth-Producing
- Foldables
- Formative Assessment
- Framing the Learning
- Graphic Organizers
- Grouping Practices
- Independent Study
- Inductive Thinking Model (Taba)
- Inquiry Model (Suchman)
- Jigsaw Model of Cooperative Learning (Aronson)

- Learning Buddies
- Learning Centers
- Learning Mats
- Manipulatives
- Mental Imagery/Visualization
- Mini-Lessons/Focus Groups
- Mnemonics
- Models of Process and Product
- Movement and Music
- Note-Taking Formats
- Pictures and Pictographs
- Practice and Rehearsals
- Prior Knowledge
- Props/Realia: See Real-World Connections.
- Questioning
- Reading Materials, Variety of: See Real-World Connections.
- Real-World Connections
- Reciprocal Teaching: See **Chapter V: Literacy Across the Curriculum**.
- Rigor and Relevance Framework® (Daggett): See **Chapter III: What Do You Do When...?**
- Role-Playing and Simulations
- Sheltered Language
- Social Skills Training
- Strategy Instruction
- Student Choice
- Student Self-Assessment
- Task Cards: See giving directions.
- Technology Integration
- Think Alouds
- Tiered Assignments
- Time Management and Organization
- Time Templates
- Tip Sheets: See Learning Mats.
- Visuals
- Vocabulary Development: See **Chapter V: Literacy Across the Curriculum**.
- WebQuests (Dodge): See Technology Integration.
- Word Walls
- Writing Support: See **Chapter V: Literacy Across the Curriculum**.

IV

Analogies, Metaphors, Similes, and Synectics
Figurative Language

Analogies allow students to work from a familiar area into a new area of study. Since understanding involves connecting new learning to something already understood, analogies can be quite useful for some learners. It is important to emphasize the points of comparison so that other similarities and differences do not distract from student learning.

Metaphorical thinking can cause the familiar to become strange or unique as well as promote divergent thinking. If the topic is one which students have studied before, and may suffer from "delusions of familiarity," a metaphor may be just the way to re-energize their thinking around the topic.

While metaphorical thinking provides great opportunities for extending learning, figurative language, especially idioms (colloquial metaphors), can cause language learners huge problems. It is essential that teachers are purposeful in their use of figurative language and recognize when it is being used in text and classroom discourse. Only then can action be taken to maximize learning.

Scaffolding with Analogies
Paragraphs and Hamburgers
A paragraph is a group of sentences that tell about one main topic. A good paragraph is like a good hamburger. It has a fresh bun on the top (a topic sentence), a fresh bun on the bottom (a conclusion), meat (main idea), and a lot of extras in between (details and transition words).

Bubble Gum and Muscles
What happens when you try to **blow a bubble with a fresh piece of bubble gum**? It pops, of course, or at the very best, a small bubble can be created. You have to **soften up the bubble gum** before it is pliable enough to form into large bubbles. **The same "softening up" is needed for your muscles** when you are getting ready for strenuous exercise in physical education class. It's important to "soften up" or warm up your muscles before making big movements...or you could pull a muscle and seriously injure yourself.

In addition to responding to teacher-created analogies, metaphors, and similes, students, with modeling and instruction, can learn to create their own.

Analogies, Metaphors, Similes, and Synectics
Figurative Language

Extending Learning with Analogies

Direct Analogy (comparison of two objects or concepts)
How is the solar system like an orchestra?

Personal Analogies (description of yourself as the object or concept)
How would you feel if you were a computer?
"Even though, as a computer, I am not alive, I do appear to have a mind of my own. I tell those interacting with me to, "Please Wait." I throw tantrums by ringing bells and flashing warning signs to those who try to force me to work faster than I can or to do a new task when I am already busy!"

Symbolic Analogies or Compressed Conflicts
These analogies are also known as oxymorons; that is, they are descriptions of objects with two words that are opposites or contradict each other.
- What would be an example of thundering silence?
- What would a slow chase look like and why might it occur?

Synectics (Gordon)
This process requires that students move through the types of analogies described above. Select the topic and then have students:
- Create direct analogies
- Then create personal analogies
- Next create symbolic analogies or compressed conflicts
- Then create a new direct analogy
- And, finally return to the original topic to write about that topic using the rich language the analogies have generated.

Four-Box Synectics Review
See the next page for an example of **Four-Box Synectics Review** and a template to use in having students process their learning by creating analogies related to either the concept or information under study or the process being used.

Ask students to name four inanimate objects. Be sure that one has moving parts. Then ask students to compare the concept of being studied to each of the four items. After pairs or small groups have created their analogies, ask them to share one or two which they think best captures the essence of the item under discussion.

Four-Box Synectics Review

A _____is like a_____because_____.

A _____is like a_____because_____.

A _____is like a_____because_____.

A _____is like a_____because_____.

A _____is like a_____because_____.

A _____is like a_____because_____.

A _____is like a_____because_____.

A _____is like a_____because_____.

Four-Box Synectics Review template is on CD-ROM.

Anchoring Activities

Anchoring activities are a series of learning experiences that students have as their "go-to" work whenever they have any available time. Because anchoring activities can be designed to review, remediate, enrich, or elaborate, all students can be expected to complete a packet or series of tasks at centers in a given amount of time. They are useful in the differentiated classroom because they:

- Maximize time on relevant tasks and allow the teacher to work with individuals or small groups in focus groups and mini-lessons
- Facilitate students making connections between concepts
- Provide appropriate practice
- Allow students to explore areas of interest
- Provide opportunities for building test-taking skills

Possibilities

- Fish bowl with problems or questions related to a key area of study on slips of paper: Students draw a slip at random and work, write, or speak on the topic listed. Spoken responses can be tape recorded.
- Centers: The centers can be an actual location in the room or the center can be self-contained in a folder or small box.
- Packets: The most efficient way to create packets is to create identical packets (in hard copy, online or on a flash drive) and designate on the cover sheet the exercises a given student is to complete. Promote engagement by allowing the student to select some of the exercises they would like to complete.
- Journals
- Web-based exercises

Ways to Differentiate

- Create identical packets accompanied by a cover sheet which tells students which problems, projects, or tasks to complete.
- Analyze student work to determine benchmarks and indicators that need to be addressed by whom and create packets of materials for accelerated students who are doing independent study or are on a compacted curriculum and for students who need to revisit identified benchmarks.
- Tape record directions that can be listened to as often as necessary.
- Use task cards in learning centers.

Resources

- Elementary examples can be found on pages 136 and 138 and secondary examples are on pages 136 and 137.
- All four examples are on the CD-ROM at the back of the book.

Anchoring Activity Exemplars

Bell Work

When students arrive to class each morning, they are expected to follow the "Ready for School" routine and then begin working on this anchoring activity:

- A picture is placed on each student's desk (or pair of desks), or children are told to select from a set of pictures.
- They respond to a simple writing prompt and are expected to write for 10-15 minutes in their journal.

This morning routine provides students practice writing coherent sentences. Differentiation is achieved using sticky notes on each child's journal page. See samples below of the differentiated tasks.

- 5+ sentences - Descriptive	- 10+ sentences - Cursive! - Newspaper Article
- 10+ sentences - Cursive - Narrative	- 5+ sentences - Descriptive 5 transition words

Roseann Vignola, Lincoln Public Schools, MA

Physics Dictionary

Directions

- Choose a new physics vocabulary word that we are working with this week.
- Find a magazine picture that can help you define and explain the vocabulary word.
- Paste the picture in the box below.
- Write a three to five sentence caption for the picture. Be sure that the caption includes a definition of the new vocabulary word in your own words, as well as an explanation of how the picture demonstrates the definition.

Vocabulary Word:_____

```




```

Caption:_____
_____
_____
_____

Anchoring Activity templates are on CD-ROM.

Anchoring Activity Exemplar
French Cultural Awareness

Directions

- When you have finished your work, go to the section of the room designated Cultural Awareness.
- From the list of famous Frenchmen, choose one person you would like to know more about. You may not use the same category twice until you have used at least four different categories.
- Using the available resources, list five facts about the person you have chosen on a 3 x 5 index card. (Be sure to put your name on the card.)
- Share the name and information you have found with a classmate who is in the area with you.
- File the card in the green file for future discussion with the entire class.

We spend one-half hour a week discussing these cards. Students go to the file, find their information and share it with the whole class in any way they choose. Students are notified in advance when they will be asked to make a presentation. If more than one student has chosen a particular person, students are given time to consolidate any information they have. Consolidation usually results in more in-depth information and discussion.

Categories of French People

- Actors/Actresses
- Architects
- Authors
- Aviators
- Composers
- Criminals
- Economists
- Fashion
- Monarchs

- Musicians/Singers
- Painters
- Philosophers
- Politicians
- Resistance workers
- Scientists
- Sculptors
- Sportsmen and Sportswomen

IV

Anchoring Activity Exemplar
Recommendations for Independent Reading List

Over the next two weeks choose 6 books that you have read this year as independent reading books. List the name of each book, the author, and the illustrator. In addition, describe each book including what caused you to choose the book in the first place. Next, tell why it should/should not be considered as a part of an independent reading list for students next year.

Title of the book:

_____

Author:

_____

Illustrator:

_____

Description of the book:

_____

_____

_____

_____

_____

Why it should/should not be on the list:

_____

_____

_____

_____

_____

_____

Anchoring Activity templates are on CD-ROM.
Created by a teacher in Louise Thompson's **Meeting the Needs** workshop series.

Assistive Technology

According to the *Family Guide to Assistive Technology*, assistive technology includes all resources that:

- Enable an individual to perform functions that can be achieved by no other means
- Enable an individual to approximate normal fluency, rate, or standards - a level of accomplishment which could not be achieved by any other means
- Provide access for participation in programs or activities which otherwise would be closed to the individual
- Increase endurance or ability to persevere and complete tasks that otherwise are too laborious to be attempted on a routine basis
- Enable an individual to concentrate on learning or employment tasks, rather than mechanical tasks
- Provide greater access to information
- Support normal social interactions with peers and adults
- Support participation in the least restrictive educational environment

While many of the assistive technology tools are ones we would expect to be listed as technology tools, special educators include tools that they describe as low-tech technology.

Low-Tech Assistive Technology

The tools listed below provide a sampling of assistive technology that is easily useable in general education classrooms and require little, if any, specialized training. The use of these tools should not be limited to students with special needs as there are many students who might benefit from using them.

- Pencil Grips: These can help students grip pencils and pens correctly, relieve hand and finger fatigue, and provide fine motor support.
- Paper Options
  - Raised line paper
  - Grid paper
  - Colored paper

Assistive Technology

- Lined paper turned sideways can help students line up math problems correctly
- Primary paper with dashed line: This paper may be an important tool for older students who enter our classrooms having never been in school.
- Reading Aids
  - Reading strips: These ruler-size devices have a window that reveals only the line to be read. These strips are useful for both beginning and experienced readers who have tracking or attention problems. Reading strips, marketed as EZC Readers, have colored and transparent plastic inserts.
  - Colored transparency film: Dyslexic readers are often better able to track when the entire page of text is covered with this film.
  - Large print books
  - Increased font size on handouts
  - Student tools for highlighting (flags, sticky notes, highlighters, highlighting tape): See pages 141-142.
- Calculators
- Tape recorders
- Digital recorders: See page 155.
- Audio books
- Podcasts
- Summaries of notes from interactive white boards printed out or posted on class website
- Captions on computers, television, and DVD programs
- Magnifiers

High-Tech Assistive Technology

Special educators work closely with general educators when these high tech technologies are used. The case managers have specialized training in their use and the requirements for their use will be written into a student's IEP.

- Switches, special keyboards or mice, and remote controls
- Wireless microphones worn by the teacher to amplify voice for the hearing impaired
- Hearing aids
- Picture boards, battery-operated communication devices, communication software and computers
- Speciality software for students with learning difficulties
- Walkers, manual or powered wheelchairs
- Adjustable chairs, desks, and straps

Bookmarks and Highlighting

Bookmarks and highlighting provide students tools that help them identify, mark, and then later readily access important information. These tools can also help students note their reactions, questions, and connections to the information they are studying.

Just as we often bookmark Internet sites that we want to reference later, students can bookmark Internet sites and pages in texts for the same purpose. We can scaffold instruction for them by bookmarking websites or pages in texts where the most essential information or clearest explanations are found.

Depending on the learning needs of the students, teachers can assist students by modeling the use of highlighting tools in text. Because textbooks are so expensive we need to have a large repertoire of ways to highlight text without permanently marking up the text. Possibilities include:

- **Erasable crayons:** Crayola and Faber Castell market erasable crayons that younger children can use to highlight text in books or on their own papers.
- **Wide white-out tape:** The placement of wide white-out tape in the margins of textbooks allows teachers to note important points in the text and/or provides students a place to note questions, vocabulary words that are confusing, or possible main ideas or definitions.
- **Sticky-notes and flags:** Both of these tools provide a place for students to mark key pages and capture key points and note questions. Teachers can preview the text and then use sticky-notes and flags to indicate where students should focus their attention, provide "on the spot" definitions, or pose questions.
- **Removable sticker dots:** These dots that are available at office supply stores are another tool useful in marking key points. The transparent variety pack with multiple colors facilitates categorizing and sorting. They could be used by either teacher or student to highlight specific parts of speech, particular points of punctuation, the required operations in a problem, or the types of errors in answers.
- **Transparency film:** Cut the transparency film to fit the page in the text or to fit student papers. Directions can be written on the transparency using different colors as appropriate, or students can place the transparency film on the text, note the page number and highlight the text by using wet erase markers on the transparency film.
- **Clear plastic sleeves:** Maps and other documents on which students cannot write can be placed in the clear plastic sleeves often used in project reports. This tool allows students and teachers to write on the plastic sleeve while the original paper is protected and held straight during use.

Bookmarks and Highlighting

- **Highlighter tape:** The Teaching Resource Center lists the Top 10 Classroom Uses for Removable Highlighter Tape. You can access it at www.trcabc.com/resources/teachers-corner/top-10-classroom-uses-for-highlighter-tape/ The bottom line is that highlighter tape which comes in one-half and one-inch widths is a great alternative when the use of permanent highlighting pens is not acceptable. Although not usually available in office supply stores, a Google search on highlighting tape will provide multiple online sources for this tool.

- **Wikki Stixs:** These bendable pieces of yarn covered with wax can be used to highlight text on a chart or on a page in a book, to make diagrams and cross sections, as well as to form letters and numbers.

- **Teacher or student-made bookmarks:** Bookmarks placed in texts to mark the reader's place as they study provide an opportunity to focus the learning process on comprehension. These bookmarks can provide either scaffolding or extensions depending on what the students are asked to have as their focus as they work the text. Tom Loftis, former high school English teacher, created **Essential Questions Bookmarks** for students to use in the books they were reading. Having the questions in front of them at all times helped him and his students stay focused on why they were reading the text.

Resources

See the **Book Club Bookmark** and **Non-fiction Journal Prompts Bookmark** on the following pages. Templates are also available on the CD-ROM. These tools were designed by Sharon Edwards, St. Vrain Valley School District, Longmont, CO.

Book Club Bookmark

Name _____

Questions I have before I read:

1. _____

   _____

2. _____

   _____

   _____

3. _____

   _____

   _____

Questions I have while I am reading:

1. _____

   _____

2. _____

   _____

3. _____

   _____

Book Club Bookmark

Questions I have after I read:

1. _____

   _____

2. _____

   _____

3. _____

   _____

Choose one question that you can now answer. Answer the question with evidence from the text. Include page numbers.

_____

_____

_____

_____

_____

_____

_____

_____

_____

Book Club Bookmark template is on CD-ROM.

Non-fiction Journal Prompts

Read the assigned selection and write a journal response. Begin each response with the book/chapter title and the date of your journal entry. Example:

Book/Chapter
Title_____

Date_____

Before you read the book/chapter...
- What do you know about the topic before getting started the book/chapter?
- What do you want to learn?

While reading the book/chapter...
- What information surprised you?
- How can you use this information in your life?
- What information do you question or think might not be correct? How might you check it out?
- What is the most important thing you have learned? Why?
- What is the most interesting thing you read?
- What techniques does the author use to make this information easy to understand?
- Where do you think you could look for more information on this topic?

Non-fiction Journal Prompts

Read the assigned selection and write a journal response. Begin each response with the book/chapter title and the date of your journal entry. Example:

Book/Chapter
Title_____

Date_____

Before you read the book/chapter...
- What do you know about the topic before getting started the book/chapter?
- What do you want to learn?

While reading the book/chapter...
- What information surprised you?
- How can you use this information in your life?
- What information do you question or think might not be correct? How might you check it out?
- What is the most important thing you have learned? Why?
- What is the most interesting thing you read?
- What techniques does the author use to make this information easy to understand?
- Where do you think you could look for more information on this topic?

Non-fiction Journal Prompts template is on CD-ROM.

Good for All But Especially for Gifted and Accelerated Students
Concept Attainment Model (Bruner)

Purposes
- To develop inductive thinking skills
- To practice identifying patterns and forming hypotheses

Set-Up
- Identify the concept to be studied.
- Locate positive and negative examples of the concept. A minimum of twenty sets of examples is recommended with at least two-thirds positively representing the concept.
- Sequence the examples starting with several positive examples.

Procedure
Phase One
- Inform learners that they will see positive and negative examples of an idea you want them to discover.
- Present data to the learners in pairs and label the data sets as positive or negative examples.
- Ask students to develop hypotheses about what attributes or patterns they are seeing. Prompt them to try out several hypotheses and extend their thinking by focusing attention on specific features of the examples.
- Track and record on the board or chart paper the possibilities they generate and delete those proven incorrect by the presentation of additional examples.
- Have students name the concept and the rules or definition of the concepts according to their attributes. If the students do not know the name of the concept, provide the name in phase two when student hypotheses are confirmed.

Phase Two
Students confirm their thinking about the concept by:
- correctly identifying additional unlabeled examples of the concept as positive or negative
- by generating their own positive examples

Phase Three
Students analyze the processes and strategies they used, what they did when strategies did not work, and whether or not they explored more than one hypothesis at once.

Access more information at
http://imet.csus.edu/imet4/lalldrin/ca_lesson/links.html

Small Group Work
Cooperative Learning

Cooperative learning is more than small group work. Without structure one person can do all the work and the rest can hitchhike. According to Johnson and Johnson whose meta-analysis Marzano references in his work, the basic tenets of cooperative learning are:

- Face-to-face interaction: See pages 170-171 for information on grouping students.
- Interdependence: This variable can be structured by limiting time and resources so that it is impossible for one person to do the task alone.
- Social skills training: In this component, students are explicitly taught norms of behavior for working collaboratively. Social skills training provides a rich opportunity for scaffolding and extending learning. See pages 210-213.
- Group processing: The most neglected facet of cooperative learning is having students analyze and reflect on how well they worked together as a group and how each member contributed to the success of the group. Once again, this is an excellent opportunity to scaffold learning.
- Individual accountability: While teams may experience success and perhaps win friendly competitions, it is essential that students mastery of content be individually assessed.

When these variables are not present, small group work is less productive. Purposeful structuring of groups and the use of flexible grouping enhance the learning possibilities.

Formal Cooperative Learning Models

- Learning Together and Alone (Johnson and Johnson): See www.co-operation.org
- Jigsaw (Aronson, Gonzales): See page 147.
- Student Teams Achievement Division-STAD (Slavin): See http://sitemaker.umich.edu/356.berman/cooperative_classrooms
- Jigsaw II (Slavin)
- Team Games Tournament-TGT (Slavin): See www.aea267.k12.ia.us/cia/files/teaching_strategies/ttourn_t.pdf
- Group Investigation (Thelen, Sharon)

Spencer Kagan writes about dozens of cooperative learning structures which can, if carefully planned, include all the variables cited in the Johnson and Johnson research.

Jigsaw Cooperative Learning (Aronson)

Set-Up

1. Identify content that could be divided into segments and taught by students to other students.

2. Divide the material to be studied into meaningful chunks. Identify the number of segments of material to be learned and place the same number of students in each base group (Three to five segments/students in a group is workable).

3. Assign a segment of the material to be learned to each person in the base groups. Each person in the base group has different material to study.

Student Tasks

4. Each student studies his material independently. This can be done in class or as homework, depending on the material and age of the students.

5. Students meet in "expert" groups to study the material and plan how to teach it to their base groups. All the 1s who have independently studied the same material meet together, the 2s meet together, etc. Because you want to ensure that the "expert" groups are identifying significant points, you may want to prepare "expert sheets" for them use in their planning. You can build in requirements for visuals and checks for understanding.

6. Students return to their base tables and teach the material they studied to their base group.

Assessment and Individual Accountability

7. Ensure individual accountability by some means. This can range from a traditional quiz to **Numbered Heads Together** to a random oral check for understanding.

Helpful Hints

- If this process is completely new to your students, use it first with simple content. A general rule of thumb is to avoid introducing complex material and complex processes at the same time.

- Analyze the social skills needed for your students to work successfully in this way. Identify which skills they have and which you will need to explicitly teach prior to their working in two different cooperative groups.

- Provide opportunities for students to discuss not only their content learning, but how they worked together in their groups.

 ©Just ASK Publications

Cubing and Think Dots

Cubing and Think Dots ask students to explore processes, concepts, and events from a variety of perspectives. The six-sided cubes feature a different activity on each side of the cube. Students roll the cubes and complete the exercise(s) that comes up.

When cubing was introduced in 1980 by Cowan and Cowan the strategy was used as a writing prompt and the original six sides of the cube were: describe it, compare it, associate it, analyze it, apply it, and argue for/against it.

Over the years teachers have greatly expanded the use of cubes to include not only Bloom's taxonomy but Williams' taxonomy, McTighe and Wiggins Facets of Understanding, DeBono's thinking hats, and Gardner's Multiple Intelligences. Originally used as writing prompts, cubes are now used across the curriculum because they provide novelty and tactile learning opportunities and promote various levels and kinds of thinking about a process, concept, generalization, or event.

Cubes can be made using the template depicted in miniature below or by gluing stems on the side of large foam dice or on small square gift boxes. Variations include cards on a ring or a numbered task list and a regular die.

Access more ideas at
http://daretodifferentiate.wikispaces.com/Cubing+and+Think+Dots

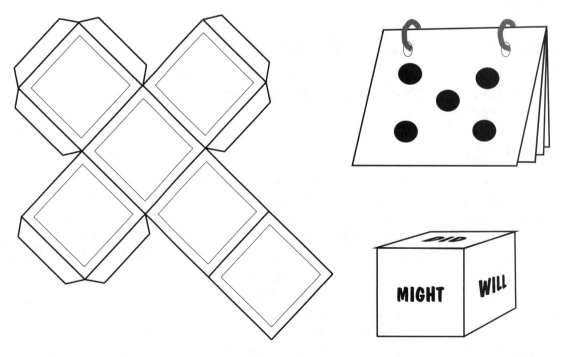

Cube template is on CD-ROM.

Cubing in Math

Donna Roberts of the Oswego City School District, New York has posted eight math teaching strategies, one of which is cubing in math. Access those strategies at: www.regentsprep.org/Regents/math/algtrig/teachres/TeachRes.htm. Donna explains how to create "math sentences" in a way that is applicable across the grade levels.

Develop two cubes whose sides contain mathematical expressions. Develop a third cube that represents the various operations that the students might be asked to perform on the two expressions.

Have the students roll the three cubes and record their answers on an answer sheet.

Differentiation

- Determine the operation to be used based on readiness of student(s).
- Vary the operations listed on the Cube #3 to extend or scaffold learning.
- Modify the expressions on Cubes #1 and #2 to extend or scaffold learning.

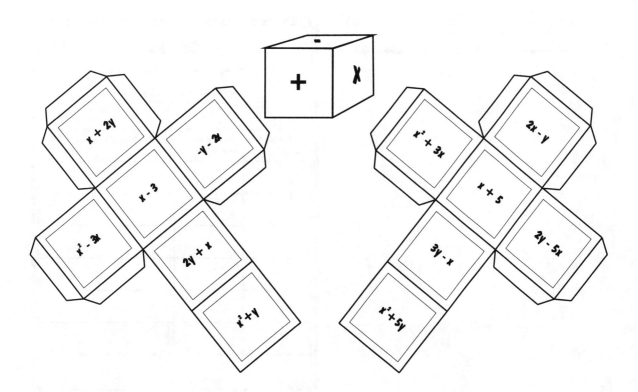

IV Cubing Templates

Math Cubes

Expression From Blue Cube	Operation (+,-,x, etc.)	Expression from Green Cube	=	Answers

©Just ASK Publications

On a Roll

The topic you are investigating/exploring today is

_____
Fill in the chart as you roll the Question Cubes.
Generate at least five questions.

First Word From the Green Cube	Second Word From the Blue Cube	Body of Question

©Just ASK Publications

Cubing templates are on CD-ROM.

Cubing: On a Roll

Process

- Provide students with the two cubes pictured below and the recording sheet pictured in miniature on the previous page.
- Announce the topic or concept that students are to study.
- Have them roll the two cubes recording the who, what, when, etc. word that comes up in the first column and the verb **On A Roll** in the second column. Then have students create a question using those two words as sentence starters.
- Have students record their sentence on the **On A Roll** recording sheet pictured on the previous page.

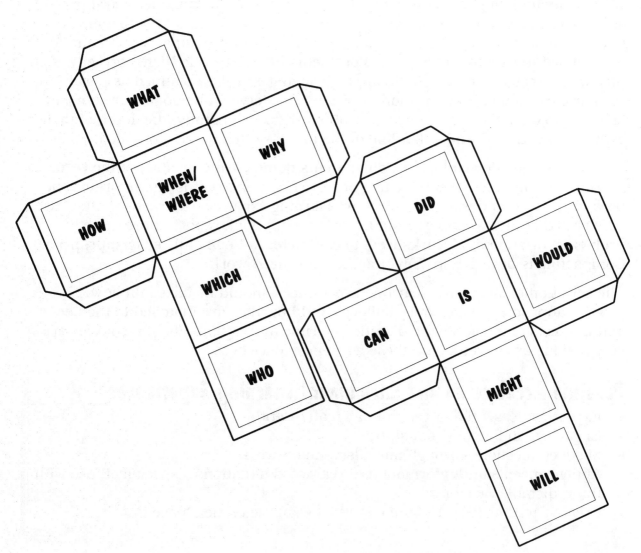

On a Roll Cube templates are on CD-ROM.

Curriculum Compacting

Developed by Joseph Renzulli and Linda Smith in 1978, the process of compacting the curriculum to accelerate learning is directly aligned with the standards-based planning process (backward design) that drives curriculum and instructional planning today.

The first step in both models is to identify what students are to know and be able to do and to then determine what it looks like when they know and can do it. After those parameters have been established, the next tasks are to identify which students already know all or some of the identified knowledge and skills and those who will need scaffolding to master that knowledge, and plan appropriate learning experiences for them.

When contemplating how to advance the learning of accelerated learners, pre-assessment data can come from pre-tests or observation. One way to identify mastery of basic skills is to ask potential candidates for compacting to complete the two or three most difficult tasks/problems; if they can do them correctly, then there is no reason for them to do all the learning exercises planned as part of the regular curriculum. Identification of content mastery can be done by reading or listening to comments students make about the area of study; the depth of their experience with and understanding of the topic is often quickly revealed.

Once it has been determined which students demonstrate mastery of the regular curriculum, the work of compacting begins. This construct is an important one because instead of designing alternative learning experiences, teachers often give accelerated students more work such as an extra book report, more math problems, or additional worksheets to complete. Not one of these is appropriate. Compacting is designed to "buy time" for advanced work.

The selection of alternative learning experiences should be based on how they provide appropriate academic challenge and how they are matched to the needs and interests of the accelerated students. Time and availability of resources are very real factors in setting up these learning experiences.

Possible Accelerated and Enrichment Learning Experiences
- Explore an essential question to a greater depth
- Engage in an independent study
- Make connections through interdisciplinary work
- Apply concepts and information in real-word situations, especially those with unpredictable variables
- Creative writing (See 4th grade student example on next page.)

Heaven on a Plate
Reviewed By Will Rutherford

Artie's is a restaurant located at 3260 Old Lee Highway in Fairfax, Virginia. It is an excellent restaurant with classic American fare and part of the Great American Restaurant Group.

Artie's has a call-ahead list which allows you to state the time you expect to arrive and they will put you on a waiting list at the time you call. This is not a formal reservation but it definitely saves you time.

When we arrived the hostess said "right this way" and we were off to our table. Less than thirty seconds after we sat down our waitress scurried over and asked us if we wanted to order drinks. I was just sitting there gawking with my mandible nearly touching my knees, thinking what great service this place has. She handed out the menus and I ordered a Shirley Temple. It came about three minutes later. Shirley Temples are made out of Sprite, ice, and red food coloring. They taste exactly like Sprite just are cooler. Our waitress came back a couple of minutes later to ask if we wanted to order appetizers. We ordered the Tex-Mex Egg Rolls and the Spinach Artichoke Dip. After the waitress left I watched her go and saw that she went to four other tables and got their orders too.

The Spinach Artichoke dip was fair. It was cheesy and you could definitely taste the spinach in it. It was better hot than cold and the chips you dip in it were very good and lightly salted. The Tex-Mex Egg Rolls were great.

They had tons of ingredients you would find in Mexican food and were mildly spicy and filled with flavor.

We then ordered bread and butter. When the bread arrived I noticed it was arranged in an interesting way. Right around the same time we got the bread Artie's started to get crowded. The bread came in a basket with rolls, raisin bread, nut bread and a couple of other kinds of bread and herb butter. The bread was very soft and warm and had herbs in it. I thought it was superb.

The waiters and waitresses were nice and alert. Our waitress was at our table right when we were finishing the bread. It was now time for the entrée. Our waitress had memorized the specials and recited them flawlessly while making eye contact with me. In the end I ordered the Hickory burger.

The food arrived about twenty minutes later. When I saw the Hickory burger my mouth started watering. It had cheese, BBQ sauce, ketchup, onions, lettuce and was dripping wet. The Hickory burger came with a side of fries. They were thinly sliced, lightly salted and peppered, and were delicious. The Hickory burger was excellent, like heaven on a plate. The filet mignon (steak) was awesome. It was tender and juicy. It came with mashed potatoes and a crab cake. The Boathouse Steak Salad was also good. It had corn, beans, steak, blue cheese, red onions and more with a light dressing. If you like more subtle

Heaven on a Plate

flavor and not tons of different tastes then the Boathouse Steak Salad is not for you. The halibut was good. When you first receive it, it looks like chicken on mashed potatoes. Don't be tricked. Take one bite and you will know it is fish but this was prepared with great flavor.

Now for the desserts...The White Chocolate Bread Pudding was surprisingly fantastic. It had a breaded outside and contained caramel, ice cream and whipped cream with raspberry sauce drizzled in a circle around the pudding. The Warm Flourless Chocolate Waffle was terrific. It's exactly what it is called, a warm flourless chocolate waffle with ice cream and whipped cream. The

Hot Fudge Sundae was fair. It was a typical hot fudge sundae with ice cream, hot fudge, whipped cream, and nuts but it didn't compare to the other two desserts.

Artie's is a great restaurant. It can sometimes be a little pricey but overall it is worth it. If you are ever trying to find a place to eat on a Saturday night definitely pick Artie's. You won't be disappointed, guaranteed!

For more information visit their website at www.greatamericanrestaurants.com/arties where you can find menus, directions, the call-ahead number, etc.

Digital Recordings

Provide Directions
- for centers
- for students who are absent
- for second language learners so they can hear the directions multiple times
- for students to play one step in a sequence of directions at a time and clarify the directions and point out potential pitfalls
- for student self-assessment at completion of the learning exercise

Deliver Lectures/Explanations
- for second language learners to listen to lectures/explanations as often as necessary
- for students who are absent for initial presentation
- with a slower pace of delivery by having students stop the tape and respond or react to what they have heard
- with clarification or elaboration on a subject and build in background knowledge or vocabulary work as appropriate

Read Alouds of Fiction and Non-Fiction
- to orally support reading with vocabulary work embedded in the tape
- to structure reading with 10:2 processing time and comprehension questions built into the tape
- to present reading passages read by expert readers with directions for students to follow expert reader by recording their own read aloud, listening to both, and self-assessing

Low-Tech Approach
Locate several small inexpensive audio cassette tape recorders. Send out a request in a classroom newsletter or post your request in the faculty workroom or at several community locations. There are hundreds of these recorders sitting around in closets in schools and homes. After you locate the tape recorders, order or purchase inexpensive cassette tapes. When digital technology is not readily available at school or in student homes, these recorders can provide a highly effective and low-cost scaffolding tool.

Giving Directions

The greatest cause of chaos/conflict is unmet expectations. The greatest cause of unmet expectations is unclear expectations or directions. Clarity and reasonableness of directions and expectations can make more difference in the classroom than almost any other factor. This is the ultimate scaffold.

Top Ten Tips for Giving Directions That Will Be Followed

- Before you start, be sure you have the students' complete attention. **Do not talk over the students**. If they need to get out materials, ask them to do so and then wait until they are all on the "right page" before you continue.
- Plan directions carefully and picture exactly what you want the students to do.
- Run a mental movie and picture what could possibly go wrong. Make plans for avoiding these potential pitfalls.
- Do a task analysis and identify which of the behaviors embedded in the task have been done successfully before, which ones the students have had trouble with, and which are new. Review, clarify, or model as appropriate.
- Use written as well as verbal modes if more than two steps are involved. A flow chart is a powerful tool for reducing questions about what to do next.
- If sequence is important in completing the task use 1st, 2nd, and 3rd instead of 1, 2, 3, or a, b, c.
- Point out new vocabulary and stress difficult or possibly confusing points in the process.
- Show models of processes, products, and problems.
- Give students time to think about the task ahead and then check for understanding by having them turn to a neighbor and explain what they think they are supposed to do.
- If you expect problems, let students coach each other with a sample.

Potential Problems

Pacing and Planning: If you assign homework as students are walking out the door, only half of them hear you and half of those who do either don't remember or think it is multiple choice about whether or not to do it.

Repeat performances: Expect recurring problems if you ask any students to do something they struggled with the last time you assigned such a task without intervention on your part.

Unclear or vague directions: You know that you were not clear when more than two students or two groups of students call you over for clarification!

Giving Directions

Minimize Confusion and Questions

Give a signal when you are about to give directions or announce an assignment. Five steps increase the likelihood that students can productively start to work. These steps can be used with the entire class, in small groups, or with an individual student.

- Announce that you are going to give the directions.
- Give the directions.
- Summarize the directions.
- Have students paraphrase the directions.
- After the student begins the assignment, check back to see if he is on the right track. You can remember this important fifth step if you visualize the restaurant server checking back on your satisfaction with the food about two minutes after the food is delivered to your table.

Directions for the Whole Class

- Use the white board, interactive white board, or charts to post directions and agendas the whole class is to follow. Place these important pieces of information in the same place each day.
- Use the class website as a communication tool so that both students and their parents know exactly what work is expected. Using the class website also provides an opportunity to include exemplars and rubrics.
- Even though the directions are posted, some students will need personalized desk copies to minimize visual tracking and visual memory problems.

Task Cards for Learning Centers and Group Work

Prepare task cards to provide directions for learning centers, small groups, and individuals. That way, the directions, sources of information, and/or tasks can be differentiated without making public announcements about who is doing what work. It makes no sense to give three different sets of directions to the entire group so task cards can help solve that problem.

Recorded Directions

- Recorded directions can be a life saver because students can have as many instant replays as they need. Some students will need to listen to part one of the directions, complete that part, and then listen to the next step in the directions before completing that step.
- Student work in learning centers can be guided via recorded directions as well.

Giving Directions

Use Graphic Organizers to Give Directions and Communicate Expectations

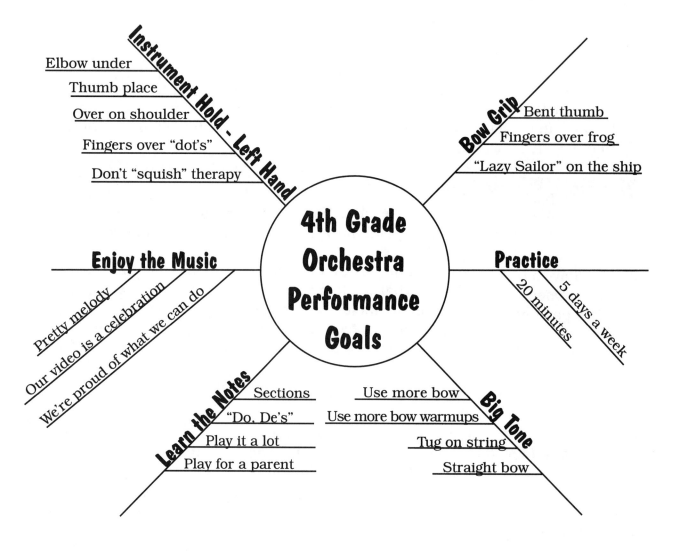

Mary Louise Veremeychik, West Irondequoit Central School District, NY

Growth-Producing Feedback

Feedback is an incredibly powerful teaching tool; Grant Wiggins writes that when growth-producing feedback is provided, most students can achieve at the same level as the top 20% of students. He also asserts that feedback has a positive impact on student engagement. Put quite simply, students who are given specific information about the accuracy and quality of their work will spend more time working on their academic assignments.

Grades Are Not Growth-Producing Feedback

It is important to have a clear definition of growth-producing feedback. Wiggins says that feedback is not about praise or blame, approval or disapproval. Good feedback describes what a student did or did not do for the purpose of changing or maintaining a behavior or performance. Robert Marzano and associates concur that effective feedback should provide students with an explanation of what they are doing correctly and what steps they must take to continue to make progress. Typical feedback includes such comments as "Nice work," "Unclear," "You need to improve your study habits," "C+," or "75%." These types of statements or grades show either an approval or disapproval of what a student has done, and are evaluative in nature. This type of feedback has very little effect on student learning and can have a negative impact on student motivation to learn. Students tend to ignore comments when they are accompanied by grades or numerical scores. Students pay much closer attention to written comments when they are not accompanied by a grade. Stephen Chappuis and Richard Stiggins found that "replacing judgmental feedback with specific, descriptive, and immediate feedback benefits students." Productive feedback tells students where they are on the continuum of mastery of given standards or benchmarks, what they are doing right, and next steps to take toward mastery.

Following Growth-Producing Feedback

Providing students growth-producing feedback is not enough. Students must have the opportunity to respond to the feedback, make adjustments in their work, and resubmit their assignments for further comments. When students are given these opportunities, they begin to develop skills of self-assessment and self-adjustment. We do not want students to be completely dependent on teachers to let them know if they are learning. We want them to develop skills that result in their having greater aspirations to succeed in the future, enjoying greater satisfaction from their learning, and setting future performance goals.

Adapted from the October 2006 *Just for the ASKing!* by Bruce Oliver. ©Just ASK Publications. All rights reserved.

Growth-Producing Feedback

> Feedback is not about praise or blame, approval or disappointment. Feedback is value-neutral. It describes what you did and did not do. … Praise is necessary but praise only keeps you in the game. It doesn't get you better.
>
> Grant Wiggins

Positive Examples

- Take a look at the example on the board. Look at my second step and compare it to what you have done.
- Remember that the objective is to make all your letters touch the line. Go back to your seat and fix the letters that don't follow that pattern.
- You must follow the steps in the recipe precisely. Go over the steps in the recipe and identify the step you missed.
- It's clear from your explanation that you have grasped the main ideas. I would recommend one change. Think about your third statement and see if you can make a better argument for your thesis statement.
- In number four, you are dividing fractions. Remember to invert the fraction and then multiply.
- Review the footnote format I gave you at the beginning of the assignment. Check to verify that all your footnotes match the guidelines and fix the ones that do not.
- I want you to listen to the tape again. Listen to how the narrator pronounces his words. Then come back and try your recitation with me again.
- Remember… *i* before *e* except after *c*. Using this rule go back and correct your spelling words.

Negative Examples

- I'm not sure you studied very long or hard on this test. I expected better results from you.
- There are just too many careless errors here. Take your paper back and correct your mistakes.
- I feel that I have presented this information in a clear cut manner. I've done my part. You just are not paying attention.
- Your work is showing great improvement. You're doing much better.
- C+ (without a rubric)
- Your writing lacks clarity and focus.
- Great work! You are becoming an excellent student.
- Your book report was just superb this time. I enjoyed reading it so much.
- You did not sound very good today. I hope you improve before next week's concert.

Formative Assessment

If It Hasn't Been Caught, It Hasn't Been Taught!

Leaders cannot be called leaders if no one is following. The same is true for teachers. Presenting or telling information is not teaching. In order to call ourselves teachers, our students have to be learning from the learning experiences we orchestrate. A significant component of our teaching repertoire has to be checking to see if our students are with us on the learning journey, or if we are going on the trip alone.

Strategies to find out where to "pick them up" for the learning journey are essential. Many of the active learning strategies we use to help students make meaning of the work can provide us with important assessment data. When we do a task analysis, access prior knowledge, or surface misconceptions and naive understandings, we gather a great deal of information about what students know and at what levels they can use that knowledge and those skills. In fact, we may find that we do not need additional pre-assessment data, but simply need to use the data we collect through those exercises.

In order to facilitate learning, we have to adjust the design of the learning experiences based on the data we collect not only at the beginning of the learning experience but throughout the work. In many instances the data is right in front of us, but we are not seeing it as "data" that can inform our decisions.

Formative or Summative?

Formative assessment results inform teachers about how well students are learning and inform students about where they are in the learning process. Summative assessment results reveal how students can apply the key concepts and essential understandings they are studying.

Any assessment can be formative or summative. While many forms of formative assessment are informal, it is not the format that determines its status; it is, instead, the way the results are used.

When we use assessment for formative purposes, students should receive growth-producing feedback and have the opportunity to make adjustments to their work based on that feedback. Of course, that means averaging grades is not an option.

Formative Assessment

We are not checking for understanding when we ask:
- "Are there any questions?"
- "Are you all with me?"
- "Am I going too fast?"
- "This is an adverb, isn't it?"

Given that the above are negative examples, what is checking for understanding? It is asking questions that can only be answered if students understand. Using Howard Gardner's definition of understanding, this would mean that students are able to use knowledge and skills in new situations in appropriate ways. While recall of significant information is an important part of learning, checking for understanding is not the same as checking for recall or memorization.

Another classroom dilemma is one that we all experienced as students. We sat in classrooms where the teacher asked many questions to the entire class and called on one student to answer. Given the number of students and the limited amount of time, the chances were pretty good that any one student was called on only once during the period. There are two big problems with that approach. One problem that the teacher only knows if the one student who answered the question knows or does not know the answer to, or, has or does not have an informed opinion on the point being discussed. The other problem is that the rest of the students can tune out if only volunteers are called on, or if the teacher makes it a practice to call on all students one by one. After students have answered they are off the hook. Why do we, as teachers, even consider continuing this practice year after year? If we want to scaffold or extend learning, it is essential that all students are actively engaged in demonstrating their current level of understanding so that we can match our interventions to their learning needs.

There are ways to check across many students on the same concept or skill in a relatively short time. As we incorporate **10:2 Theory** into our practice, a strategy that is easy to implement is **Think-Pair-Share**. This strategy meets the needs of the introverted learners who want time to think before talking because there is a short think time before any answers are accepted. Other possibilities include signal cards, slates, sort cards, journal entries, and homework. It also meets the needs of extraverted learners who need to talk to create meaning. See pages 238 and 202.

Resources
- See **Student Self-Assessment** on pages 222-228.
- See **Questioning** on pages 200-203.
- See **Making Assessment a Learning Experience** on the next page.

Making Assessment a Learning Experience
Formative Assessment

Try-Angle

Give each student a triangle with each side five inches in length. Have students write inside the triangle important information that they want to remember for an upcoming test. Students bring their "try-angle" to the testing situation and use the information as they complete the test.

Sharon Boudreau, Fairfax County Public Schools, VA

Chris' Test

Design a multiple choice test similar to the state or district test format. Acting as a fictional student named "Chris," take the test and distribute copies of the test that "Chris" took to the students. Have students work in pairs go through the test, question by question, and determine if Chris has answered each question correctly. In short, each pair of students grades the test. As they work together, students are reviewing content as well as discussing test-taking skills. Administer a similar test to the students the next day.

Brian Mandell, Fairfax County Public Schools, VA

Extra Inning

Collect test papers at the end of the period and announce that students will be able to have an extra inning tomorrow...ten minutes at the beginning of the period. They are to go home and study whatever they could not remember or figure out during the test. As promised, the next day they can work on their tests for an additional ten minutes. If you want to track what they struggled with have them use a different color ink or pencil. Do they get full points? Absolutely! We are into learning here and even those who had everything correct the first time are checking one more time!

David Brinkley, St. Vrain Valley School District, Longmont, CO

2 x 2

Correct two tests simultaneously. Mark only those questions that both students answered correctly. Return the papers for the two students to go over. They have to decide if they are both incorrect or which one is correct and submit a new consensus answer to the problem.

David Baker, St. Vrain Valley School District, Longmont, CO

Dump Your Brain

Prior to distributing an assessment, have students quickly write down the important information they remember from their studying. They can use that information as they complete the assessment.

Foldables

Foldables are three-dimensional graphic organizers that are widely used with English Language Learners. Dinah Zike has written several books describing various formats to use. The graphics below and the mind map on page 169 convey purposes, kinds, materials, content, and storage.

Resources

- The Catawba County Schools, North Carolina website provides examples of and directions for shutters, envelopes, shape books, matchbooks, layered books, accordion books, lapbooking, door folds, and tri-folds. Access the site at www.catawba.k12.nc.us/C_i_resources/Foldables.htm
- Directions for Foldables: http://newsouthvoices.uncc.edu/files/nsv/institute/Foldables.pdf
- Foldables for Math: http://pages.sbcglobal.net/cdefreese/foldables

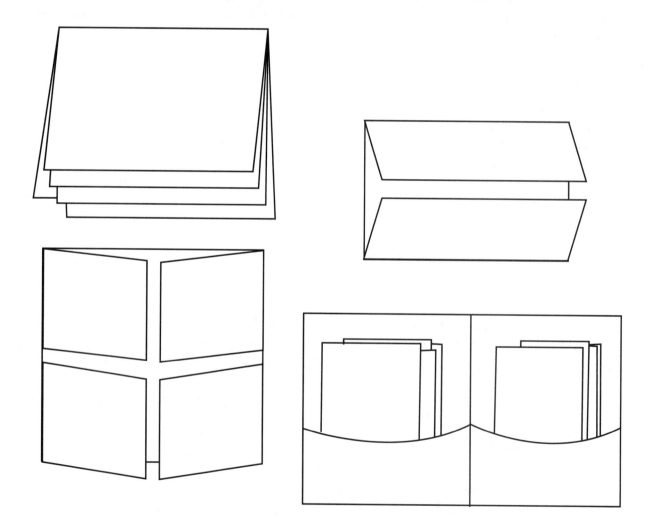

Framing the Learning

Providing context by framing the learning is essential scaffolding for all learners. When teachers include the following actions in their lesson plans, student learning increases by leaps and bounds. How we orchestrate these actions is a matter of matching to student needs. That we include these components in our instructional plans is simply not multiple choice. We must:

- Communicate standards, the learning process, and assessment by
  - Explaining what students need to know and be able to do.
  - Clarifying why students need to know and use what the standard targets.
  - Delineating the activities and assessments students will experience in order to process their learning.
  - Articulating how students will demonstrate learning and the criteria to be used for assessment.
  - Providing models for processes and products.
- Provide the agenda/outline for the day, unit, and year.
- Identify student naïve understandings and misconceptions and help students re-frame their thinking as appropriate.
- Help students access prior knowledge and make connections.
- Have students process, use, and summarize learning in meaningful and rigorous ways that promote retention and transfer.

Framing the Learning
Anticipation/Reaction Guide

Before Reading   **After Reading**

_____ 1. Accessing prior knowledge helps level the playing field for learners.   1._____

_____ 2. It is extremely difficult for students to give up misconceptions.   2._____

_____ 3. Providing exemplars for the learning of processes looks like what Madeline Hunter called guided practice.   3._____

_____ 4. Students in primary grades do not need to be informed of the learning standards.   4._____

_____ 5. Student achievement increases when students know what excellent work looks like.   5._____

Note: 4 is false.

Anticipation/Reaction Guide template is on CD-ROM.

Graphic Organizers

There is no doubt that graphic organizers are essential scaffolding, organizational, and thinking tools. Teaching students to use them independently should be a goal of every teacher. They are important to the learning process because by using them, teachers and students:
- Graphically display ways of thinking
- Organize ideas for discussions and writing
- Have tools for tackling and outlining text: See pages 276-277.

Types of Thinking Represented by Graphic Organizers
- **Compare and Contrast**: Venn Diagram, Matrix, Semantic Feature Analysis: See page 167 and 277.
- **Descriptive and Expository**: Mind Maps, Concept Maps, Story Maps, Fishbone, and Frayer Model: See pages 158, 169, 272, 277, and 287.
- **Sequence and Chronology**: Flow Charts, Time Lines, Story Boards, and Cycles; See page 168 and 277.
- **Classification and Taxonomy**: See page 167-168 and 277.
- **Cause and Effect**: See page 277.

Steps in Building Student Independent Use
These steps of the Gradual Release of Responsibility model are repeated as each new type of graphic organizer is introduced. The type of graphic organizer and the kind of thinking it represents is explicitly communicated in each step.
- Teacher points out and uses graphic organizers found in texts.
- Teacher uses completed graphic organizers to present information.
- Teacher presents an almost completed graphic organizer and students work with teacher to complete the organizer.
- Teacher uses graphic organizers that are less and less completed and students collaboratively, and eventually independently, fill in remaining information.
- Students are presented with a blank graphic organizer and use it to record ideas or capture information.
- After students have built expertise at using several graphic organizers, they are encouraged to select, with guidance, the one that best represents the kind of thinking required by the task they are to complete.

Student independent use of graphic organizers is the goal because they provide students the opportunity to use both nonlinguistic and linguistic representations of their thinking.

Inspiration and Kidspiration are popular technology tools for creating graphic organizers. For information go to www.inspiration.com.

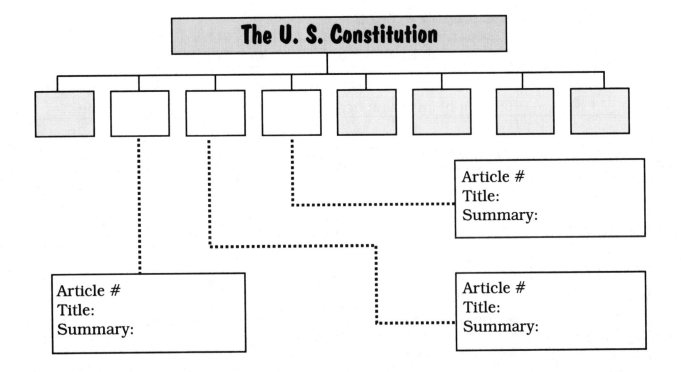

The U. S. Constitution

Article #
Title:
Summary:

Article #
Title:
Summary:

Article #
Title:
Summary:

From Sea to Shining Sea: The U.S. Grows Stronger and Larger 1800 to 1850

	Louisiana Purchase	Florida	Texas	Oregon	Mexican Cession	Gadsden Purchase
Date						
How?						
Why						
What It Is Like						

Graphic Organizer templates are on CD-ROM.

Scaffolding Learning
Graphic Organizers

Possessive Adjectives in French

		in front of masculine nouns. e.g., Mon papier
	Mon	in front of any noun beginning with a vowel. e.g., mon amie
		in front of any word beginning with an "h". e.g., mon hotel

My

Ma   in front of all feminine nouns, except those beginning with a vowel. e.g., ma poupee

Mes   in front of all plural nouns. e.g., mes papiers, mes amies, mes hotels, mes poupees.

Writing a Research Paper

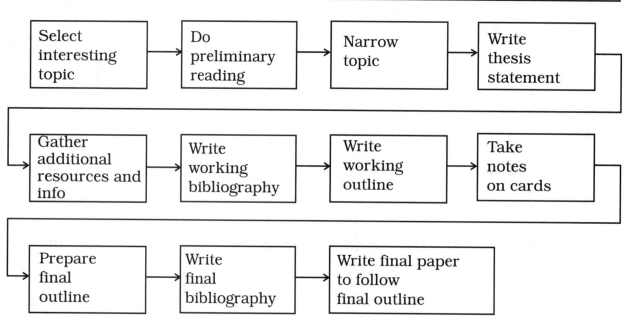

Select interesting topic → Do preliminary reading → Narrow topic → Write thesis statement

Gather additional resources and info → Write working bibliography → Write working outline → Take notes on cards

Prepare final outline → Write final bibliography → Write final paper to follow final outline

Graphic Organizers templates are on CD-ROM.

Scaffolding and Extending Learning
Class Mind Maps

Process

- Ask students to create a mind map of what they already know or remember about the concept or information they are learning.
- After the students have had a few minutes to work individually, have them work with a partner to build on what they recalled on their own.
- As a third step, have students work in table groups to create a table mind map on chart paper or have the entire class work together to create a class mind map on the board or Smart Board.
- To complete the exercise have students review the work of other students and note patterns and trends. Use the student-created work to point out significant information, to gather formative assessment data about what to re-teach or extend.

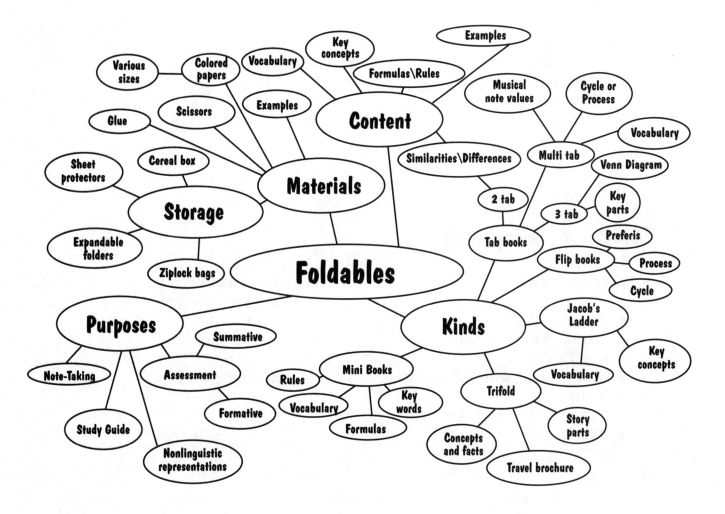

©Just ASK Publications

Grouping Practices

General Guidelines
- Grouping configurations include large group, small group, partnerships, and individually.
- Purposefully use a wide range of grouping configurations.
- Base grouping decisions on the complexity of the information and task as well as the familiarity of the students with the process.
- Rick Wormeli suggests a model in which students begin class in a whole group configuration, then move to small group work, and end the class by returning to the large group to share and summarize their learning.

Flexible Grouping Possibilities
- Student Choice
- Interest
- Homogeneous
- Heterogeneous
- Information processing style
- Readiness/skill level
    - Reading
    - Writing
    - Listening
    - Organizational
    - Social
- Random

Structuring Group Work
- Base groups
- Focus groups for
    - Extension
    - Remediation
    - Strategy Instruction
- Group Size
    - One-on-One with the teacher
    - Pairs
    - Groups of four or five
    - Whole class
- Assign Roles
    - Discussion Director
    - Materials Manager
    - Summarizer
    - Fact Checker
    - Encourager
    - Illustrator

Application for Group Membership

Name_____ Section_____

The information you provide on this form will be used to assign you to the group in which your special talents will be best utilized. Please be as honest and complete as possible.

Please mark an **S** on the line if the category describes what you consider to be a **strength** for you. Please mark a **W** on the line if the category describes one of your **weaknesses**. If you consider yourself **average** in the category described, please mark an **A** on the line.

S = Strength   W = Weakness   A = Average

_____ Reading

_____ Writing to be understood

_____ Writing mechanics

_____ Gathering materials

_____ Creative ideas

_____ Like to work hard

_____ Organizing time

_____ Organizing ideas

_____ Following directions carefully

_____ Careful printing

_____ Speaking in front of a group

_____ Cleaning up, putting things away

_____ Art work

_____ Listening

_____ Getting along with others

_____ Organizing people

In the space below, write a sentence or two that tells what is unique about you and why you would be a positive, contributing member of a group.

Independent Study

Compacting the curriculum for gifted, talented, and advanced learners not only minimizes student boredom and disengagement, it provides opportunities for students to engage in enriched learning either individually or in small groups. While the term independent study is most often used when discussing instructional programs for advanced learners, such study should be our goal for all of our students. This discussion of independent study is focused on how it can be a part of the instructional program in a general education classroom.

Giving students an independent task to do or letting them choose a task to do (watch a DVD clip, read a book, do Internet research and answer questions on a worksheet or summarize what they saw, read, or found) does not fit within the parameters of independent study. In fact, without purpose and thoughtful planning, it is simply bad practice. When planning for independent study there are three levels at which students might work:

- Guided
- Independent
- Self-initiated

According to Tomlinson, an independent study, be it guided, independent, or self-initiated, requires that students:

- Identify a question or a problem to investigate
- Put together a plan for that investigation
- Clearly articulate criteria for evaluating the process and the resulting product
- Complete the investigation
- Plan and implement a presentation of the product/results of the investigation

Needless to say, for independent study to function smoothly and productively, the teacher must know the students well and have a keen sense of their readiness to do each of the above tasks. Additionally, students must be able to or be taught how to self-assess, task analyze, and evaluate the effectiveness of their efforts, as well as build the capacity to self-adjust. Even the most advanced students may need scaffolding and structure as they move toward more independence.

For information useful in coaching students in the selection, design, and implementation of independent studies:

- See **Rigor and Relevance Framework** on page 95.
- See **Suchman's Inquiry Model** on page 174.
- See **RAFTs** on pages 205.
- Access the Study Guide for Problem-Based Learning at www.studygs.net/pbl.htm.
- Access the study guides for time management, problem solving/decision making, cooperative learning and more: www.studygs.net/index.htm.

Good for All But Especially for Gifted and Accelerated Students
Inductive Thinking Model (Taba)

Stage One   Concept Formation
Phase One   Creating and listing of data set
Phase Two   Grouping of data
Phase Three   Labeling and categorizing of data

Stage Two   Integration of Data
(Interpreting, Inferring, and Generalizing)
Phase Four   Identifying relationships
Phase Five   Exploring relationships
Phase Six   Making inferences

Stage Three Application of Principles or Ideas
Phase Seven   Predicting consequences and hypothesizing
Phase Eight   Explaining and/or supporting the predictions and hypotheses
Phase Nine   Verifying predictions

Implementation Guidelines
- Teachers may organize the data set or have the students create and organize the data set. If time is limited, the process can be shortened by teacher preparation of the data.
- During the process, teachers ensure that the stages occur in the right order. It is common for students to try to label the categories and then try to force items into their predetermined categories.
- Teachers plan and ask questions designed to help students move to the next stage at the appropriate time.
- When first using the process, the teacher decides when to move on to the next phase; as students gain experience with the model, they can make decisions about when to move on to the next phase.
- Props, or other visual cues, help to focus students on the topic to be studied. For example, when the lesson is based on current events, the covers of news magazines can be posted to remind students of specific events and of the kinds of events that make the news as they generate the data set.

Inquiry/Problem Solving Model (Suchman)

Steps in the Inquiry Model
- Identification of a content-based question/problem
- Presentation of process and the question/problem
- Formation of hypotheses
- Data gathering via questioning
- Analysis of data and formation of conclusions

Putting the Inquiry Model to Work

Identification of a Content-Based Problem
- The **problem/question** that serves as the basis of an inquiry lesson may surface as a result of ongoing study, or it may be identified by teacher and/or students as an appropriate focus of study.
- Teachers and students working in a **standards-based classroom** often organize their study on **essential questions** that are complex and, more often than not, have more than one "right" answer. This process is a powerful one for focusing student learning on the essential questions.

Presentation of the Problem
- The use of an **anticipatory set** or **props** helps students focus the problem. This increases the likelihood that students will make connections between this problem and their life experiences.
- Present an explicit statement of the problem/question orally and in writing.

Formation of Hypotheses
Students may spontaneously volunteer **hypotheses**, as well as ask the teacher or student leading the process questions that can be answered "yes" or "no."

Gathering Data
- In many instances, the teacher organizes the **data-gathering** process. As students build skills in organizing the process, more responsibility can be turned over to them.
- Who does the gathering of the data depends on the age of the students, the complexity of the problem, and the amount of time the teacher wants to spend on the **inquiry process** as compared to the time spent on the **content**.

Analysis of Data and Formation of Conclusions
- The data can be organized in a variety of ways. Students can be taught to use **graphic organizers** to organize data so it can be evaluated and patterns identified.
- Original hypotheses need to be revisited, revised, and perhaps eliminated, if the data does not support original conclusions.

Learning Buddies

Learning Buddies provide students with opportunities to develop verbal fluency, build in movement, access prior knowledge, process their learning, and to peer edit and check work.

Structuring the Process
- Announce a processing time.
- Provide a focus question or process directions to define the task.
- To build in movement, have the partners stand together as they follow the teacher's directions or answer the question. The time for these processing discussions is generally brief; 2-4 minutes is the norm.
- Circulate and listen in on the discussions to check for understanding and to hold the students accountable for talking about the designated topic.

Ways to Structure Partnerships
- Pairs can be carefully crafted by the teacher or randomly partnered by pulling names out of a hat, matching cards, counting off, etc. Formats for partnerships could be:
    - Heterogeneous by skill level, interests, and/or information processing style
    - Homogeneous by skill level, interests and/or information processing style
- **Clock Buddies**, **Element Buddies**, **Parent Function Partners**, etc. are efficient, long term, content specific adaptations of this structure. Students are given a graphic with slots for four to twelve "appointments." At each slot, two students record each other's name. This sign-up period takes about four to five minutes and provides an efficient way for students to interact during the next few weeks. Whenever the teacher announces a time for students to process learning, a partnership is identified and students meet with their partner. To further structure the partnerships, preassign one of two of the partnerships with heterogeneous or homogeneous skill levels. See examples on the next page.

Clock Buddies

Learning Buddy Exemplars

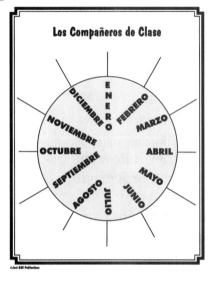

Los Compañeros de Clase

ENERO
FEBRERO
MARZO
ABRIL
MAYO
JUNIO
JULIO
AGOSTO
SEPTIEMBRE
OCTUBRE
NOVIEMBRE
DICIEMBRE

©Just ASK Publications

South America Learning Buddies

©Just ASK Publications

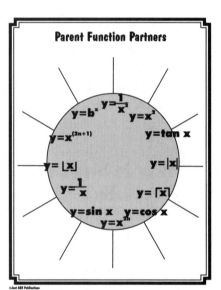

Parent Function Partners

$y=b^x$ $y=\frac{1}{x^3}$ $y=x^2$ $y=\tan x$ $y=x^{(2n+1)}$ $y=\lfloor x \rfloor$ $y=|x|$ $y=\frac{1}{x}$ $y=\lceil x \rceil$ $y=\sin x$ $y=\cos x$ $y=x^n$

©Just ASK Publications

Clock Buddies

Make an appointment with 12 different people (one for each hour on the clock). Be sure you both record the appointments on your clocks. Only make the appointment if there is an open slot at that hour on both of your clocks.

Tape this paper inside a notebook, or something that you
Bring to Class Each Day!

©Just ASK Publications

Canadian Collaborators

Yukon
Northwest Territories
British Columbia
Alberta
Saskatchewan
Manitoba
Ontario
Quebec
Newfoundland
Prince Edward Island
Nova Scotia
New Brunswick

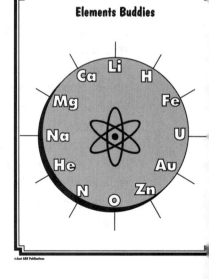

Elements Buddies

Ca Li H
Mg Fe
Na U
He Au
N O Zn

©Just ASK Publications

Learning Buddy templates are on CD-ROM.

Learning Centers

Learning centers provide rich opportunities to extend and enrich learning, a myriad of ways to fill in learning gaps, and allow students to pursue related areas of interest in more depth. While the term is most often used in an elementary context, centers can play an important role in the secondary classroom as well.

While learning centers can be actual locations in a classroom, when classroom space is limited, folders or boxes that can be taken by students to their seats or other available space. Directions for either kind of center can be recorded on differentiated task cards.

Types of Centers

Social Studies: Current events, travel brochures, historical investigations, maps and globes, artifacts contributed by the community or class members, careers in the social sciences, *National Geographic for Kids* and other magazines, web-based research and games

Math: Logic puzzles, stock market exploration, materials such as pictures and postcards that can be used to create word problems, careers in math, web-based research and games, math manipulatives

Science: Brain teasers, *Guinness Book of World Records* information and games, history of science, careers in science, current events, scientific journals, web-based investigations and games

Literacy: Poetry, puns, limericks, and other neglected genres to read and write, vocabulary development games to be played or created, literature from other countries, books at various reading levels

Interest: Developed for or by students who have expressed interests related to but not directly addressed by the standard curriculum

Enrichment: Creative writing, web-based investigations, primary sources, newspapers and journals, music, multiple intelligences opportunities (See pages 66-67 for ideas.)

Skill Building: Reading, math, fine motor

Primary: Art, language development, dramatic play with costumes and props, sand and water table, puppets, reading corner
www.mrsmcdowell.com/centers.htm and www.teachingheart.net/LC.htm are good resources for primary centers.

The possibilities offered by learning centers make them interesting and engaging learning opportunities for students. The chance to work in a learning center may encourage students to more fully attend to and complete other assignments. The range of materials selected and the complexity of the tasks developed and assigned make learning centers an outstanding opportunity for differentiation.

Learning Mats

The next time you are in a restaurant notice the placemats that serve as children's menus and provide younger diners activities to keep them engaged until the food arrives. Picture them 12 x 18 inches in size with learning tips as the border of the placemat. Bingo! You have learning mats. You can make yours using construction paper or poster board which you laminate after adding the learning tip borders. Possible borders include:

Math Borders
- small multiplication table in the upper right hand corner
- a ruler with both standard and metric measurements along the lower edge
- number facts
- equivalent fractions
- algorithm for converting percentages to decimals
- examples of distributive, associative, and commutative properties
- algorithm for the four operations on fractions and/or mixed numerals
- liquid, volume, and weight equivalents
- algorithm for the operations on whole numbers written as problems and as equations
- parent functions
- frequently used formulas
- examples of angles
- examples of polygons
- examples of shapes

English/Language Arts Borders
- punctuation marks
- examples of when to use capital letters
- upper case and lower case letters
- transition words
- paragraph organization
- graphic organizers for different kinds of thinking
- genres of literature
- types of poetry
- parts of a book

Learning Mats

Social Studies Borders

- graphic organizers for different kinds of thinking
- names of continents
- names of oceans
- directions on maps and globes
- geography terminology
- time line

Science Borders

- frequently used formulas
- liquid and volume measurements, equivalents, and abbreviations
- a ruler with both standard and metric measurements
- plant parts
- habitats
- body systems
- parts of a microscope
- water cycle
- kinds of clouds
- periodic table
- systems and interactions
- changes and patterns
- properties and measurements
- models and evidence

Variation: Tip Sheets

Tip Sheets are smaller scaffolds that can be carried in a three-ring binder or book bag and can range in size from 3" x 5" to 8 ½" x 11". These laminated tip sheets might be hole-punched for transporting in a three-ring binder or placed on a circle clamp for handy use. They could be stored in an index card box but that would make for more difficult transport between school and home.

Content might include any of the items listed above as well as formulas, translations, algorithms, maps, models of graphic organizers, templates for book responses, etc.

Ⅳ Manipulatives

Manipulatives allow learners to move from the concrete to the semi-abstract and then to the abstract word. To better understand this process think about first having a real or plastic apple, then a picture of an apple, and then finally the word apple. Or, better yet, think about yourself as a learner. When you are learning a new application or software package, how much does it help you to have an actual computer and the software package as learning tools, or, at least, have the explanation accompanied by models, pictures, charts and diagrams? When possible we want to provide our students opportunities to handle the information.

Most Used Manipulatives

- Cuisenaire Rods
- Tangrams
- Magnetic words, letters, numbers and/or mathematical symbols
- Tiles: These tiles are often used in math classes at both the elementary and secondary levels. Their use allows students to better visualize the mathematical operations they are performing. Tiles also come with words or letters on them that students can arrange into sentences.
- Sort cards: These cards can have vocabulary words, parts of math equations, historical events to sequence, coins and their value, digital clock faces and standard clock faces, word families to group, words and pictures to match, translations, etc. The act of sorting the cards allows students to handle and manipulate the information.
- Signal Cards: Provide students with red, yellow, and green cards that they can use to signal answers to questions posed by the teacher or other students. The universal languages of traffic lights, soccer, and car racing give immediate meaning to the three colors.
- Foldables: These three-dimensional graphic organizers are great favorites of kinesthetic learners and of teachers of second language learners. See pages 164 and 169.
- Wikki Stixs
- Models
- Bodies: Students often do body math such as illustrating angles with their arms, or signaling the operations to be completed.
- Virtual versions of concrete manipulatives typically used in mathematics education, such as Base 10 Blocks, Cuisenaire Rods, and Tangrams, are now available at no cost online. They can be manipulated with the mouse. Start your investigation at http://nlvm.usu.edu/en/nav/topic_t_1.html.

Mental Imagery/Pictures in Your Mind's Eye

The Power of Mental Imagery

Marzano reviews the literature and writes about the power of nonlinguistic representations. He includes the following learning experiences as examples of nonlinguistic representations:

- Generating mental pictures
- Creating graphic representations
- Making physical models
- Drawing pictures and pictographs
- Engaging in kinesthetic activity

Zimmerman and Hutchins list creating mental images as one of the seven keys to comprehension and Davey lists the lack of mental image formation as one of the habits of unsuccessful readers.

Leveling the Playing Field

Prior knowledge and life experiences greatly influence the mental pictures we create. Our task as teachers is to figure out how to build in our learners the capacity to visualize as they read and listen. We face a huge challenge with readers who are still struggling with decoding text and are therefore handicapped in their capacity to form mental images while reading. It is essential that we explicitly model forming visual images and monitor our students' use of this practice to aid in comprehension.

Instructional Process

- Explain that just as successful athletes form mental images of what a successful performance looks like, successful readers form mental images when they read.
- Introduce the process with short segments of highly descriptive text. As students become skilled at forming mental images, introduce more complex texts as well as expository texts that have students form mental images about abstract concepts and ideas, very large or small objects, and life in other lands or times.
- While reading text aloud, do a think aloud explaining the mental images you are seeing.
- Allow students to ask questions about what you are seeing.
- Have students describe their own mental images and encourage different perspectives.
- Have students draw their mental pictures and share them with classmates. A scaffolding tool called a Draw Aloud Organizer is available at: www.readwritethink.org/lesson_images/lesson792/draw2.pdf.

IV

Mini-Lessons

Mini-lessons are short lessons designed by the teacher for an individual or small group of students; they focus on content or a process that classroom data indicates needs to be pre-taught or re-taught. This classroom data may come from a task analysis, a pre-assessment, an error analysis, or a formative assessment. Formative assessment data can come from quizzes, journal entries, earlier assignments, homework, listening in on cooperative groups at work, conversations, student questions, or student responses to teacher questions.

Using Differentiated Packets to Structure Mini-Lessons

Prepare packets of materials that focus on a given concept or process and have them ready to use in mini-lessons. One way to use such packets without an inordinate amount of preparation time is as follows:
- Put together a packet of instructional materials or references to where the materials can be found in the classroom or on the Internet.
- Include in the packet learning experiences aligned with the standards that use the identified instructional materials.
- Include in the packet a table of contents of all materials.
- Based on data, indicate on the table of contents which of the materials and related learning experiences a given student or small group of students should complete by highlighting the tasks to be completed.
- Place students with similar learning needs in small groups.
- As the students work together, circulate among the groups and assist as appropriate. In some instances you may stop to lead the discussion or do some direct teaching.

Resident Experts or Coaching Corners

This approach to mini-lessons is student led. Identify students who have demonstrated mastery of the key concepts and processes that will be assessed in the near future or that have just been assessed. Place the "experts" in a section (corner) of the room. Either assign students to specific groups or have students, with training, go to the area where they participate in a mini-lesson on concepts or processes around which they need further study. In order to accelerate the learning of other students who have also demonstrated mastery, set up stations or corners where the discussions are structured to enrich and extend the thinking about the key concepts under study.

See page 183 for an example of how a Spanish III teacher used pre-assessment to establish focus groups for mini-lessons on the preterit and imperfect tense.

Pre-Assessment and Mini-Lessons
In Focus Groups

Objectives
- To see what students know and/or remember about preterit and imperfect tense
- To strengthen writing skills using the past tense

Process
- Have each student write answers to pre-assessment (See below.)
- Place students into appropriate group based on skill level
- Have each student write ½ page about his/her life at six years of age
- In their groups they edit papers together
- Work with each group as needed

Results
After students completed the pre-assessment, I had three groups.
- Group 1: Did not understand the questions or could not answer
- Group 2: Understood the questions but had multiple grammatical errors in the response
- Group 3: Had no or few errors in response

¿Quíen Soy Yo? ¿Quíen Era Yo?

1. ¿Dónde naciste? ¿Y cuándo?
2. ¿Dónde vivías cuando tenías 6 años?
3. ¿Qué hacías cuando tenías 6 años?
4. ¿A qué escuela asistías cuando tenías 6 años?
5. ¿Jugabas a unos deportes?
6. ¿Hiciste un viaje cuando eras más joven? ¿Adónde fuiste?
7. ¿Tenías un animal domestico cuando eras mas joven?
   ¿Qué tenías?
8. ¿Qué jugabas caundo eras más joven?
   ¿Qué juegos?¿Tenías unos juguetes favoritos?
9. ¿Qué hiciste el año pasado?¿En la escuela?
   ¿Y en tu tiempo libre?
10. ¿Trabajabas el año pasado? ¿Y dónde?
11. ¿Qué haces este año...?

Created by a teacher in Louise Thompson's **Meeting the Needs** workshop.

Ⅳ Mnemonics

Mnemonics are memory techniques that help many learners memorize factual information. Students can use some of the tried and true ones listed below or invent their own.

Jingles
- Thirty days hath September, April, June, and ...
- Spring forward, fall back: to remember how to change clocks to and from daylight savings time

Songs
- The Alphabet Song... Complete with a "lmnop" right in the middle
- New lyrics to songs like "Twinkle, Twinkle Little Star," or "Wheels on the Bus" to capture the key points to be remembered (See next page for example.)

Rhymes
- I before E except after C and in words like neighbor and weigh.
- In fourteen hundred and ninety-two Columbus sailed the Ocean Blue.

Acronyms
- ROY G. BIV for the order of the colors in the light spectrum: Red, Orange, Yellow, Green, Blue, Indigo, and Violet
- HOMES for the Great Lakes: Huron, Ontario, Michigan, Erie, and Superior
- PAW: Pour Acid into Water

Acrostic Sentences
- Never Eat Slimy Worms for N, E, S, and W on a map
- Every Good Boy Does Fine for the notes on the treble clef line
- Please Excuse My Dear Aunt Sally: Order of solving algebra equations - Parenthesis, Exponents, Multiplication, Division, Addition, and Subtraction
- My Very Energetic Mother Just Served Us Noodles for the order of the planets: Mercury, Venus, Earth, Mars, Jupiter, Saturn, Uranus, and Neptune.

Loci Method
The Loci Method is a mnemonic strategy that takes practice to master. In essence you remember a list of items by mentally placing them in a room or along a pathway you know well. You can remember more words if you can visualize the items in familiar locations.

Pegword System

One bun
Two shoe
Three tree
Four door
Five hive
Six sticks
Seven heaven
Eight plate
Nine line
Ten hen

When students need to remember a list of items or steps the pegwords listed to the left can be useful. Have students learn the pegwords and then have them draw a picture (or at least visualize) of the item attached to the pegword. For instance, if a student was memorizing the Bill of Rights she might draw a bun with a face on it with an open mouth and a speech bubble to represent freedom of speech. To represent the right to bear arms a student might draw or visualize a shoe with a gun sitting in it or draw human arms on the shoe. The key is the use of imagination and exaggeration to promote remembering the image and the information.

Formula Follies
Sing to the tune of "Wheels on the Bus"

For **perimeter** of a figure you add the sides, add the sides, add the sides
For **perimeter** of a figure you add the sides, all the way around!

Circumference of a circle is π x d, π x d, π x d,
Circumference of a circle is π x d, π is 3.14!

Area of a rectangle is length x width, length x width, length x width
Area of a rectangle is length x width, only for this shape!

Area of a triangle is 1/2 bh, 1/2 bh, 1/2 bh,
Area of a triangle is ½ bh, that's 1/2 times base times height!

Area of a circle is πr^2, πr^2, πr^2,
Area of a circle is πr^2, that's π x r x r!

The **volume** of a rectangle is lwh, lwh, lwh,
The **volume** of a rectangle is lwh, that's length times width times height!

Sue Quinn and Joanne Fusare-White, Rush-Henrietta Central School District, NY

Models of Process and Products

Models provide guided practice and clarity about expectations and directions. They may come in the form of teacher, student, or technologically-generated demonstrations, analysis of work by previous students, examination of professional work, work scored against a rubric, or teacher and class doing a run-through of the process together with no grades assigned.

Frequently used processes and products such as algorithms in math, formulas in science, paragraph or essay structure are best posted in the classroom for easy access. Some students may need copies at their desks. Posting such visuals or using podcasts on the classroom website can also facilitate student success and support parents in working with students.

The Right Stuff!

A third grade team in West Irondequoit Central School District, Rochester, New York, published a booklet titled: **The Write Stuff**. It included the district writing learning standards for third grade, exemplars of each type of writing the students would be asked to complete during the year, and rubrics for each type of writing. Students used this tool to guide their own writing and parents had access to exemplars of quality third grade writing.

Biography PowerPoint Presentation Exemplar

The outline of your PowerPoint presentation will help you select and present information about your book in a five-minute oral report.
In preparing the PowerPoint slides use:
● background colors that contrast highly with the text.
● a text font at least 24 points or larger.
● graphics that are appropriate to your text.

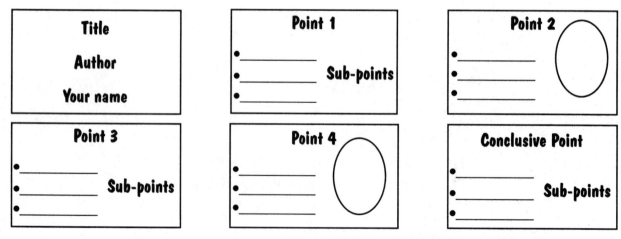

Suzanne Kisielica, New Trier High School, Winnetka, IL

Music and Movement

Ways to Build in Movement

- Use role plays, skits, and pantomimes.
- Have students play charades to communicate big ideas.
- Have students use their bodies to represent the continents, the equator, the Tropic of Cancer, etc. The waist line would be the equator and the chest the tropic of Cancer. Have students chant continent names or set the names to a song like Frère Jacques.
- Have students create short commercials in which they act out/advertise exciting points of learning.
- Use active learning strategies like **Corners** and **Inside-Outside Circles**.
- Use a ball toss process to call on students to answer questions.
- Paint map of USA and map of the world on playground and have students play hopscotch on the maps.
- Create human bar graphs.
- Have students signal math operations, angles, punctuation, and responses to questions.
- Organize contests in which students "mail" pictures or words in paper bags. Create mailboxes (paper bags) labeled with beginning sounds, parts of speech, continents, and distribute lots of pictures or words to be mailed (sorted) into the mailboxes.
- Place a number line on the floor and have students practice adding and subtracting by moving on the line.

Musical Moments

Have students write new lyrics to childhood favorites and, on occasion, choreograph movements to go with the new lyrics. (Yes, high school students will like it no matter how loudly they complain.) Song possibilities include:
- Twinkle, Twinkle, Little Star
- Frère Jacques
- Home on the Range
- Three Blind Mice
- This Land is Your Land
- Mary Had a Little Lamb

Total Physical Response (TPR)

Access information about TPR created by James Ascher at:
- www.tpr-world.com/ABC.html: The ABC's of The Total Physical Response
- www.tprsource.com/asher.htm
- www.dupage.k12.il.us/_includes/services/doc/3-TOTAL%20PHYSICAL%20RESPONSE.DOC

Note-Taking Formats

Each of us uses a variety of formats to take notes. What works for one does not work for another and what works in one situation does not work in another. The same is true for our students. Our tasks are to teach students what information should be included in notes and to introduce them to multiple ways to take notes and then work with them as they determine which note-taking formats work best for them and when each is best used.

Graphic Organizers and Mapping

See pages 276-277 for information on the selection of graphic organizers based on text structure and/or the kind of thinking to be used in the paper or presentation they are preparing. Also see pages 166-169 for examples and how to model and scaffold the selection and use of graphic organizers so students build expertise in selecting and using the best one for the text they are reading.

Newspaper Notes

Mildred Gore's method uses a matrix format on which the students outline events in sequence recording about each: when, where, who did what, how, to whom, why, and the effect. See template on page 192.

Five-Column Notes

See miniature template on next page.
This note-taking format can be completed in either columns or boxes with each column or box representing one of the following:
- The big idea
- Details
- Connections to other texts
- Connections to world
- Connections to self

Interactive Notebooks

See page 193.

Cornell Notes

This two-column note-taking format requires that students draw a line the length of their paper about three inches from the left side. They take notes to the right of the line and then use the space to the left of the line to make connections, ask questions, record vocabulary words, etc. This note-taking format can be scaffolded by providing an outline of the notes with selected words missing and some questions and points already noted in the left-hand column. See miniature template on next page.

Note-Taking Formats

Customized Formats

See page 191 for a template designed to match a particular assignment. This assignment could be scaffolded by providing access to easy-to-read newspapers like *USA Today* and can be extended by having students design their own note-taking format and use newspapers like *The New York Times* and *The Wall Street Journal* in either hard copy or online.

Resources

Jim Burke, HS English teacher in Burlingame, California presents many templates for note taking on his website. Permission is expressly given to teachers to use them in their instructional programs. Access these at www.englishcompanion.com.

Cornell Notes

Key Points	Lecture, Discussion, or Reading Notes
Students put summaries, questions, vocabulary words, connections and graphics in this section.	Teachers can scaffold this section by providing a note taking outline with information already inserted. Desktop publishing makes it easy to prepare two or three versions with more or less information provided. The key points section can also be scaffolded by providing guidance as to a few of the ideas to be included in that section.

Five-Column Notes

The Big Idea	Details	Connections to Other Texts	Connections to World	Connections to Self

Note-Taking Format templates are on CD-ROM.

Note-Taking Formats

Strategy Log

Use a strategy log to help you think about the strategies that you use.

Page/Paragraph/ Problem	Problem I Had	Strategy I Used	How It Worked
Page 210 "Principles in Geometry"	Couldn't remember the difference between a line and a ray	Words in bold type. Glossary. Illustration of each concept in my notes	Worked well. I refer to my notes as a quick reference to keep these terms straight

Making Connections Log

What I Already Know About the Topic/ the Process/the Procedure	Questions I Have About the Topic/Process	What the Text Says About the Topic/Process	How I Can Connect This to Other Ideas or Texts	How I Can Use This Information

Listening Log for Civil Rights Supreme Court Cases

As you listen to group presentations, fill in the chart below.

Case	Year	Issue	Outcome

Note-Taking Format templates are on CD-ROM.

The Bill of Rights in Action

Find newspaper articles to prove that these rights are at work in the United States today. Put the date of the article, name of the article (the headline), and the page on which you found it in the boxes labeled for the various rights. You may need to use several different days' papers to complete the activity.

Right to Bear Arms	Right to Legal Counsel	Right to a Jury Trial
Right to Freedom of the Press	**Right to Protection from Cruel and Unusual Punishment**	**Right to Peacefully Assemble**
Right to Freedom of Speech	**Right to Privacy**	**Right to Freedom of Religion**
	Right Protecting Self-Incrimination	

Sue Betham, Jeanne Hamel, and Bryan McKinnley, Rush-Henrietta Central School District, NY

Gore's Newspaper Notes

When	Where	Who	Did What	How	To Whom	Why	Effect

Gore's Newspaper Notes template is on CD-ROM.

Interactive Notebooks

One of the most exciting innovations to promote student processing of new learning is the **Interactive Notebook** described in Addison Wesley's **History Alive!** and widely used by teachers of history and other social sciences. The uses of the **Interactive Notebook** extend to all areas of study because the structure and potential contents capture the essence of active participation, multiple intelligences, and the variables of the brain-compatible classroom.

To get started with the **Interactive Notebook** process, ask students to purchase and bring to class each day an 8½ x 11 inch spiral notebook with at least one hundred pages and a container holding a pen, a pencil with an eraser, at least two felt tip pens of different colors, and at least two highlighters of different colors. Other desirable equipment includes a small pair of scissors and a glue stick. If the cost is prohibitive for some students, create classroom supply kits.

Students are taught productive methods of note taking during lectures, readings or other presentations that they record on the **right side of their notebooks**. They are encouraged to vary size of letters, boldness of letters, use of capital letters and lower case letters, indentations, underlining, bullets, colored markers, and highlights in the note-taking process.

The **left side of the notebook** is reserved for student processing of the information recorded on the **right side**. Students can be asked to review and preview, draw maps, think of a time when..., summarize in a sentence, create graphic organizers, create a metaphor, respond to "what if" questions, or take a stand. Additionally, encourage them to add newspaper clippings or political cartoons, drawings and illustrations, or other such personal touches. The use of color and visual effects is highly encouraged! The left or processing side, can be completed in class or as homework.

Access a PowerPoint on Interactive Notebooks at http://teachers.henrico.k12.va.us/fairfield/saunders_d/batcave/interactive+notebook.ppt

Pictures and Pictographs

A picture is worth a thousand words. The 15,000-year-old paintings in the Altamira Cave near Santillana del Mar, Spain are the most acclaimed examples of Paleolithic art works. As that previous sentence is read, without pictures or prior experiences with the Altamira Cave, it has absolutely no meaning for the reader. Thus, the power of pictures and pictographs. It is our responsibility to provide visual representations if we want our students to truly understand what they are studying. The Internet provides limitless access to the world so there is no excuse for not providing students with all the visual reinforcement they might need.

A pictograph uses pictures or symbols to represent an assigned amount of data. Directions for how you or students can turn an Excel spreadsheet into a pictograph are available at www.microsoft.com/education/createpictograph.mspx.

Pictures and pictographs support the learner as they move from the concrete to the semi-abstract to the abstract spoken and written word or number. Using programs such as KidPix, Inspiration, Kidspiration, and Excel give students the opportunity to draw pictures or create pictographs (symbols) to represent ideas, events, places or objects. Students can:

- Illustrate a process (life cycles, writing process, solve an equation, science concept, government process, etc.)
- Create a story web
- Make a map
- Create pictographs for math

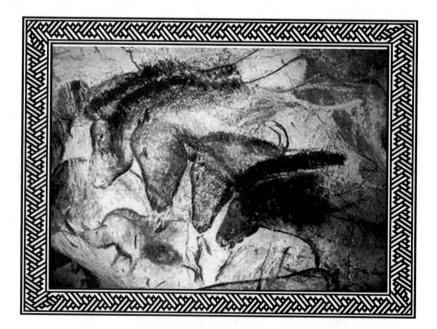

Practice and Rehearsal

Bands and orchestras do it. Football and soccer teams do it. Actors and actresses do it. Tennis players and golfers do it. Teenagers learning to drive do it. Singers and dancers to it. They all do it with coaches, and their practices and rehearsals are not averaged into the game or match score or reported in the review by the theater or movie critic. We need to use the same process in the classroom. Since practices and rehearsals are an important part of the learning process we need to figure out how to make practices and rehearsals learning experiences rather than tasks that are averaged into final grades or the game score.

Practice Points to Ponder

- **Guided practice with feedback**: This type of practice takes place in the classroom right after new processes have been introduced. Students should be sent home to practice only processes that they can complete with a 80 to 90% success rate. Practice does not make perfect; practice makes permanent. That means that we do not want students doing homework that they can not do independently.

- **Practice of discrete parts with feedback**: When a musician is playing a piece and makes a mistake, there is a tendency to start over. That practice is ineffective because the musician is practicing the part played correctly the first time. The way to learn the musical piece is to practice the component that was problematic and then go back to the beginning adding the newly mastered next step to what was already mastered. It is imperative that the teacher work with students to identify where processes are breaking down and help them build expertise with that discrete part rather than continuing to do what they already know how to do.

- **Backwards chaining**: In this format of practice and rehearsal, all the steps except the last one are completed by the teacher and the student is required to do only the last step. When the last step is mastered, the task is presented again with the last two steps left to the student, and so on until the student can do the entire task. Ths approach is especially useful with students who have trouble completing multiple-step processes.

- **Independent practice with feedback**: This practice format is like a dress rehearsal. It is not time for the curtain to go up or for a grade as if it were show time/the summative assessment. It is the time for students to attempt to complete the task without assistance from the teacher or parents. Immediate and growth-producing feedback for the teacher is an important component of this format. The length of time and the guidance that occurs to get to this point is representative of how we scaffold learning.

Prior Knowledge

According to the landmark 1984 *Handbook on Reading Research*, accessing prior knowledge has more to do with student achievement than does native ability as we currently measure it. Having students access and use prior knowledge yields a variety of results. The data is clear that this is one of the non-negotiatables of best practice because it:

- Levels the playing field
- Surfaces misconceptions and naive understandings
- Promotes personal meaning-making
- Provides the teacher with pre-assessment data so that the teacher can use students' experiences, stories, examples, and mistakes to frame the upcoming learning

Accessing prior knowledge can be scaffolded by modeling, previewing topics or concepts via technology, providing a word bank or providing three possible responses for student use. Accessing prior knowledge can be extended by building on the rich and diverse experiences and thinking academically advanced students bring into the classroom. The four strategies described here and on the next three pages, **Sensational Sentences**, **Frame of Reference**, **Stir the Class**, and **Sort Cards**, are strategies that provide opportunities for advanced learners to build on their own and each other's background knowledge; at the same time, all four strategies can easily be scaffolded.

Sensational Sentences

This strategy is one way to access prior knowledge, surface misconceptions and naive understandings, have students make predictions, set purpose for reading, and introduce new vocabulary all at once. See the template on the following page and on the CD-ROM.

To set up the exercise:

- Select 10 words related to the upcoming lesson. Include both known and unknown words and concepts.
- Place or have the students place those words in the Word Box.
- Have students create five sentences by using two words in each sentence until all words are gone.
- Provide input of new information (text, visual, guest speaker, etc.)
- Following the lesson, have students reread the sentences they wrote and correct those that are incorrect.
- For active engagement, have students use some form of a silent signal or cheer when they encounter information that matches what they predicted.

Sensational Sentences

_____

Topic/Concept

Word Box

```
_____        _____
_____        _____
_____        _____
_____        _____
_____        _____
```

___ 1. _____

_____

_____

___ 2. _____

_____

_____

___ 3. _____

_____

_____

___ 4. _____

_____

_____

___ 5. _____

_____

_____

Sensational Sentences template is on CD-ROM.

Accessing Prior Knowledge

Frame of Reference

- Place the topic or issue to be discussed in the center of the matted frame where a picture would be placed in a picture frame.
- Give students several minutes to individually jot down words or phrases that come to mind when they hear or see the term "pictured." These words go in the "mat" area of their frame of reference.
- Ask students to then jot down how they came to know what they know or think...that is the sources, people, events that have influenced their thinking. These reactions go in the "frame" area of the graphic.
- Following the individual reflection and writing, ask students to share their **Frame of Reference** with a partner or a small group.

Stir the Class

- Provide each student with a data collection sheet containing ten to twenty lines, or have them number their own sheets.
- Have each student write, as directed, three reasons, three causes, three points of interest, etc., about the topic/concept to be studied. Ask them to make the third one on their list unique.
- At a signal, have students move around the room collecting/giving one idea from/to each student. Ideas received from one student can be passed on to another student.
- After an appropriate amount of time, ask students to return to their seats. Have them compare lists, prioritize, categorize, design research projects, etc.
- At this point, continue with the lesson being sure to include the ideas students generated.

Sort Cards

- Have students, working individually, generate words and short phrases that come to mind when they think of a designated topic. Ask them to record each idea on a separate index card.
- Have students share ideas, clarify similar ideas and eliminate duplicates
- Have students sort the ideas of the group into categories. The categories can be created by the students or the teacher can identify categories for student use.
- When the sorting and labeling is completed, have students take a tour around the room to observe and analyze the work of other groups. Ask one student to stay behind at the base table to answer questions.
- To extend thinking: Ask students to do metacognitive processing; that is, have them process how they went about their thinking as they generated, sorted, categorized, labeled, and analyzed the work of others.

See miniature templates for Frame of Reference and Stir the Class on page 199.

Accessing Prior Knowledge Tools

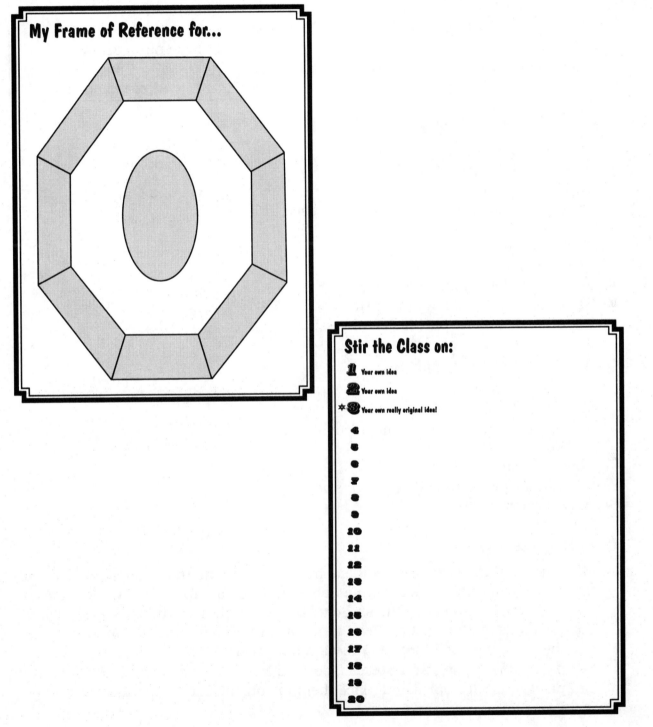

My Frame of Reference for...

Stir the Class on:

1. Your own idea
2. Your own idea
3. Your own really original idea!
4.
5.
6.
7.
8.
9.
10.
11.
12.
13.
14.
15.
16.
17.
18.
19.
20.

Frame of Reference and Stir the Class templates are on CD ROM.

Questioning and Prompts

> Most teachers waste their time by asking questions which are intended to discover what a pupil does not know whereas the true art of questioning has for its purpose to discover what the pupil knows or is capable of knowing.
>
> Albert Einstein

Purposes of Questioning
- To initiate a discussion
- To pique student curiosity
- To focus students on a new concept or a different aspect of a concept
- To access prior knowledge and experience
- To consolidate previous learning
- To surface misconceptions
- To check for understanding
- To help students make connections
- To promote retention and transfer
- To break down complex tasks and issues

Questioning Considerations
- Level of thinking required
- Wait Time I and II
- Response to incomplete or incorrect answers
- Probing questions
- Advance notice
- What to do when students don't answer

See page 81 for suggestions.

Questioning Tips
- McKenzie and Davis suggest that teachers tell students that a question is a one-minute, five-minute, or ten-minute question. Such an approach would lead not only to deeper thinking by the students but to much more thoughtful design of the questions by the teacher. Read more at http://fno.org/toolbox.html
- See the next page for **Bloom's Question and Task Wheel**.
- See page 203 for **Question Stems Bookmark**. It is also on the CD-ROM so you can print multiple copies and place them in your teacher's manuals and other texts.

Questioning and Prompts

Extending Learning with Prompts

Ask students to go beyond summarizing what they learn. Expand the prompts you give them to include:

- Alter... the variables, the setting, the context
- Analyze... the causes, the effects, the alternatives
- Categorize
- Classify
- Compare and contrast
- Compose
- Construct
- Critique
- Defend
- Develop
- Expand
- Imagine
- Invent
- Rank
- Recommend
- Suppose
- Transpose

Bloom's Taxonomy Question and Task Design Wheel

Bloom's Taxonomy Worksheet template is on CD-ROM.

Scaffolding Questioning
Think-Pair-Share

Purposes
- To provide processing time
- To build in wait time
- To provide rehearsal
- To enhance depth and breadth of thinking
- To increase level of participation
- To provide opportunities to check for understanding
- To allow the teacher to intervene with one or two students without an audience

Process
- Ask a question.
- Ask students to think quietly about possible answers to the question; this is usually only thirty seconds to one minute, unless the question is quite complex. (**think**)
- Have students pair with a neighbor or a learning buddy to discuss their thinking. The discussion usually lasts two to three minutes. (**pair**)
- Ask students to share their responses with the whole group or with a table group. Not all students have to share their answers with the large group. (**share**)

Some teachers use hand signals, pointers, bells, cubes, etc. to mark transition points during the cycle. When appropriate, students can write notes, web or diagram their responses during the "Think" or "Pair" time. Students can either explain their own thinking, that of their partners or the consensus they reached. **Think-Pair-Share** can be used 2-5 times during an instructional period.

Think-Pair-Share in Action
Traci Thorstenson, a first grade teacher in Prince William County Schools, Virginia, used **Think-Pair-Share** in her first grade classroom during a math lesson on measuring length using non-standard units of measure. In reflecting on its impact on learning she wrote: When I asked the students why they got different answers when they measured the same object using three different units of measure, only a few students raised their hands to answer the question. I then asked all students to think of their answer in their heads and then tell a neighbor what they were thinking. After a couple of minutes of students discussing their thinking with their neighbors, I signaled for their attention and asked my initial question again. This time, almost all the students raised their hands to answer. The use of **Think-Pair-Share** led to an immediate increase in both my capacity to access their understanding and in the likelihood that all students grasped the concept.

Questions Stems
That Promote Student Thinking

- What should we be asking about ...?
- What do you need to do next?
- Based on what you know, what can you predict about...?
- Does what...said make you think differently about...?
- Tell me how you did that?
- How does...tie in with what we have learned before?
- Suppose...what then?
- How does this match what you thought you knew?
- What might happen if...?
- When have you done something like this before?
- What might...think about this?
- How would you feel if...?
- How did you come to that conclusion?
- How about...?
- What if...?
- What do you think causes...?
- Yes, that's right, but how did you know it was right?
- When is another time you need to...?
- What do you think the problem is?
- Can you think of another way we could do this?
- Why is this one better than that one?
- How can you find out?
- How is...different (like)...?
- What have you heard about..?
- Can you tell me more?
- What else do you see?
- How does that compare with...?
- What do we know so far?

Questions Stems
That Promote Student Thinking

- What should we be asking about ...?
- What do you need to do next?
- Based on what you know, what can you predict about...?
- Does what...said make you think differently about...?
- Tell me how you did that?
- How does...tie in with what we have learned before?
- Suppose...what then?
- How does this match what you thought you knew?
- What might happen if...?
- When have you done something like this before?
- What might...think about this?
- How would you feel if...?
- How did you come to that conclusion?
- How about...?
- What if...?
- What do you think causes...?
- Yes, that's right, but how did you know it was right?
- When is another time you need to...?
- What do you think the problem is?
- Can you think of another way we could do this?
- Why is this one better than that one?
- How can you find out?
- How is...different (like)...?
- What have you heard about..?
- Can you tell me more?
- What else do you see?
- How does that compare with...?
- What do we know so far?

Question Stems Bookmark is on CD-ROM.

Real-World Connections

Keene and Zimmermann, in **Mosaic of Thought**, recommend that readers be taught to make three kinds of connections: **text-to-self**, **text-to-text**, and **text-to-world**. This easy to remember yet powerful construct is easily extended beyond text to all learning experiences be they writing, speaking, listening, or creating.

Text-to-Text Connections

Tom Loftus, Greece Central School System, New York, used the essential question, "Is the world a fair and just place?" He has his students discuss and write about that question from the perspectives of The Pearl Buyer from Steinbeck's **The Pearl**, of Cora and Juana from Langston Hughes' "Cora Unashamed," and Romeo and Juliet from Shakespeare's **Romeo and Juliet**.

Text-to-Self Connections

The social studies assignment described on page 291 calls for students to translate the events of the American Revolution into their lives in their own elementary school.

Text-to-World Connections

The student exemplar "Heaven on a Plate" on pages 153-154 is an example of taking the learning beyond the classroom and having students write about their experiences in the world. The author of this restaurant review had an audience beyond the teacher's in-box because he sent the review to the restaurant and was invited to take a tour of the kitchen the next time he ate at the restaurant. For this assignment, students had a choice of a restaurant review, a theatre, movie, or television show review, or an article about a sporting event so all students had access to a real-world source.

RAFT

To make real-world connections, students need audiences for their work that extend way beyond the teacher's in-box. That is, they need opportunities to create real products for real audiences. One strategy for designing learning experiences that promote that kind of student work is **RAFT** which is explained on the next page.

Real-World Connections

RAFT

RAFT requires students to engage in scenarios and create products for real audiences. It allows them to consider information from a variety of perspectives and to use a wide range of formats to present information to limitless audiences. This brain-compatible approach causes students to rethink, rewrite, and discuss an event or concept in another place or time or through the eyes or voice of the famous or familiar. An array of online possibilities can be included. There is a list of potential products and perspectives (roles and audiences) on the CD-ROM.

Using the planning template pictured below, teachers created the following **RAFTs** for their students.

Role _____

Audience_____

Form (product) _____

Time _____

Elementary Science

Role: You are a member of Bat Conservation International.

Audience: Your audience is community leaders.

Form: Your job is to write an article for the ***Greece Post*** on behalf of Bat Conservation International. You are to convince the people in the community that we should do all we can to save the bats.

Time: You must complete this assignment by Friday, April 1st so that it can be printed in Monday's edition of the ***Greece Post***.

Barb Bedner, Greece Central School District, NY

AP Statistics

Role: Project manager for small overnight delivery company

Audience: Employees in the shipping department

Form: Memo based on a computer-generated regression formula for the cost of shipping during the last month: Language used has to be accessible to non-mathematicians.

Time: Current

Randy Zamin, New Trier Township High School, IL

A list of perspectives and products and a template for creating RAFTs are on CD-ROM.

IV Real-World Connections

Props, Realia, and Physical Models

Realia, a term used in the field of language acquisition, means actual (real) objects used as instructional tools. The use of realia and physical models allows learners to see, hear, and in some cases, handle the objects. Recently the term virtual realia has come into use to represent digital images of artifacts used to help connect abstract concepts to the world beyond the classroom, especially as related to culture. All of us learn from having models and artifacts readily available for up close examination. Why else would we devote leisure days to trips to museums and art galleries? Our task as teachers is to be constantly looking for concrete materials and technology-based virtual realia and field trips to enhance our instructional programs.

The Wonderful World of Reading

Tovani writes about the importance of having accessible reading materials available in the classroom. That means, in addition to gathering props, realia, and physical models to help our students make real-world connections, we need to gather words, words, and more words for our students to interact with every moment of the day. Sources of materials include doctors' offices, grocery stores, airports, train stations, community centers, restaurants, city offices, concerts, etc. Gathering such materials can become a class project. Possible materials to gather include:

- Comic books
- Catalogs
- Children's literature
- Magazines and newspapers
- Cliff Notes
- Abridged versions
- Word games
- Board games
- Poetry
- Puns, jokes, and riddles
- Books in other languages
- Books from around the world
- Logic puzzles
- Maps and atlases
- Posters and charts
- Menus
- Recipes
- Flyers
- Online games and interactive materials
- Content specific journals
- Multiple genres of books
- Dictionaries
- Encyclopedias
- Brochures: travel, real estate, wellness, automobiles, motor cycles, etc.
- Labels and signs
- Schedules
- Technical how-to directions
- Student work
- Books of music
- Books with CD-ROMs
- Books and materials by and about a variety of ethnic groups

There are language arts, math, science, and social studies possibilities in each of these!

Role Playing and Simulations

Powerful learning can occur if we have students make meaning of their learning through real-world connections and the use of complex thinking skills. Assuming the persona of a character from literature or a person in history and/or creating products for such people causes students to process the learning at a much deeper and more enduring level.

Discussions over Time and Place
- Place an essential or focus question in the square in the middle of the page.
- Place the names of characters from various pieces of literature, people from various countries, people from various time periods, or any set of people who would have differing viewpoints on the question under study.
- Students speak, discuss, debate, or write about the question from the perspective of one or more of the persons.

Simulations
A simulation is a learning experience in which students create an "as if" environment. Simulations cause learners to move into another time period, another place, or assume the perspective or role of another person. Such learning experiences move from the contrived nature of readings and worksheets to situations that help students make personal meaning of the concepts being studied.

Simulations can be brief and spontaneous ("Pretend you have just landed at the Cairo airport") or highly structured and ongoing (a recreation of the Renaissance or a simulation of life in a rainforest). The latter requires considerable preparation and orchestration. Fortunately, there are many commercially prepared simulations available to supplement your creativity and that of your students. Before creating or selecting and using a longer simulation, be sure to ask yourself if it is worthy of the instructional time that will be consumed. Be sure that you review the standards and check your pacing plans to ensure that this engaging exercise is the best use of time.

Sheltered Language

Just as an umbrella protects us from rain and a house protects us from all elements of weather, sheltered language should be used to protect English Language Learners (ELLs) from the elements of English that might unnecessarily interfere with language and content learning. Just as we have to remember to take an umbrella with us or close the windows to keep out wind, rain, or snow, we have to be purposeful in sheltering our language in the classroom so that ELLs can safely and successfully engage in high levels of learning. Many of the suggestions listed in **Chapter III: What Do You Do When...** section on English Language Learners on pages 104-107 are useful in sheltering language.

Key Points to Remember

- Use a sequence of simple sentences rather than a compound or complex sentence.
- Speak in complete sentences and ask English-speaking students to do the same. This provides a model of sentence structure for ELLs (and practice for the English-speaking students).
- Monitor your rate of speech.
- Pause for processing, word retrieval, and translation.
- Repeat rather than rephrase. Students have to start the translation process over when the directions or information is presented using different wording.
- Be cognizant of words with multiple meanings and point out those multiple meanings to students as appropriate.
- Point out signal words such as first, second, third, and on the other hand which explain process.
- Avoid pronouns; use nouns instead.
- Be mindful of idioms, jargon, and slang.
- Include both content-specific and language-development objectives in instructional design.
- Use props and realia.
- Use nonlinguistic representations such as graphic organizers, charts, and pictures.
- Demonstrate.
- Role play.
- Label objects in room.
- Consider Total Physical Response (TPR).
- Remember that it takes much longer to do homework in a second language and plan assignments accordingly.
- Create a library of supplementary reading materials written in simpler language.

Sheltered Language

Best Practices That Work Well with ELLs

- Select from scaffolding and extension tools
- Use manipulatives
- Activate prior knowledge
- Consider cultural frames of reference
- Provide a clear explanation of tasks
- Engage high-level thinking
- Provide direct instruction in thinking strategies
- Provide growth-producing feedback
- Using cooperative learning
- Involve students in evaluating their learning
- Use formative and summative assessment to drive instruction

SIOP ®

The most widely acclaimed program for sheltered instruction is the **Sheltered Instruction Observation Protocol (SIOP) Model** which, according to the SIOP Institute website, was developed to facilitate high-quality instruction for English Language Learners in content area teaching. Now owned by Pearson Education, Inc. the protocol was developed by Jana Echevarria and Mary Ellen Vogt, researchers at California State University, Long Beach, and Deborah Short of the Center for Applied Linguistics under the auspices of the Center for Research on Education, Diversity & Excellence (CREDE), a national research center funded by the U.S. Department of Education. The model consists of eight interrelated components: lesson preparation, building background, comprehensible input, strategies, interaction, practice/application, lesson delivery, and review/assessment. Visit www.cal.org/resources/digest/sheltered.html to learn more about the model and research project.

Resource

www.gips.org/programs/ell/guiding-documents3/sheltered-instruction
This Grand Island, Nebraska, website provides extensive information on teaching ELLs.

IV Social Skills Training

Many of the strategies discussed in this book have students working in small groups. For example, **Reciprocal Teaching**, **Jigsaw**, **Discussion Partners**, **Literature Circles**, **Socratic Seminars**, **Think-Pair-Share**, and **Learning Buddies** require that students know and use appropriate interaction and communication skills.

As you design lessons that include these strategies, identify the essential interaction and communication skills the students will need to work well together. Consider the following lists of skills and decide those that are essential for the grade you teach and the lessons you design. Identify the social skills that might be problematic for some of your students and plan how you will teach them.

- moving into groups quickly and quietly
- giving positive nonverbal feedback
- avoiding put-downs
- disagreeing with ideas not people
- checking for understanding
- staying on task
- waiting to talk without interrupting
- using please and thank you
- ignoring distractions
- respecting the opinions of others
- asking probing questions
- asking clarifying questions
- encouraging others to participate
- sharing materials

- making eye contact
- summarizing
- agreeing to disagree
- checking for agreement
- taking turns
- listening to the speaker
- paraphrasing
- using low voices
- staying with the group
- not interrupting
- using names
- building on ideas of others
- reaching consensus

You can construct **T-Charts** with students on which you list what you would see and hear if they were using one of the skills listed above. This is a valuable exercise for the class to complete together. Write the behaviors on chart paper and post chart for review at the end of the lesson and periodically in the future. You may also want to use the **Small Group Work Observation Form** to track skill use. See miniature versions of these templates on page 213 and full-size templates on the CD-ROM. Yet another alternative is to use **Talking Tokens** described on the next page.

Each of the above skills can be assigned as a role. Additionally, you may identify other roles such as materials manager, illustrator, timekeeper, scribe, or reporter. It is important to ensure that the roles rotate throughout the students so that all build expertise with each.

Promote Equal Participation

Give each student one to three tokens with each student's set of tokens a different color from those held by the other students. When a student talks in the group, she "spends" a token and places it in the middle of the table. When a student has spent all of her tokens she cannot talk again until everyone else in the group has spent their talking tokens. Once all the tokens are spent, they are retrieved and the process begins again.

Develop Social Skills and ELL Language Skills

Assign different responses to different color tokens. For example, each student might have a blue token that means "Ask a Question," a red token that means "Give an Idea," a green token that means "Encourage Participation" and a yellow token that means "Summarize Progress." The students have to make each of the four responses during a designated time period.

An alternative to plastic colored tokens or chips is to create **Talking Tokens** sets for each student and have them "spend" their **Talking Tokens** during the group work. See the template on page 212 and on the CD-ROM. Consider establishing the rule that once you have spent your tokens you cannot speak again until all members of the small group have spent their tokens. This promotes the use of oral language by second language learners and keeps the loquacious group members from totally dominating.

Another alternative is to announce that you will be **Clipboard Cruising** and name the responses for which you will be listening. Make note of student use of those skills on the **Small Group Work Observation Form** and share your findings at the end of the class. See the template on the CD-ROM.

Assign Roles

Have each student in the group select a different color token from their collection. You then announce what role each color represents. These roles might include scribe, timekeeper, summarizer, encourager, cleanup person, or materials manager.

Jigsaw Information

Have all the students holding a certain color token meet together to trade information and to compare and contrast their findings.

©Just ASK Publications

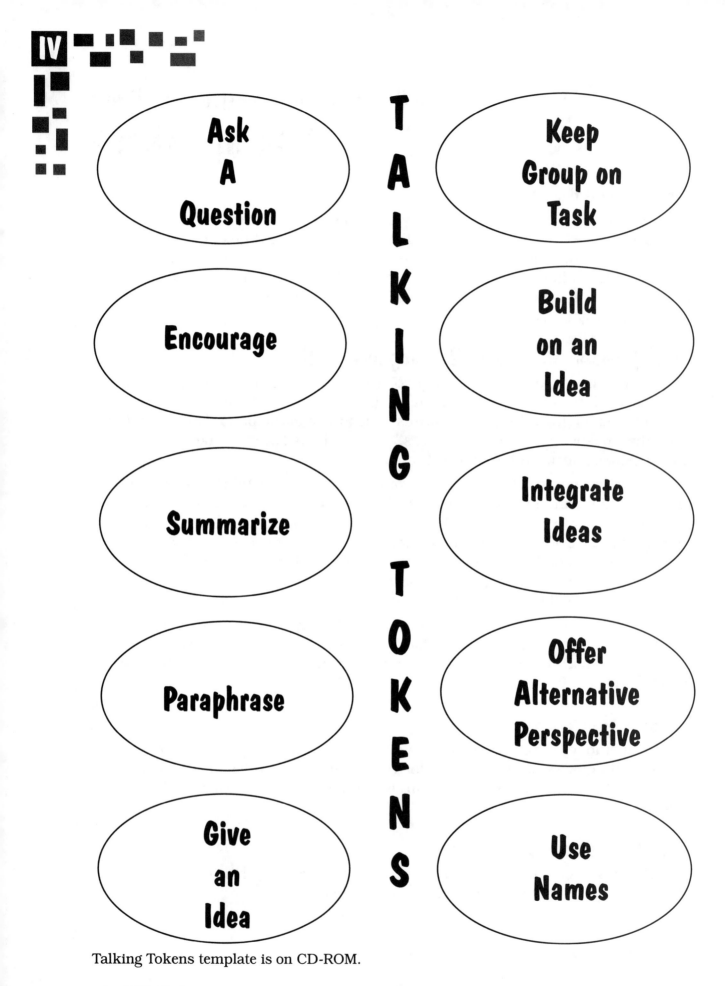

IV

Ask A Question

Keep Group on Task

Encourage

Build on an Idea

Summarize

Integrate Ideas

Paraphrase

Offer Alternative Perspective

Give an Idea

Use Names

T A L K I N G   T O K E N S

Talking Tokens template is on CD-ROM.

Social Skills Training Tools

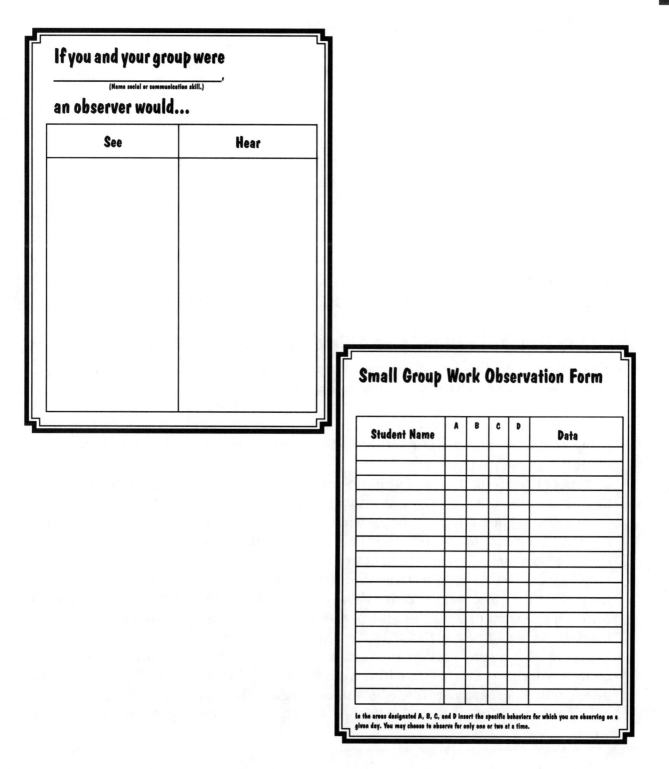

If you and your group were

_____,
(Name social or communication skill.)

an observer would...

See	Hear

Small Group Work Observation Form

Student Name	A	B	C	D	Data

In the areas designated A, B, C, and D insert the specific behaviors for which you are observing on a
given day. You may choose to observe for only one or two at a time.

See and Hear Chart and Small Group Work Observation Form templates are on CD-ROM.

IV

Strategy Training

Strategies All Students Need to Know

- The Six-Step Problem Solving Process: See page 215.
- Metacognition (Thinking about Their Thinking).
- Reading Strategies: See **Chapter V: Literacy Across the Curriculum**.
  - Using prior knowledge: See page 196.
  - Predicting
  - Inferencing: See page 278.
  - Text structure: See pages 276-277.
  - Word meaning
- Self-Assessment and Goal Setting: See pages 222-226, 250-252, and the CD-ROM.
- Pattern Awareness and Analysis
  - Words
  - Events
  - Error Analysis: See chart on page 227 and on the CD-ROM.

Points to Ponder in Building a Thinking Skills Repertoire

- Student use of a thinking skill does not mean that they know which skill they are using. We need to explicitly teach the names of the skills they are using. This is a vital part of the academic vocabulary development process.
- Students need multiple opportunities to reflect on and label the skills they are using so we need to ask students to analyze assignments and projects to identify the skills required.
- Just because students use a skill doesn't mean that they recognize where else that skill can be used. They not only need to use skills in a variety of situations, we need to help them focus on where else they might be able to use the skill both inside and outside the school setting. This is essential if we want them to become independent users of the skills.
- Just because learners can name and define the skills they are using does not mean that they know how to use those skills well or efficiently. Have them keep a running record of skill use and perhaps even use a longitudinal rubric to track their level of expertise with the skill or strategy.
- Learners also need to reflect on the usefulness of each of the skills, and analyze what actions or behaviors were the most effective and why. As students develop their repertoires of skills and strategies, they should be given opportunities to analyze and reflect on which works best when, and why that is so.

The Six-Step Problem Solving Process

Step One: Identify the Problem

A great deal of time is spent solving the wrong problem. Often people try to "fix" a symptom rather than getting to the problem. Once the problem can be written in a problem statement that says, "The problem is that...", write a goal statement describing what a successful remedy would accomplish. It may be that the problem is so big and complex that the components of the problem may need to be tackled one at a time.

Step Two: Generate Potential Solutions

This step calls for divergent thinking and brainstorming. The goal is to generate as many potential solutions as possible. Consider doing individual brainstorming before you share ideas. Do not judge solutions as they are generated, but jot them down for later consideration as a solution or as a component of the solution. Do not stop too soon. Often the best ideas come toward the end of the brainstorming because ideas begin to be integrated.

Step Three: Evaluate the Solutions

Some suggested solutions may need to be eliminated because of the time, energy, or money they would require. Others may be eliminated because of policies and rules. After those have been eliminated, examine the remaining possibilities and rank order them by criteria you design. Identify the two or three solutions that have the best potential and analyze them further as to how feasible it would be to implement them and the possible impact each might have.

Step Four: Select a Solution to Try

In this step, a solution to try is selected. If the solution involves the assistance of other people, they will need to be consulted as to their willingness to participate. Once a solution is identified, decide on the criteria to be used to evaluate the effectiveness of the solution after the implementation.

Step Five: Make a Plan and Implement It

Using the description of the ideal situation, the solution selected to try, the time frame for implementation, and the criteria to be used to evaluate the effectiveness of the solution, make an action plan and implement it.

Step Six: Evaluate the Solution

Use the criteria established in step five to decide whether or not the solution is working and determine if the plan should be modified. Use the problem-solving process to plan any needed modifications.

Skill Building and Meaning Making for Me

Directions for student: Use this form at the beginning of each unit to maximize your own learning experiences. These are questions you need to ask yourself whenever you are trying to learn or make meaning of something.

1. What should I know and be able to do at the end of this lesson/unit or experience?

2. What do I already know that will be useful in learning this new material or working in this way?

3. How are these skills and this knowledge important in the world outside of school?

4. When are the important checkpoints and deadlines?

5. How will I be able to tell when I have done a really outstanding job?

Skill Building and Meaning Making for Me template is on CD-ROM.

Student Choice

Glasser identified choice as one of the four most sought after variables in our lives. The other three are a sense of belonging, freedom, and having fun. Given that, if we want our students to come to school eager to engage in learning, we have to continuously ask ourselves about the ways we are providing students choice in their learning and, at the same time, are ensuring that they are learning to make good choices. As a side note, we should never ignore the fact that a little fun makes us all enjoy our work more. Questions to consider are:

- What choices do students have around sources of information, processes for making meaning, and for demonstrating their learning?
- How often do students feel in control, in charge of themselves? What causes them to feel in control? Think beyond "They decide whether or not to get involved and to do the work."
- What decisions that really count are students allowed to make? Consider issues like pacing, contracts, order of study, and depth and breadth of particular areas of study.
- What structures are in place to help students learn how to be responsible for their own learning? Consider variables like error analysis, rubrics, self, peer, and group assessment, time management, study skills lessons, and reflections.
- How purposeful are you in planning and asking all students questions that have more than one right answer? How often do the students ask you and each other complex questions?
- How often do students feel important in your classroom? What makes them feel important?
- How often do you and your students share laughter and pleasure?
- How do the students react when they walk into your classroom? Happy? Calm? Safe? Excited? Assured? Afraid? Bored? Anxious? What goes on in this learning environment that contributes to that reaction?

The exemplars on the next three pages demonstrate how students can be asked to do rigorous and relevant work while being given choices based on their interests and information processing styles.

> "In all my 25 years of teaching secondary students and training teachers, I have never known teachers who are having trouble with discipline or motivation to say that their students have choices, control, or true responsibility for their own schooling."
>
> Carolyn Mamchur

How I Used Student Choice
Algebra: Linear Regression

Tasks 1-4 were completed by all students. Student choices for the next task are displayed on the following page.

Suppose that you have designed a style of tote bag that your friends think is practical and unusually attractive. You start to wonder if you might be able to start a business making and selling the tote bags through mail orders. So far, you have gathered the following information.

- The cost of materials to make one bag is $5.71
- When assembled, the bag weighs 1.25 pounds.
- Shipping cartons cost $ .89 and weigh 12 ounces. Each carton can hold from one to six bags.
- It takes you 45 minutes to make one bag.
- Advertising brochures cost $25.00 for any number up to 100. For each brochure over 100, there is an additional $.15 cost.
- The monthly rental fee for a post office box is $35.00
- Your parents will let you work out of a spare room in your house, but they ask that you contribute $50 per month for the use of the room and for your business' share of utilities (heating, electricity, and so on).
- A package delivery service will ship your packages at the rates listed on the attached chart.

1. Write an equation or set of equations to model each of the following:
   a) The total weight in pounds W of a carton that contains n tote bags
   b) The cost of regular delivery R for a package whose weight does not exceed p pounds
   c) The number of full cartons C needed to ship an order of n tote bags.
   d) The advertising cost A for printing b brochures
   e) The cost of materials M to make n tote bags

2. Choose two of the situations in number 1 and represent each on a graph.

3. Assume 150 brochures are printed each month. Then the fixed expenses for your business each month are the cost of brochures, the rental of the post office box, and the $50 paid to your parents. The sum of your fixed expenses and the cost of materials is considered to be your total expenses. Write an equation that represents your total expenses E in the month when you make n tote bags. Graph your equation.

4. Decide on a price for each tote bag. Then write an equation that represents the total amount of the income I that you will receive from the sale of n tote bags. Graph your equation on the same set of axes that you used in number 3. What information can you read from this graph?

Algebra: Linear Regression

The class worked in groups of two or three on the first part of this assignment. For the second part of the assignment students selected one of the three choices below. Completion of the extension exercise was optional.

Graphers
- Graph the other equations from number 2 that you did not graph in class with your group. Graph all equations on a graph paper with appropriate scales and labels. Title each graph.
- Make a chart or poster showing all the data you have collected on the various costs to run this business.

Reporters
- Graph all equations stated on the worksheet.
- Suppose that you are going to apply to a bank for a loan to start your business. Prepare a report that you can submit to the bank along with your application for the loan. In your report include information about costs, the amount you plan to charge your customers, the amount of profit that you expect to make, and the amount of the loan you are requesting. Include at least one graph.

Futurists
- Graph all equations as stated on the worksheet.
- Decide on how much you should charge your customers and defend why you chose that amount.
- Based on that cost, explain how much profit you expect to make and how much money you would need to start up your business. Use your math knowledge, graphs, and equations to support your answer.
- Think about what effect it would have on your business plan if you incorporated the cost of shipping and packaging into the price of the item. Explain the advantages and disadvantages of doing this. Which would you chose and why?

Extension
Research how you might run this business over the Internet. Think about costs, procedures, etc.

Carol Frey, Hamilton High School, Sussex, WI

Biography Unit Presentation Approval Sheet

Name_____   Date_____

Please read over the following list of famous people from Massachusetts.

- Paul Revere
- Clara Barton
- Susan B. Anthony
- John Hancock
- Squanto
- Miles Standfish

- Ben Franklin
- Dr. Seuss
- Abigail Adams
- Phillis Wheatley
- Alexander Graham Bell
- Robert Goddard

I choose to study_____for my biography presentation.
I am interested in studying this person because

_____

_____

_____

Please read over the following list of presentation options. You are not limited to this list. If you and your parents think of a presentation idea that isn't on this list, that is fine. Please have all presentation options approved by Ms. True.

- Poster
- Song/rap
- Poem (use a form we know)
- Video
- Journal entry
- Children's book
- Skit/puppet show

- Timeline
- Dress up as your person
- Newspaper article/News report
- Essay
- Interview
- PowerPoint slide show

I choose_____as my
presentation option. I choice this presentation option because

_____

_____

_____

_____

Biography Unit Presentation Approval Sheet template is on CD-ROM.

How I'll Show What I Know

To demonstrate what I have learned about _____ I want to:

___ write a report   ___ do a photo essay

___ compile a scrapbook   ___ build a model

___ put on a demonstration   ___ do a statistical chart

___ set up an experiment   ___ design a mural

___ produce a videotape   ___ write a song

___ develop an interactive computer presentation

___ create a series of sketches, diagrams, or graphic organizers

___ other _____

This would be a good way to demonstrate understanding of this concept because:

_____

_____

To do this project, I will need help with:

_____

_____

Action Plan: _____

_____

_____

_____

_____

The criteria/rubric that will be used to assess the finished product is:

_____

_____

_____

My projected completion date is _____

Student Signature   _____ Date ___/___/___

Teacher Signature   _____ Date ___/___/___

How I'll Show What I Know template is on CD-ROM.

Student Self-Assessment

While advanced and gifted students are often asked to self-assess and set learning goals, student self-assessment is an often neglected learning experience for struggling or resistant students. That is most unfortunate because they would benefit from such analysis. Below, two teachers reflect on how they used student self-assessment with their students and how honest the students were in analyzing themselves. On the following pages there are six different teacher-designed student self-assessments. There are additional ones on pages 250-252. Note that some of the self-assessments include a goal-setting component. As Grant Wiggins says, self- assessment alone is not enough; we have to learn to self-adjust.

Student Self-Assessment in 3rd Grade Math

The students in my 3rd grade classroom have been studying many mathematics concepts. At this point in the year, they are struggling with all different topics. Most students who are demonstrating difficulties stay for extra help one-half-hour a week to receive more individualized instruction. Although some students struggle more openly than others, it can be hard to gauge their confidence on different concepts. Using the Mathematics Self-Assessment allowed the students to rate their strengths and weaknesses and communicate their needs to me. (See page 224.)

I am thinking of creating a math workshop once a week to individualize instruction. I can tell my students that they will be working on skills they have noted as areas for improvement, and the reason they are in certain groups is because they indicated a strength or weakness on the concept. As a classroom teacher, I have made similar observations of the strengths and weaknesses of my students that they have made about themselves. Their responses on the surveys were honest and overall accurate.

Eileen Whitney, Newburyport Public Schools, MA

Student Self-Assesment in Middle School

I did my survey with nine 8th grade students with learning disabilities. I gave the survey during academic support time and explained I wanted their input on where they see themselves as having strengths and weaknesses to help plan their high school program. I also put in some other categories beyond academics to look at more than just classes and have a little fun. I went through it with an overhead and did it for me first, showing them I have strengths and weaknesses, too.

The results were very honest and interesting to see. The students appreciated me asking. The surveys can help me look at the students through their eyes and be sensitive to how they feel and see their own learning skills.

Karen Caves, Newburyport Public Schools, MA

My Independent Writing Rubric

4 Outstanding!	3 Wow!	2 So-So!	1 Oops!
• I wrote the whole time.	• I wrote most of the time.	• I wrote some of the time.	• I wasted precious writing time (not focused).
• I stayed in a "just right" writing spot the whole time.	• I stayed in a "just right" writing spot the whole time.	• I moved around some.	• I moved around a lot.
• I am thinking about my meaning as I write.	• I thought about my meaning sometimes.	• I thought about my meaning a little.	• I don't know what my meaning is for my writing.
• I have narrowed my focus.	• I have narrowed my focus.	• I know what I am making and I know my idea.	• I know what I am making and my idea is big.
• I know my audience and purpose.	• I know my audience and purpose.	• I thought about my audience and purpose.	• I did not think about my audience or purpose.
• I respected the writers around me.	• I respected the writers around me.	• I respected the writers around me a little.	• I did not respect the other writers around me; I was off track.
• I stopped and reread my writing a lot to make sure it made sense.	• I stopped and reread my writing some to make sure it made sense.	• I reread my writing once to make sure it made sense.	• I did not reread my writing.
• I put capital letters at the beginning of sentences.			
• I used ending punctuation.	• I thought about my capitalization, ending punctuation, and spelling.	• I thought a little about my capitalization, ending punctuation, and spelling.	• I am not thinking carefully about my capitalization, punctuation, and spelling.
• I made sure my spelling of small words was correct.			
• I thought about my writing goal.	• I thought about what I am working on as a writer (my goal).	• I thought about my goal in the beginning and at the end.	• I did not think about a goal.
• I met with another writer on my writing.	• I met another writer.		
• I tried something new today.	• I tried something new today.		
• I did not repeat the same word(s) over and over.			

My Independent Writing Rubric template is on CD-ROM.
Shawn Hays, Mesa County Valley School District, CO

Mathematics Self-Assessment

	Subtraction	Subtraction with Regrouping	Addition	Addition With Regrouping	Multiplication	Division	Area and Perimeter	Problem Solving
Very Confident								
Almost There								
Sometimes I Get It								
Feeling Confused								
I Really Need Help								

Mathematics Self-Assessment template is on CD-ROM.

Learner Responsibilities Questionnaire

Please answer the following questions with the following ranking:

4- Almost Always
3- Most of the time
2- Sometimes
1- Rarely

1. I place all papers and notes in correct folders/notebooks. _____

2. I bring all required materials to class. _____

3. I clean and organize my locker on a regular basis. _____

4. I hand in my assignments on time on a regular basis. _____

5. I use work time wisely when given time in class. _____

6. I break long-term assignments down into manageable pieces. _____

7. I display on-task behavior during class. _____

8. I actively participate in groups when appropriate. _____

9. I complete homework and turn it in on time. _____

10. I take in-class notes when expected. _____

11. I ask the teacher for help when necessary. _____

12. I set short and long-term goals for myself. _____

13. My short-term goal is:

_____

14. My long-term goal is:

_____

Learner Responsibilities Questionnaire template is on CD-ROM.

Self-Assessment for School Success

Use this scale to record your strengths and areas for improvement.

1-2   Please help me!   8   Competent - I don't need instruction
3-4   I try but do not always follow through   9-10   Excellent - I feel great about this!
5-7   Good but still working and improving

1. Rate your organizational skills - keeping track of papers, notes, homework,
    handouts, agenda, etc._____
    Comment:_____

2. Rate your self-reliance and strategies for preparing for test and quizzes._____
    _____
    Comment: _____
    _____

3. In general, did you pass in assignments on time last year?_____
    Comment:_____

4. How well do you plan and manage long-term assignments?_____
    Comment:_____

5. Are you comfortable approaching teachers for extra help or guidance? _____
    _____
    Comment:_____

Please list any individual goals you hope to accomplish by the end of the year in
this history class?
Please rate your interest level in the following history topics. The scale is 1-10 (10
being the highest.)

_____ Monarchs   _____ Enlightenment

_____ French Revolution   _____ Latin American Revolution

_____ Industrial Revolution   _____ Imperialism

_____ World War I   _____ Interwar years

_____ World War II   _____ Cold War

Is there anything you want to ask me?

_____

Self-Assessment for School Success template is on CD-ROM.

Error Analysis

Maintain this error analysis chart so that you can become aware of the patterns of errors you are making. This chart is easily adaptable to science, writing, spelling, and the study of foreign languages. Use the variables identified in a task analysis or those provided by your teacher.

List types of errors above the columns in the chart.

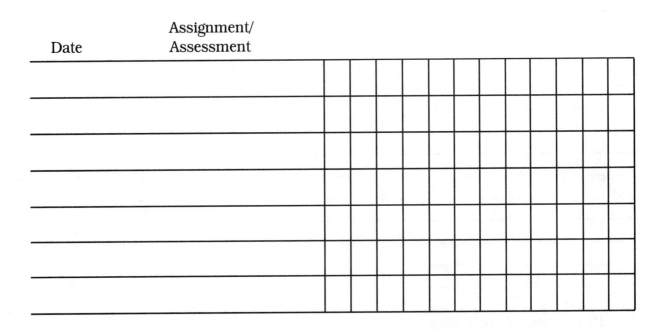

Date	Assignment/Assessment												

Directions:
For each assignment or assessment completed, write the name and date of the assignment or assessment on the lines to the left of the grid. Identify the type of errors made and check the appropriate boxes. At the end of each unit, identify the pattern of errors.

Error Analysis template is on CD-ROM.

Contract for Improvement Points

Name:

Class Period: Date:

Title of Work to Be Improved:

I,   agree to re-work/re-write the work named above. I will improve the work by addressing the following specifics agreed upon by my teacher and myself. The points I might earn have been assigned and I understand that I must complete the work according to the contract requirements in order to receive full credit.

Specific Improvements   **Points Possible**

1.

2.

3.

4.

5.

6.

Date Improved Work Due: Total:

Signatures:

Contract for Improvement Points template is on CD-ROM.

Technology Integration

The discussion of technology integration is embedded throughout this chapter in the discussion of other scaffolding and extension tools and in **Chapter V: Literacy Across the Curriculum**. Additionally, you will find dozens of suggested websites throughout the book and find them featured on the second page of each chapter in a section titled Best on the Web.

The first two resources that are the focus of this two-page review, CyberGuides and WebQuests, have great potential for scaffolding and extending instruction; they also support the construct that there is no need to reinvent the wheel because while these powerful learning tools are based on California standards of learning, they are very closely aligned with the learning standards across the country.

CyberGuides

www.sdcoe.k12.ca.us/score/cyberguide.html provides hundreds of standards-based web-delivered units based on core literature studied K-12. Examples of CyberGuides include **The Lord of the Flies**, **The Odyssey**, **Tuck Everlasting**, **The Old Man and the Sea**, **The Trumpet of the Swan**, **Freedom Train**, **Charlotte's Web**, and **Abuela**.

WebQuests and Quest Garden

- http://webquest.org
- www.slideshare.net/yvette21/creating-a-web-quest
- www.slideshare.net/andella/all-about-webquests-presentation
- http://questgarden.com

Bernie Dodge, creator of WebQuests, writes on the Quest Garden website: (I developed) the WebQuest model in 1995 for a course at San Diego State University. The goal then, and now, was to create lessons that make good use of the web, engage learners in applying higher-level thinking to authentic problems, and use everyone's time well. Since that beginning, one of the ongoing challenges has been to make it faster and easier for teachers to do all these things. QuestGarden is the end result of that effort. The lessons on this site are available for use by educators everywhere. A free 30-day trial of the lesson creation tools is available and a two-year subscription that offers searches by grade level and content areas costs only $20.

Resources

www.azk12.org/technology.html at the Arizona K-12 Center focuses on key technologies that are engaging, easy to implement, and inexpensive. Making podcasts, using blogs, manipulating digital images, and including wikis in instruction are featured.

Technology Integration

Interactive Whiteboards

We must not use this tool as an electronic worksheet. The "gee whiz" aspect is certainly appealing to our digital native learners but we, as the adults in the room, have to be sure that we are designing lessons that focus on standards-based rigorous and relevant learning when we use them.

Classroom teachers around the country and the Instructional Technology Department of the Wichita Public Schools, Kansas, suggest using interactive whiteboards to:

- Save lessons to present to students who were absent. Notes can be put on a server or posted on a web page or in a blog.
- Present multi-media presentations created by students or teachers. Video clips can be embedded into these presentations.
- Have students create e-folios including samples of their work and narration.
- Do digital storytelling.
- Annotate or take notes directly into PowerPoint presentations and video clips.
- Take virtual field trips to galleries, museums, and on site locations.
- Teach proofreading and editing skills.
- Highlight key steps, big ideas, parts of speech, patterns of errors, similarities and differences, etc.
- Create graphic organizers that teach text structure and pinpoint higher levels of thinking.
- Teach students how to navigate, research, and assess information on the Internet.
- Illustrate and write a book as a class. Use the record feature to narrate the text.
- Analyze and critique complex math problems. (Complexity is relative.)
- Teach vocabulary.
- Act as an interactive electronic Word Wall.
- Have students create class mind maps. Save them for later review.
- Use Windows Media Player or QuickTime to show streaming video or video clips.
- Print notes so that students can concentrate on the learning process rather than trying to take notes at the same time.

Think Alouds

A **Think Aloud** is a strategy in which the teacher assumes the role of a student "thinking aloud" about how to comprehend a passage or how to work through complex or confusing tasks or problems. The purposes of this strategy are to point out potential pitfalls, common misconceptions or behaviors of learners, and to model strategies, ways of thinking, and working through the problems.

Our students think that we were born knowing how to write bibliographies and knowing all the rules of capitalization and punctuation. Why? They think so because we always seem to do it right the first time. When we do demonstrations, we show our students how a task or process is to be done; we seldom demonstrate the trial and error nature of accomplishing tasks. To help fill that void, **Think Alouds** were originally discussed in the reading literature (Davey, 1983) as a way to help students with reading comprehension; their use has been extended to demonstrating the perils and pitfalls of any multi-step or obscure task. (Saphier, et al. 2008) As Brian Ludiwig reports on the Greece Central School District, New York, website, Jeffrey Willhelm, in his book, ***Improving Comprehension with Think-Aloud Strategies***, adds yet another layer to our thinking about and practice with **Think Alouds**.

The Original Process
- Identify points you want to make with a **Think Aloud** prior to presenting it.
- Assume the role and talk out loud about your thinking and feelings as you attempt to complete a task. Tasks to model include reading, taking a test, doing homework, problem solving, listening carefully, or speaking clearly.
- Do not interact with the audience (your students).
- Model the following as appropriate:
  - confusion about what you are supposed to do
  - failure to recall all of the steps in the directions
  - false starts
  - weighing alternatives
  - making predictions
  - reviewing what you've done in similar situations
  - remembering what you've read or been told to do
  - possible frustrations
  - thinking of places to get help
  - fix-up strategies
  - persistence and recognition of effective effort
  - feeling of success
- When you are finished with the role play, have students identify the strategies you used in working through the task.
- Coach your students, or have students coach each other, in using the same process.

Think Alouds

Using Think Alouds to Model Reading Strategies

Possible fix-up strategies to model include:

- Making predictions
- Building in pauses for processing during which you jot down key points and questions
- Trying to identify connections between what is being read and your own life, to what is going on in the world, and to other books, videos, movies, programs you have seen or read
- Analyzing text structure and transition words
- Using context clues
- Using SQ3R: See page 262.
- Reviewing possible decoding strategies to use with unknown words

Wilhelm offers alternative ways to conducting **Think Alouds**. He recommends using the Gradual Release of Responsibility model (Pearson and Gallangher) which includes demonstration, shared demonstration, guided practice, and independent practice.

- Teacher does think aloud; students listen. (Original model)
- Teacher does think aloud; students help out.
- Students do think alouds as large group; teacher and other students monitor and help.
- Students do think alouds in small group; teacher and other students monitor and help.
- Individual student does think aloud in forum; other students help.
- Students do think alouds individually; compare with others. (Using this approach, the students record their thinking in writing.)
- Teacher or students do think alouds orally, in writing, on an interactive white board, on an overhead, with sticky notes, or in a journal.

As noted above, Wilhelm extends the notion of **Think Alouds** by having students write about their thinking. He notes that "written think alouds have the advantage of providing a record of reading activity that can be shared, manipulated, saved, assessed, and compared to earlier and later efforts to gauge and demonstrate improvement, etc."

Tiered Assignments

Tiered assignments are perhaps the most sophisticated form of differentiation because they require:
- a deep understanding of the essential understandings and content standards
- knowledge of students' learning strengths, background knowledge, and interests
- skillfulness in task analysis
- a well-developed and ever-expanding repertoire of instructional strategies
- access to a variety of instructional and learning resources

Tiered assignments are not about more or less work. The goal is to provide multiple pathways to student success and mastery of the identified outcomes. While the entry points on the learning journey are different, the destination is the same. That means, even tasks that appear to be less demanding must be designed so that learning is scaffolded so all students have access to the same rich curriculum and are held accountable for the same high level of learning. Tasks designed for advanced students must not be perceived as more work, but rather, as different work aligned with the same learning goals in ways that extend the thinking of those advanced students.

Design Variables for Tiered Assignments
- A clear picture of the learning goals and what success will look like (This requires the design and communication to students of the essential understandings, the summative assessment, and the assessment criteria.)
- The use of task analysis results and pre-assessment data to design learning experiences
- Teacher knowledge of and access to a variety and range of materials and resources
- Flexible grouping
- Learning and information processing styles of students
- Student interests
- Individual, small group, and large group instruction and work
- Decisions about:
  - The degree of independence in work and decision making
  - Frequency and degree of teacher support
  - Pace of learning and production
  - Role of student choice
  - The accessibility and complexity of the materials and resources used

Consider how these variables are embedded in one or more of the three examples of tiered assignments on the following pages.

Tiered Assignment
Differentiating a Research Project

In this tiered assignment, the task is the same for all students. They are to
- Research and rank order ten_____
- Provide the rationale for the selection and ranking of each entry
- Explain how the entries might have an impact on_____

The task can be differentiated by varying the accessibility of sources, the complexity of the process, and the product choices.

Differentiating Accessibility of Sources
- Identify books, journal articles, websites, and past papers prepared by students. Place print materials in a dedicated area in the library or on a cart in the classroom and bookmark websites in dedicated folder.
- Provide a bibliography of recommended books, journal articles, websites and past papers prepared by students.
- Have students go to the library and the Internet to find reference materials

Differentiating Complexity of Process
- Provide a list of ten _____. Have students research the listed _____. Based on their research, have them rank order them, provide their rationale, and identify potential impact on _____.
- Provide a list of 20 _____ to consider. Have students research them, identify the ten most likely to impact _____, rank order them, give their rationales for their selections and the rank ordering, and identify potential impact on _____.
- Do not provide a list. Have students research _____ that are most likely to have an impact on _____. Have them then identify the ten most likely to impact _____, rank order them, provide rationale for their selections and rank ordering, and identify potential impact on _____.

Differentiating Product
- Students are given a choice of presentation modes with all presentations to include participation of all group members, active learning opportunities for the audience, checking for understanding, and technology integration.
- All products will be assessed against the criteria listed in the rubric distributed at the beginning of the research project.

Tiered Assignment: Library/8th Grade Science Project
Evaluation of Internet Sites

Objective of the Lesson

Students will consider the importance of and the means of evaluating the quality of information found on the Internet. Emphasis will be placed on discovering the source of information, its scope, and currency.

Students will do searches related to one of the following:
- NASA's most recent launch
- Developments in the treatment of AIDS
- Effects of pollution on the Great Lakes

The Firefox Finders

Using three pre-selected sites, students will locate and print out the home pages. They will highlight information that enables them to determine who posted information, the date of posting or revising of the information, and the types of information available at the site. The students will complete a chart comparing the information on the three sites and rank the sites for quality of source, currency, and scope.

The Internet Explorers

Students will develop at least three search strategies designed to locate the best sites available for gaining information on one of the topics listed above. Students will execute their searches and print out the first 20 hits for each search. Using the printouts, students will select the five sites which they think will best meet their information needs. They will highlight and explain the information or clues in the search results which led them to select those particular sites.

The Whole Class

After completing the tiered assignments, the two groups will share their findings with each other. The **Firefox Finders** will have worked with more concrete information while the **Internet Explorers** will have drawn conclusions based on inference. Both steps are necessary in the overall evaluation process. The final sharing gives all students a chance to experience the entire evaluation process.

Gail Grinnell, West Irondequoit Central School District, NY

Tiered Assignment
3rd Grade Reading Lesson

Students in my third grade classroom study areas of the world as part of the social studies curriculum. I try to incorporate this social studies emphasis into the reading program as much as possible. This is sometimes difficult, given the range of reading skills.

I found a book called **Polar Lands** that would be at the independent level for most, instructional for a few, and difficult for a few. One major outcome was to teach all my students to use the strategy "**Stop and Think**" while reading. Interestingly, I do this and similar comprehension techniques with the majority of my children but the children who find reading difficult get far too few experiences with "**Stop and Think**." Differentiating instruction forced me to include these children in this valuable strategy.

Group One was composed of the struggling readers who needed a great deal of modeling as well as the most teacher contact throughout the exercise. I decided that having them read chorally would work best. Once we got into it they were able to read it more fluently than I expected, so it turned into individual reading. After modeling quite a few examples of "**Stop and Think**," their task was to draw a picture to share what they predicted the next paragraph would be about. After reading the text, they needed to summarize by drawing a picture of what they remembered. The last step was to draw a picture of information that needed to be clarified. Once again they surprised me by asking if they could write their responses instead.

Group Two was asked, after much modeling and guided practice, to independently record into a tape recorder their predictions, summaries, and clarifications. They did an excellent job using the tape recorder to express their thoughts.

Group Three worked with the most independence. After completing a form on "**Stop and Think**" they had to go to the library and try to find answers to their clarification questions, using resources such as the computer and encyclopedias.

All three groups did an excellent job. I did not find that differentiating instruction took more time to prepare, but it did make me rethink my expectations.

Laurie Sullivan, West Irondequoit Central School District, NY

Organization and Time-Management Aids

Let's Get Organized... the Bottom Lines

- The first time-management tools that come to mind are a wrist watch, an alarm clock, and other readily accessible clocks at school and at home. Knowing what time it is makes a great starting point.
- Next, one or more time-management and organizational tools such as computer-based or written calendars, task lists, planners, or personally designed to-do lists; more and more people are using iPhones or Blackberrys to send themselves reminders about tasks to complete and have programmed reminders of tasks and appointments on their computers.
- An assigned place for all school materials; students should be able to determine where to keep their materials as long as they can find them when they need them or teachers ask them to use them. Should they not be able to organize their "stuff" in an efficient way, scaffold their organization with an eye to withdrawing that support as they gain skillfulness and confidence.

Helping Students Learn to Organize Themselves

- Work with them in identifying the component parts included in assignments and in establishing goals and timelines with appropriate checkpoints.
- In the beginning, establish interim checkpoints for what appears to be even straightforward and simple tasks. As students begin be able to handle those tasks, encourage their independence, and then gradually add to the complexity of the tasks while still providing support and scaffolding.
- Provide verbal prompts and cues to ensure the student is prepared to complete homework. For example, ask the student what needs to be done on the given night. If he answers math, ask what is needed to complete the math and what math needs to be done. It may be that the student even needs these questions in written or picture form.

Possibilities

It is counterproductive to require universal organizational systems without periodic analysis of what is working and is not working. It is possible to end up spending way too much time managing student organizational systems and far too little time planning and delivering solid instruction. We serve our students best if we offer and teach them a variety of ways to organize themselves and then have them access the effectiveness of the plan based on clearly established and public criteria. Some strategies to introduce are:

- Tables of contents for three-ring binders with assignments, dates assigned, date due, and date completed listed
- Color-coded folders
- Study logs listing starting and finishing times and tasks accomplished

Time Templates

It has often been said that time is the currency of education. Each of us has the same amount of teaching and learning time to "spend" and it is up to us to budget wisely to make ends meet. Much has also been written about the importance of time on task. It seems, however, that the additional question has to be, "Is the task worth doing?" As you design worthwhile tasks for your students, keep the following templates in mind as you budget your time on a yearly, monthly, weekly, and daily basis.

Wait Time

Pause three to five seconds after asking a question to give all students time to process the question. Pause three to five seconds again, after a student answers, so you and the other students can process the response and the responding student can add more as appropriate. This is especially important for English Language Learners who must go through a multi-step translation process and for the students with special needs who have word retrieval challenges.

10:2 Theory

Pause after small meaningful chunks of information for student processing. Have pairs or trios discuss the most important points, confusing points, connections, etc.

Sequence

We remember best that which occurs in the first few and last few minutes of instruction. Maximize that time. Create lots of beginnings and endings. That which is just after the middle of a list is the hardest to remember. When possible, reorder the list to place the difficult items at the beginning or end.

Movement

Legitimize movement. The brain can only absorb what the rear end can endure. Have students stand for the two-minute processing in 10:2. Have students move to meet with a partner or use various signals to indicate understanding or agreement.

Practice

Divide new skills into the smallest meaningful chunks and mass short practice sessions at the beginning of new learning. Always move to real and meaningful use of the skills as soon as possible.

Forgetting

Most forgetting occurs within just a few minutes of learning. Build in recitation, review, processing, and practice immediately. As Madeline Hunter said, "Slowing down is a way of speeding up," because learning increases with immediate processing.

Notice

Warn students of upcoming transitions. Think of the "two-minute warning" before the end of professional football games and use the same technique in the classroom. This practice models respect for student input and allows students to finish their thoughts. It is especially important for students on the Autism Spectrum and for students diagnosed as ADHD.

Pace of Speech

The more complex the concept and the more unfamiliar the vocabulary, the slower the pace needs to be. Be particularly aware of the pace of your speech when there are English Language Learners in the class.

Pace of Lesson

Consider the complexity of the concepts being presented and pace accordingly. Given that attention spans are short, provide a variety of learning experiences, and build in movement and processing time. Include large group, small group, and paired work.

So that students can learn how to use time effectively, share with them how you make instructional decisions related to time and ask them to consider the implications for their independent study.

"Learning is the constant; time is the variable." ...Vermont teacher

IV

Visuals

Student-Made Visuals

Marzano writes about the significance of nonlinguistic representations in learning. We should use student-created visuals whenever we can because active, hands-on learning leads to higher levels of engagement. Possibilities are:

- Student-created graphic organizers: See pages 166-169, 276-278, and the CD-ROM.
- Student-generated mental pictures: See page 181.
- Student-drawn pictures and pictographs: See page 194.

See the examples below for ways to engage students in creating visuals that can serve as teaching and learning tools.

In My Mind's Eye

Have students draw their vocabulary words rather than write definitions. See page 265. Marzano includes the student-created visuals in his six-step process for learning vocabulary. Also see page 275 for a template students can use to create their own deck of vocabulary cards.

Through the Eyes Of

Distribute four or five pictures or postcards that represent the work of a particular artist (Picasso, Monet, Klee, and Degas are good choices.) to each small group of students. Have students draw the concept, process, or event under study through the eyes of the artist, replicating the artist's style. Post the charts and have students explain how their drawings represents both what they are studying and the style of their artist.

Graffiti

Post charts around the room with a key concept, formula, or process on each. Have students move around the room in small groups writing or drawing pictures that capture the construct on which they are working. After each group has had the opportunity to work at each chart, use the charts as teaching tools.

Walking Tour

Post pictures or display objects, preferably student-created or selected, that are related to the area of study around the room and have students take a **Walking Tour** or **Gallery Walk**. Have them discuss how the pictures and physical models communicate important information about or are related to the area of study. The objects might represent such areas of study as the use of fractions, the history of Chile, emotions, or community helpers.

Connection Collections

The ultimate visual is the "real thing." Models, props, artifacts, and realia add richness to the learning process. To set up these **Connection Collections** either the teacher or the students collect objects that represent literal or metaphorical connections to the content under study and place them in a bag, baggie, or box. The objects can be pictures or actual artifacts. Students are tasked with identifying the connections between the items and the content under study or making predictions about an upcoming study.

If there is any possibility that your students would not have objects to bring from home, prepare a tub of pictures and artifacts from which those students could choose so that they can be full participants in engaging learning experiences like those described below.

The Renaissance
Joanne Fusare White, Rush-Henrietta Central School District, Henrietta, New York, used **Connection Collections** with her middle school students in their study of the Renaissance. She prepared bags of artifacts connected in some way to people like Michelangelo, the Medicis, and Leonardo da Vinci. She gave each small group a bag of artifacts. After they examined the artifacts they read short biographies of selected figures and determined which person was represented by the bag they had. When they had established the connection for their first artifact bag, they circulated the artifact bags until they had linked each artifact collection with a Renaissance person.

Books in a Bag
Linda Denslow, second grade teacher, Rush-Henrietta Central School District, New York used **Connection Collections** as a culminating activity for the books and stories she and her students had read during the year. She created a model connections bag for one of the stories, then asked students to choose a favorite story for which to create a bag. She wrote the directions so she could keep the bags to use the next year when she introduced each story.

Phoetry (photo poetry)
A third grade teacher in Chapel Hill-Carrboro City Schools, North Carolina, had her students create connections or artifacts bags as a pre-writing assignment at the conclusion of a unit on poetry. They were given small brown bags and were asked to return the next day with a picture and two other items in the bag that related to the picture but were not actually in the picture. The students then wrote their poems about the items and the picture.

Using Basic Principles of Design
Creating Visuals and Handouts

Lines, Spacing, and Boxes

- Use lines and spacing to clearly indicate the relationship between ideas.
- Create boxes with gray backgrounds to emphasize important or big ideas.

Bullets and Alignment

- Use bullets rather than numbers unless the sequence is significant. In that case, use 1st, 2nd, and 3rd.
- Use left alignment for a clean look and to indicate the most important points; indent to indicate sub-points of the main topic.

Font Selection

- Do not use "cute" yet hard-to-read fonts.
- Do not use more than two fonts on a page.
- Vary font sizes to indicate importance and hierarchical relationships.

PowerPoint Slides, Transparencies, Charts, and Whiteboards

PowerPoint presentations are widely used in classrooms today. Unfortunately, they are not always used well. We are replicating some of our bad habits with overhead transparencies and notes on the board in our use of this tool. One issue is unreadable text, because it is too small, too crowded, or too dim. A second issue is asking students to copy the information on the slides into their notes without any opportunity to process and make sense of it. In order to maximize the power of this tool (as well as charts and whiteboards) use these guidelines:

- Begin with the end in mind. Identify the two or three key concepts or the essential understandings and plan how the information will focus on them.
- Avoid too much text. Use no more than six to eight lines with no more than seven or eight words per line on each slide or chart.
- Avoid small text. The words should look oversized on 8 ½"x11" paper. When creating slides, use 40 or larger font size for headings and 24 or larger for body text. When creating charts, print rather than using cursive and make letters at least one inch tall.
- Avoid overpowering backgrounds, delayed transitions, graphics that do not support or enhance the content, and do not write in all capital letters.
- Be consistent but do not overdo consistency to the point of being boring. Possible consistent components are: color, background, border, and fonts.
- Use bold, italics, and color to emphasize key points.
- Use sans-serif fonts like Vag Rounded, Gill Sans, or Arial for ease of reading. Times New Roman is not a good choice for PowerPoint slides.

Word Walls

Creating a Word Wall
- Add five to seven words per week.
- Make word walls cumulative. Important words from previous units/areas of study remain on the wall so that students can make connections between areas of study and the teacher can intentionally spiral the learning opportunities.
- Encourage students to nominate words for the word wall and provide a rationale for why the nominated words are worthy of display.

Ways to Use Word Walls
- Use **Three-Column Chart** headings: See page 261.
- Use **Tic-Tac-Toe**. See page 274.
- Do word sorts with teacher-identified categories appropriate to the content being studied.
- Have students do word sorts in which they determine the categories.
- Encourage students to refer to the word wall when they are writing, doing lab reports, and solving problems.
- Create a class mind map connecting words within and across units of study.
- Have students maintain their own **Vocabulary Deck** of words that matches the word wall so that they can sort them, use them, compare them, and, in general build expertise in using them in their receptive and expressive language. See page 275.

Types of Word Walls
- Word families
- Cognates
- Key concepts studied in a course
- Essential terms for a unit of study
- Language Limbo: Words that have multiple meanings, both social and academic
- Language Limbo: Words that have the same meaning
- People, places, events in a geographic region or period in history
- Scientific concepts and processes
- Mathematical terms and operations
- Genres of literature
- Idioms, slang, and colloquiums
- Words/concepts organized in a taxonomy or classification-like structure
- Process words from Bloom's and Williams' Taxonomies

Literacy
Across the
Curriculum

Best on the Web

Reading Rockets

www.readingrockets.org

Reading Rockets is a national, multimedia project offering information and resources on how young students learn to read and why so many struggle. The Reading Rockets project is comprised of PBS television programs, available on videotape and DVD; online services, including the websites ReadingRockets.org and ColorinColorado.org. It is an initiative of WETA, the flagship public television and radio station of PBS, and is funded by a major grant from the U.S. Department of Education, Office of Special Education Programs.

Academic Vocabulary

www.englishcompanion.com/pdfDocs/academicvocab.pdf

A Google search on "academic vocabulary" results in a multitude of lengthy lists compiled at the state and district level. Jim Burke, high school teacher of English, presents this two-page list of 358 words students need to know in order to be able to understand and follow directions given in assignments, classroom assessments, and standardized assessments.

Literacy Without Limits - Help for Struggling Students: Grades 4-12

www.literacywithoutlimits.org

From the Kentucky Education Television website: This website is designed to be a helpful, non-intimidating, and immediately useful resource for teachers. Effective instruction is illustrated in authentic classroom videos with the featured Kentucky teachers providing insight into their planning, pedagogical reasoning, and expectations for each lesson.

Technology Integration in Early Childhood Literacy

http://www.montgomeryschoolsmd.org/departments/earlychi

From the website: The Early Childhood Technology Literacy Project is an instructional project in Montgomery County Public Schools (Maryland). The instructional focus of this project is to integrate technology into instruction and increase early childhood students' skills in reading and writing. This project was designed to help school teams, including classroom teachers, specialists, and instructional assistants, work cooperatively to develop, plan, and deliver exemplary reading and writing instruction using instructional technology.

Literacy Across the Curriculum

Using Journals
Successful and Unsuccessful Readers
Reading Strategies
Vocabulary Development
Text Structure
Discuss, Dialogue, Debate, and Present
Writing Across the Curriculum
Reading Responses

It often comes as a surprise to secondary teachers that we are indeed teachers of reading. We tend to believe that our task is to transmit knowledge in a way that instills in our learners the passion we feel for the content we are teaching. When the reality of the wide range of our students' reading and writing skills manifests itself, we can get discouraged and frustrated. As elementary teachers we can get so caught up in programs, workbooks, and preparing students for standardized assessments that we can lose sight of the bigger goal of creating life-long learners with a love of reading, writing, and other modes of communication.

It is not the purpose of this chapter to serve as a definitive text on the teaching of reading and writing. There are literally hundreds of excellent books that serve that purpose. The purpose of this chapter is, instead, to pull together in a few pages strategies that teachers across grade levels and content areas can use to support diverse students as they master content and the complexities of not only reading and writing but listening and speaking in the academic world and beyond.

> Literacy in the 21st century will mean the ability to find information, decode it, critically evaluate it, organize it into personal digital libraries and find meaningful ways to share it with others. Information is a raw material - students will need to learn to build with it.
>
> Thomas Friedman, *The World is Flat*

V

Literacy Across the Curriculum
Getting Started with Journals

Mike Schmoker and Katie Haycock have both written about the "crayola curriculum." They contend that in many elementary classrooms students spend more time coloring than they do reading and writing. On the other hand, Robert Marzano has written that visuals, graphic organizers, and other non-linguistic representations are important to the learning process. Clearly we must carefully craft the assignments we give our students and provide both variety and balance.

Easy-to-implement entry to incorporating literacy across the curriculum is the use of journals and interactive notebooks. They provide opportunities for rigor and relevance and for the use of non-lingusitic representations to extend learning. Their use appeals to verbal/linguistic and intrapersonal learners. Journaling may open learning avenues for these students in content areas that are usually presented in a more logical/sequential manner.

Journals may be kept in hard copy or on computers. Blogs are a great way to engage our students, provide a motivating and engaging writing opportunity, and create opportunities for language and communication skills development. With younger learners, create a class journal using lots of pictures and use circle time to generate charts which can be posted and serve as large scale journals for students to review at any time

Possible Uses of Journals and Interactive Notebooks

- To record daily thinking and learning...aha's and questions, implications, general musings
- To prepare for discussions...questions, key ideas, etc.
- To summarize lessons and ideas...such as 3-2-1 or "As a result of today, I..."
- As an alternative to homework assignments when unclear as how to proceed
- To make predictions about next steps, rationales, effects of actions
- To identify and solve problems
- To promote vocabulary development
- To make connections to prior learning and/or life beyond the classroom
- To respond to discussions, printed text, videos, demonstrations or lectures
- To generate possible topics for research
- To let off steam
- To set priorities and schedules
- To record and evaluate study habits, efforts, and academic progress
- To create graphic organizers, pictures, poems, charts, etc.

See Note-Taking Formats on pages 188-193 for more information on journal entries and Interactive Notebooks.
See three journal entry templates on pages 250-252.

Math Journal Entries

Collect postcards and pictures that can be distributed to students or placed in a learning center. Ask students to analyze the pictures and then write stories about the pictures that include math problems to be solved. Have students exchange the picture-based problems with classmates and solve each others' problems.

When students are unable to complete a homework assignment, have them write an entry in their math journals explaining what they tried and where they got stuck. Often, when student's write about their attempts to do the assignment, they are able to figure out how to move forward with solving the problem and complete the original task. Writing about their thinking promotes student metacognition and strategy development and leads to deeper understanding of the math concepts being studied.

Science Dialogue Journals

Kathy Yorks, Lock Haven High School, Lock Haven, Pennsylvania, uses dialogue journals throughout the school year as a tool to communicate privately with her students. She finds that they provide a window into her students' minds, promote student construction of new knowledge, and help them develop critical thinking skills. Dialogue journals can be used as often as seems appropriate. The process requires a commitment on the part of the teacher to read each journal and comment on what is written so that an ongoing dialogue is maintained. There does not have to be a comment on each entry. The journals are not graded in the traditional sense but do become a part of the data a teacher has about each student's understanding and feelings about the content, the class, and the learning process. Learn more about Yorks' use of dialogue journals at www.accessexcellence.org.

33 Ways to Use Blogs in Your Classroom

Access an incredible list of ways to use blogs in your classroom at http://web20intheclassroom.blogspot.com/2008/10/ways-to-use-blogs-in-your-classroom-and.html. Possibilities listed there include:
- A blog on which students post reviews of books they have read
- A blog where students communicate with students in another country about their daily lives and share and compare their school work
- A blog about the preparation for and participation in the school's science fair:
- A blog where students collaborate to write a class journal that captures the learning journey for a unit or the entire year

Learning Log

We have been learning about _____

One interesting thing I learned is that _____

_____

_____

Another interesting thing I learned is _____

_____

_____

_____

Here is a picture to show what I learned.

Learning Log templates are on CD-ROM.

Learning Log

Name: _____   Week of _____

M O N D A Y	**Things I Learned** 1. 2. **Opinion of My Day** **Something on Which I Want to Work Harder and What I Plan To Do**
T U E S D A Y	**Things I Learned** 1. 2. **Opinion of My Day** **Something on Which I Want to Work Harder and What I Plan To Do**
W E D N E S D A Y	**Things I Learned** 1. 2. **Opinion of My Day** **Something on Which I Want to Work Harder and What I Plan To Do**
T H U R S D A Y	**Things I Learned** 1. 2. **Opinion of My Day** **Something on Which I Want to Work Harder and What I Plan To Do**

Learning Log templates are on CD-ROM.
Stacy Holahan and Margie Cawley, Rush-Henrietta School District, NY

Reflections on My Week

Name: _____ **Week of:** _____

What I Learned This Week:

How I Can Use It:

Areas in Which I Am Making Progress:

I Need to Improve in:

My Goal for Next Week:

What I Enjoyed Most This Week:

Reflections on My Week template is on CD-ROM.
Stacy Holahan and Margie Cawley, Rush-Henrietta School District, NY

Proficient Elementary Readers

Off to a Great Start!
Sharon Lancester in Stone's ***Best Teaching Practices for Reaching All Learners*** describes how she writes color words on the board with a colored marker that matches the color word. Voila! The students are all thrilled that they can read on the first day of kindergarten.

Seven Keys to Comprehension
According to Zimmerman and Hutchins the seven keys are:
- Create mental images
- Use fix-up strategies
- Use background knowledge
- Synthesize information
- Ask questions
- Make inferences
- Determine the most important ideas or themes

These seven variables are aligned with Davey's earlier writing on the behaviors of unsuccessful readers. See pages 255-262 for more information on those behaviors and strategies to use to help students better comprehend what they are reading.

What It Means to Be Literate
According to the New Jersey Core Curriculum, to be literate means that one is able to:
- Speak for a variety of purposes and audiences.
- Listen in a variety of situations to information from a variety of sources.
- Write in clear, concise, organized language that varies in content and form for different audiences and purposes.
- Read various materials and texts with comprehension and critical analysis.
- View, understand, and use nontextual visual information.

This document goes on to say that literacy is not achieved by adding skills one-by-one, but by using and exploring these interdependent processes of language.

Literacy Across the Curriculum
Proficient Secondary Readers

Willard Daggett, President of the International Center for Leadership in Education, says "Once a student leaves high school, 90% of his reading will be information reading. Only 10% of his reading will be for pleasure." This statement from Daggett reinforces the responsibility we have to explicitly teach students how to read informational material in all our classroom settings.

Profile of Proficient Readers

Based on their review of the literature, secondary educators in Fairfax County Public Schools, Fairfax, Virginia, identified the following as behaviors by proficient readers across the curriculum. Proficient readers:

- Set a purpose for reading
- Access prior knowledge and relate it to new information
- Construct meaning
- Reread, skim, summarize a chapter
- Paraphrase and predict based on chapter headings
- Frame and re-frame focus questions prior to, during, and following reading
- Look for important ideas in charts, tables, and graphs
- Test their understanding of technical information
- Identify patterns in the text that serve as examples of the main idea
- Use graphic organizers to organize ideas
- Sequence events, e.g., in an explanation of historical facts
- Look for relationships, e.g., between math concepts
- Read ahead for clarification, e.g., of scientific terms and concepts
- Mentally execute directions in a manual
- Have a repertoire of strategies and know when to use which
- Think about reading strategies before, during, and after reading
- Monitor their understanding of difficult explanations

Secondary content-area teachers can use the components of a balanced literacy program, such as guided reading, modeled reading, and discussion groups, to help their students develop and use these skills. Other essential tasks of the secondary teacher include the teaching about, and providing practice with, content-specific vocabulary through the study of commonly used prefixes and suffixes, as well as Latin and Greek roots, and the structure and parts of the textbooks used in the study of the discipline. Information, patterns, connections, and processes that are clear to teachers who are experts in their field may well escape the learner who is encountering this material for the first time.

Supporting Unsuccessful Readers

Davey found that there are certain behaviors shared by unsuccessful readers. Starting with her list and building on it makes the task of teaching reading K-12 less daunting. See six behaviors of unsuccessful readers below followed by suggestions as to how to remediate those behaviors.

Behaviors of Unsuccessful Readers
- Poor visualization
- Little or inappropriate use of prior knowledge
- No predictions or hypotheses; therefore, no purpose for reading
- Little self-monitoring of comprehension
- Few, if any, fix-up strategies
- Form hypotheses but fail to evaluate and modify them appropriately on the basis of new information

What to Do
When students do not use visualization with either narrative or expository text:
- Teach them to use mental imagery. See page 181 for details on structuring that process.
- Use and teach students to use nonlinguistic representations. See pages 166-169, 181, 187, and 195.

When students do not use prior knowledge and/or do not monitor comprehension:
- Have students set their own purposes for reading rather than using teacher-imposed purposes for reading. For instance, rather than telling students to "read to find out why Jose was so excited about what was planned for after school," ask students to predict and speculate in their own words about what could be the cause of the excitement. Many teachers' manuals suggest teacher-imposed purposes for reading rather than providing strategies for helping learners set their own purposes for reading.
- Use **Three-Column Charts** to help students focus on the reading. They are useful before, during, and at the end of reading. See page 261 for directions for **Three-Column Charts**.
- Use **Anticipation/Reaction Guide** to model how to appropriately use prior knowledge and how to check back after reading to note how new information impacts understanding. See page 165.
- Use **Reciprocal Teaching** to build student skillfulness with predicting, clarifying, questioning, and summarizing. See page 259.

Supporting Unsuccessful Readers

When students fail to monitor their comprehension and have few, if any, fix-up strategies:

- Use **Think Alouds** to demonstrate the thinking processes used by successful readers. See pages 231-232 for possible strategies to include.
- Explicitly teach vocabulary. See pages 263-270.
- Teach text structure. See pages 276-277.
- Help students make connections. Explicitly frame questions, prompts, and assignments in ways that cause students to make connections between what is being studied in class and their life beyond the moment, beyond the classroom, to the past, and to the future. See pages 204-206.
- Use and teach students to use Raphael's **Question-Answer Relationship or QAR** strategy to teach students to ask themselves the following questions to guide reading comprehension:
  - Are all the parts to the answer in one sentence? (Right There)
  - Does the reader need to put together information found in various sentences and/or parts of the book? (Think and Search)
  - Is the reader expected to combine information from the text with his own opinions and knowledge? (Author and You)
  - Is the reader to use her own experience and knowledge rather than information in the text to answer the question? (On Your Own)

When students fail to re-frame their thinking around incorrect hypotheses:

- Point out words with multiple meanings. Hammond's **Word Splash** is a good tool for helping students realize that words are being used in multiple ways. See pages 268 and 272.
- Point out the writing patterns of authors who use contradictions as a means of hooking new information onto old, incorrectly held ideas (i.e., "Most people think that..., but..."). The problem here is that the topic sentence (or the main idea) is found in the middle or at the end of the paragraph or is never expressly stated.

> When students fail to use productive reading comprehension strategies, do not stop with telling them what to do in that particular instance. Explicitly help them develop their own repertoire of strategies, expertise in knowing when to use which, and skillfulness in determining the effectiveness of the selected strategy in a given situation.

Alert! Ineffective Reading Tactics

Inappropriate Use of Prior Knowledge and Text

Learners enter learning experiences with some prior knowledge. Often it is incomplete and/or inaccurate. Jay McTighe and Grant Wiggins, in **Understanding by Design**, describe understanding as ranging from "naive" to "sophisticated." Unfortunately, many students manage to answer questions at the end of the chapter, complete worksheets, and even pass examinations without really processing the information; that is, they read and respond without making meaning or connecting cognitively with the new information. Therefore, they fail to add to or refine their store of knowledge or their understanding of the concepts being studied. There are several approaches that readers routinely use that can fool both them and us. Be mindful of these ineffective approaches so that you can intervene as necessary.

Fill in the Blank and Call It Quits

Some students rely primarily on their prior knowledge. These students tend to read just enough to find information or concepts that resemble something they already know and determine that the material "makes sense to them." They use their prior fund of knowledge to answer the questions and, without even knowing it, attribute that information to the text. In these instances, students may "fill in the blanks" or select the correct multiple choice answer without having ever really processed the significant information in the text.

I, Too, Can Learn These Highlighted Vocabulary Words

Other readers focus on isolated words found in the text in order to complete the assigned task. They neglect to identify relationships between words or relationships to their prior knowledge. They often look for "big words" or italicized words to use as answers to teacher questions. They may even manage to satisfactorily complete the assignment without ever processing the significant information in the text. It is really no surprise that students focus on unrelated words rather than main concepts because it is often new vocabulary that textbook publishers print in bold type or italics. When these students are later asked to explain a concept studied in the text, whether it is in a class discussion or on a written assessment, they have no idea of how to respond in a thoughtful way.

If It's Listed in Trivial Pursuit, I'll Learn to Define and Explain It

Even some students who are relatively good, strong readers depend on unrelated facts to answer questions because they have found that developing lists of facts

Alert! Ineffective Reading Tactics

has led to school success in the past. They usually do not relate facts to one another or to real-life experiences, and do not distinguish between details and main ideas. These students complete school assignments without having ever processed the significant information in the text.

I Already Know This Stuff!

Many readers rely too heavily on prior knowledge when trying to make sense of textbook material. It is their belief that the text will always confirm their previously held knowledge. They look for information that matches what they already know and read with the belief that they "already know all this stuff." Even though these students do integrate prior knowledge with the new information, they often distort or ignore some of the new information in order to create the match. As a result, these students complete their reading without having processed the information in the ways the teacher and the textbook authors intended.

Checking on Their Comprehension

Do not accept the completion of questions at the end of the chapter or worksheets that ask students to locate and regurgitate information in the text. Design and ask questions that enable you to find out if learning at a deep and enduring level has occurred. Be sure that you know that they:

- Recognize and can paraphrase the most important concepts presented in the text.
- Realize that there is a conflict between their previous understanding and the information presented and are willing to re-frame their thinking and/or abandon old ideas, as appropriate, to resolve the conflict.
- Are aware of the fact that they are changing their perspective or level of understanding.
- Can make personal connections and apply the information in the text to other academic or beyond-the-classroom situations.

Confidence and Effective Effort

Confidence plus effective effort leads to the development of reading skills. Our task is to help all students build a repertoire of reading strategies, and to recognize and analyze the processes they use to comprehend what they read. This task is appropriate for all readers, advanced, successful and struggling because sooner or later all readers have to tackle material that is complex and confusing for them. Use the page references throughout this section to access strategies to use.

Literacy Across the Curriculum Strategy
Reciprocal Teaching

Predict   Clarify   Question   Summarize

Reciprocal Teaching is designed to help students develop expertise with the thinking and process skills of predicting, clarifying, questioning, and summarizing. It is a strategy that can be used with K-12 learners. It works equally well with narrative and expository texts. Anne Marie Sullivan Palincsar developed **Reciprocal Teaching** as a variation of **ReQuest**, which was developed by Anthony Manzo. Both strategies have as their ultimate goal students independently setting a purpose for reading, asking questions throughout the lesson, and summarizing.

These skills are best taught separately and then integrated into the model. The classroom teacher can model thinking aloud about each, use each of the process skills as prompts in **Think-Pair-Shares,** and as the focus of informal one-on-one discussions and quick checks for understanding.

There are several versions of the technique. In the original version, the teacher and a student take turns being the "teacher," hence the name. In this way the classroom teacher is able to model desired behavior, and the student "teacher" practices the processes immediately. Over time the strategy can be used by a teacher working with a small group, having students assigned various process responsibilities and different students functioning as the "teacher." In the elementary setting, small group guided reading sessions can be transformed into a reciprocal teaching structure. In the secondary classroom, the strategy can be used to structure small group work.

After students have developed familiarity with each of the four process skills, identify text to be read. Have students predict what the text will be about based on the cover, the headings, the first sentences, on what they know about this text or the author, or what has happened/been presented in previous chapters. Read a small section of material with the small group having the "teacher" clarify, question, and summarize. Have the students take turns being the "teacher" who leads the process. Continue the process alternating small sections of the reading material with pauses for predicting, clarifying, questioning, and summarizing.

Since the ultimate purpose is independent use of the process skills and strategies, in the most sophisticated version students would work in small groups with all students having prepared for the discussion by writing out their responses to each of the four processes. One student would be designated the "teacher" or leader of each discussion group and the classroom teacher would circulate around listening in on the discussions.

Literacy Across the Curriculum Strategy
Collaborative Strategic Reading

Klingner, Vaughn, and Schumm combined word identification, **Reciprocal Teaching**, and cooperative learning strategies to develop **Collaborative Strategic Reading (CSR)**. This strategy is used in inclusion classrooms where all students, including those with learning disabilities and English Language Learners, are working together side-by-side.

In **CSR**, students work in heterogeneous groups of 4-5 students. The four-step process they follow is:

- Given a reading, the small group accesses prior knowledge and makes predictions about what they will be learning.
- The groups then identify words or word parts that they do not understand and use a series of "fix-up strategies" to decode those unknown words that in CSR are called "Clunks." The word identification/decoding strategies they are taught to use are:
  - Re-read the sentence for key ideas
  - Look for context clues in the prior and following sentences
  - Examine prefixes and suffixes
  - Identify smaller words inside the unknown word
- Next the students ask themselves "What is the gist?" of this reading or "What is the most important person, place, or thing?" and "What is the most important information about the person, place or thing?"
- The last step in the process is that students design questions to check each other on their understanding of the reading, collaboratively answer their own questions, and then summarize their learning.

When working in their **CSR** cooperative groups, students are assigned roles that ensure engagement and the inclusion of each of the four components of the process. The roles are:

- Leader: Decides what to read and the strategy to use next
- Clunk Expert: Leads groups through the four-word identification/decoding strategies
- Gist Expert: Guides the discussion around the important people, places, and things.
- Announcer or MC: Ensures that all contribute to the process by calling on individuals to read or share their thinking
- Encourager: Provides feedback and encouragement

Literacy Across the Curriculum Strategy
Three-Column Charts

Purposes

- To access prior knowledge through brainstorming
- To identify areas of student interest or concern
- To aid the teacher in planning lessons as well as checking for understanding
- To track student learning throughout unit
- To identify areas for further student research/study

Process

- Use this strategy prior to, during, or at the close of a reading, electronic presentation, or a unit of study. The process can be done individually, in small groups, or as a class activity.
- Announce topic and column titles; post on charts or have students record in table groups.
- Have the teacher or students record student responses to the stems. The student who offers the idea tells the recorder which column to put it in.
- During the brainstorming phase, emphasize getting lots of ideas rather than debating or discussing the ideas as they are generated. Debates, clarifications, and discussion of ideas occur once the brainstorming is over. The teacher does not clarify any confusions or react in any way other than to record the data. Conflicting data may be recorded.
- During the lesson or unit of study, points of misconception, confusion, or curiosity are addressed.
- This strategy is easily scaffolded or extended by the selection of prompts, method of completion, and use of student-generated comments throughout the lesson or unit.

What I Knew	What I Now Know	What I Still Don't Know and Will Investigate
What I Know	What I Don't Know	What I Wish I Knew
Productive	Somewhat Productive	Unproductive
Most Important	Somewhat Important	Not Important at All
What?	So What?	Now What?
In Reading Vocabulary And Use in Writing and Discussions	In Reading Vocabulary Can Read, But Don't Use It	Never Heard/Saw It Before

Three-Column Chart template is on CD-ROM.

Literacy Across the Curriculum Strategy
SQ3R

Have students follow these steps to better comprehend material they are asked to read. This strategy can be used in all content areas.

Survey (S)
- Read the title.
- Read the introduction and summary.
- Check out the headings and subheadings.
- Take a look at all the charts, graphs, diagrams, maps, and pictures.
- Note points that are emphasized: enlarged font size, bolded and italicized text, etc.
- Read questions at end of chapter or on assignment sheet.

Question (Q)
Some users suggest turning each subheading into a question. In any case, for each section in the chapter, ask these questions:
- What is the main point?
- What evidence supports the main point?
- What are the applications or examples?
- How does what I just read relate to the rest of the chapter, previous areas of focus, the book, the world, to me?

Read (R)
- As you read the section/selection, search for the answers to your questions.
- Make notes in the margins. See pages 141-142 for ways to highlight school-owned text.

Recite (R)
- Verbalize the answers to the four questions and listen to your answers.
- 75% of learners are talk-processors so the best case scenario is to work with a partner and discuss your thinking. Other approaches include tape recording answers or talking out loud as if explaining your thinking to a friend.

Review (R)
- Read the text again to see if you have noted all the important points.
- As appropriate, note additional points.
- As appropriate, add more margin notes. See pages 141-142 for ways to highlight school-owned tests.

Vocabulary Development

Looking words up in a dictionary or a glossary and writing the definition, even when followed by using the word in a sentence, is most likely not the best approach to vocabulary development. Students need to work with the vocabulary words in context and in connection with other words they already know and use. They need to do so in a way that promotes mastery (the capacity to use the word in both their receptive and expressive language), retention (the capacity to use the word over time), and transfer (the capacity to use the word appropriately in other contexts).

Six Levels of Vocabulary Development

Graves and Slater, in *Content Area Reading and Learning*, identify six levels of vocabulary development. While looking up a word in a dictionary or glossary may be appropriate some of the time, it is not the best approach most of the time. When you identify critical vocabulary words to pre-teach or to emphasize during teaching, consider the relationship the students already have with the word when selecting the instructional strategy. The levels identified by Graves and Slater are:

- Learning to read words already in oral vocabulary
- Learning new meanings (content specific) for known words
- Learning new words for known concepts
- Learning new words representing new concepts
- Clarifying and enriching meanings of known words
- Using words currently in the students' receptive vocabulary (listening and reading) and in their expressive or productive vocabulary (speaking and writing).

For our English Language Learners we need to add:

- Learning the English word (oral and/or written) for words already in the student's oral vocabulary in first language
- Learning English words (oral and/or written) for academic concepts already mastered in student's first language
- Learning and using English words for new academic concepts in both receptive and expressive language
- Making sense of English language structure as it relates to other languages known by student

Vocabulary Development

Selecting Vocabulary to Teach

Beck, McGeown, and Kucan identify three tiers of vocabulary:

- Tier One: Basic words students already use in their oral vocabularies (walk, chair, are)
- Tier Two: Academic words important to understand in order to comprehend and because they are frequently found in other content areas (compare, impossible)
- Tier Three: Low frequency content specific words (photosynthesis, plateau)

They advocate focusing on Tier Two words because of their transferability across the content areas. While this is a widely accepted approach, the considerations about stages of language development put forth by Graves and Slater, as well as the language development needs of second language learners, require that in some instances we have to also explicitly teach Tier One words.

Additionally, students who are gifted and those who have exceptional verbal linguistic skills would most likely be bored silly with a focus on Tier Two words. Gifted fourth grade students at White Oaks Elementary School in Fairfax, Virginia, are challenged by words such as impromptu, tintinnabulation, serendipity, stalemate, sassafras, fortuna favet fortibus, and maxim-all related to areas of study across the curriculum. Some students even demonstrate mastery on a pre-assessment. To add to the joy of mastering complex vocabulary, the students do a silent cheer when they encounter the words in their study or hear a classmate using the words in dialogue and discussions. Tier Three words are just right for these students.

Student selection of vocabulary to learn is a powerful motivator and should be one of our ultimate goals. If students graduate from school thinking that the only time they investigate vocabulary is when the words are assigned by a teacher, we have missed the whole point of vocabulary development. Build in frequent opportunities for students to identify words they would like to learn and use in their receptive and expressive language.

Literacy Across the Curriculum
Vocabulary Development Strategies

Each of the following instructional strategies would be appropriate for some students in some situations, but not for others. By developing your repertoire of strategies, you can select and teach your students to select strategies that work best for them as they work on building vocabulary.

Frayer Model

This visual organizer helps learners separate critical attributes from interesting information about a concept. See pages 272-273 and CD-ROM for templates to use in setting up this organizer. This is a recommended approach for new words or new concepts.

Graphic Organizers

Descriptive graphic organizers, also known as **mind maps**, are particularly useful in helping students refine their understanding and use of terms, as well as to integrate the terms within a context. Students could create their own mind maps, work with a partner to refine their mind maps, and then create a class mind map on the board. This is an excellent way to review an important and complex concept that has challenging vocabulary and/or vocabulary that is being used in a new way.

Classification or taxonomy graphic organizers which look like family trees are useful in grouping words in a meaningful way. The brain can only hold a few isolated facts but when words that are related to one another are grouped the brain is able to remember far more words.

Compare and contrast graphic organizers such as the Venn Diagrams or matrices (also known as a semantic feature analysis) that provide yet another way for students to organize vocabulary words.

See the examples of these graphic organizers used in vocabulary development on the pages 168-169. Templates for these graphic organizers are located on the CD-ROM.

In My Mind's Eye (Visual Vocabulary)

Select five to ten critical vocabulary words and ask the students to draw pictures that capture the essence of the word. One seventh grade student, when given the word "wind" to illustrate, drew a picture of a flag on a flag pole blowing in the wind. This strategy is useful in the early grades all the way through AP courses.

Literacy Across the Curriculum
Vocabulary Development Strategies

Inside-Outside Circles (Kagan)

When it is necessary to have students learn definitions, but they do not need to work on glossary or dictionary skills, have each student look up one word. Have them write the word on one side of an index card and write the definition or draw a visual representation of the word on the other.

In Kagan's **Inside-Outside Circles**, students face each other in concentric circles. They present their vocabulary words or questions to one another and make sure that their partners know the definitions or answers. They then switch cards, move to the next person, and repeat the process multiple times until all the words have been studied by all the students.

At the beginning of a lesson on landforms, a middle school social studies teacher had students create visual representations of various landforms. They then engaged in **Inside-Outside Circles** teaching one another. This vocabulary development exercise appealed to both visual learners and kinesthetic learners because they were creating non-linguistic representations/pictures, handling the cards, and were up and moving around.

An additional benefit of using **Inside-Outside Circles** as a vocabulary development strategy is that many vocabulary words can be mastered in a short period of time without the drudgery of each student looking up each word.

Language Limbo Learning Logs

In order to minimize misconceptions and confusion, it is important for you and the students to identify the words that are used in a unique way in a given content area. Once you have identified the words that have important and specific contextual meaning, (such as factor, gross, mean, run, and product in mathematics) create or have the students create a three-column log in which they record the word, its definition in general use or other settings, and its mathematical use. This can become part of their own personal glossary or vocabulary/word study collection.

Meaningful Sentences (Slavin)

Success for All includes **Meaningful Sentences** in its comprehensive reading comprehension program. **Meaningful Sentences** answer three to four of the following questions: who, what, when, where, why, and how? For example, if the vocabulary word is "table" it would not be satisfactory for a student to write "This is a table." The student would need to write something like "We eat Thanksgiving dinner at the big table so that all the family can sit together." This example includes answers to the questions: who, what, when, and why.

Three-Column Charts

This strategy, which is explained in detail on page 261, is a good one for helping students identify their own level of use and expertise with words. Use the headings **I Know and Use It in My Speech and in My Writing**, **I Recognize It and Understand It When I Hear and Read it**, and **I Am Not Sure of the Meaning**.

Tic-Tac-Toe

This strategy is perfect for extending the thinking of students beyond memorizing definitions because it demands that they make creative connections between the nine words laid out in **Tic-Tac-Toe** fashion. An extra plus for this strategy is that words from previous units or from other content areas across the curriculum can be added to the mix. To simplify the process, provide the students with only three words between which they must make connections. You can think of this as the old Sesame Street "One of These Does Not Belong." For second language learners who are just learning to read in English, you can use cards that have pictures on one side and words on the other; that way they can flip the word cards over for visual support when they need it. For very young students you may want to use only pictures. You can have them orally tell you the sentence they constructed. See page 274 for complete directions for **Tic-Tac-Toe**.

Wonderful World of Words (Student-Selected Words)

We do not want students to think that the only time they should investigate definitions or uses of words is when such work is assigned by a teacher. Encourage students to create a record of the words they choose to learn, the definition of those words, and the reasons they need or want to know and use those words.

Word Association

Provide the students five to ten vocabulary words identified as critical to understanding content or directions for a task. Have the students listen as you provide hints about or a definition of one of the words by saying, "I am thinking of a word that … ." Have them select the correct word. Teach them to use the same process to quiz each other.

Literacy Across the Curriculum
Vocabulary Development Strategies

Word Sorts

The name **List-Group-Label** is used in the reading literature for the word sort strategy that is useful for helping students clarify and enrich meanings of known words. As the name implies, students list all the words they can think of related to a given topic. They then group the words and label the groupings. These three steps are the first stage in Taba's inductive thinking model, which was originally presented as an elementary social studies strategy. Another word sort useful in vocabulary development calls for providing students words on cards or cards on which to put selected words and then having them sort the cards into pre-determined categories such as same meaning, opposite meaning, paired words, or no relationship.

As an assessment, Judy Wnezloff, of Kewaskum, Wisconsin, provided her elementary students 30 words related to their study of plants. She had them sort the words into categories, label each of the categories, and write a rationale for the way they sorted the cards and labeled the cards.

Word Splash

Dorsey Hammond coined the term **Word Splash**. Early readers can use a "picture splash." The idea is to have students look at words that are known to them, and decide how they might be related to one another and to the focus of their study. This is not a strategy to use with new words, but rather with words being used in a different context or with a different meaning. See page 272 for an example.

Word Walls

Selected concept/vocabulary words from the current area of study are placed on the wall in the classroom. They may be arranged in a random angled way to encourage students to make guesses about what they mean, why they are important, and how they are related to the topic under study and to each other. Alternatively, they may be grouped by category and even printed on different color paper to explicitly identify the group to which each term belongs. The important point is to have the words on display for students to refer to in their discussions and while they are writing. This approach is appropriate for all levels of vocabulary development. It is especially useful for English Language Learners and for promoting use of the terms and concepts in written and spoken language of all learners. See page 243 for more information on **Word Walls**.

Vocabulary Development Strategies

Six-Step Process (Marzano)

Explain

In this step, the teacher gives a student-friendly, relevant, and perhaps humorous, description, explanation, or example of a new term. The explanation can be enhanced by pictures, computer images, mental images, and stories.

Restate

Next, students generate their own definition and consider how the term relates to their own life experiences. They should share their definition with a learning buddy or with their table group and discuss the similarities and differences. Students often keep a vocabulary notebook, a collection of vocabulary cards, or include their vocabulary work in their interactive notebooks.

Show

Students generate a visual (nonlinguistic representation) to capture the essence of their current understanding of the term. This visual might be a picture, a symbol, or a graphic organizer. Depending on time and resources, computer graphics could be accessed and/or created. If the term represents an abstract concept, provide multiple exemplars or other scaffolding.

Have students complete the first three steps when a term is first introduced. They will have multiple opportunities to revise both their explanations and their visuals in the next three steps which are spaced over time.

Discuss

This step uses the principle of learning, cumulative review, in that students revisit terms they have previously studied. Too often we have students study vocabulary or spelling words for a week, do multiple exercises with the terms, and take a test on Friday. We all know that two weeks later we have often forgotten the word. This step spirals the study of the terms throughout the year and asks students to find the words in context both inside and outside of school. Because 75% of our learners are talk-processors, the opportunity to use and discuss the terms over time promotes their learning.

Literacy Across the Curriculum
Vocabulary Development Strategies

Refine and Reflect

If students are expected to repeatedly use the terms in complete sentences and use them to frame questions about their learning, their ownership of the terms increases significantly.

Engage in Learning Games

This final step in Marzano's **Six-Step Process** is designed to have students "play" with vocabulary. The commercial and student-made learning game possibilities are limitless. Be sure to collect some of the student-generated games for use in future years. These games make excellent learning centers.

Resources

Dozens of computer and board-based games that support the sixth step in Marzano's **Six-Step Process** are available on the Tennessee Academic Vocabulary Project's website at http://jc-schools.net/tutorials/vocab/TN.html. Also available on that site are the words the Tennessee Department of Education has identified as critical to each grade level and subject area.

Game-board templates are available on the Jefferson County Schools, Tennessee website at http://jc-schools.net/tutorials/gameboard.htm. When using these game boards be mindful of the fact that you control the level of thinking students are required to use by the questions and clues you (and they) craft for use in the games.

Step Process · Six · Levels · Visual · Vocabulary · In · My · Minds · Frayer · Model · Eye · Vocabulary · Deck · Inside-Outside · Circles · Language · Limbo · Logs · Games · Graphic · Organizers · Three · Tiers · Learning · Column · Charts · Marzano · Splash · Word · Association · Wonderful · World · of · Words · English · Language · Learners · Refine · and · Reflect · Sorts · Walls · Tic-Tac-Toe · Meaningful · Sentences · Mind · Maps · List-Group-Label · Development

Sometimes multiple words are used for the same action. For instance, we might say "add," "find the sum," or "combine" in reference to addition. We might use the term "subject complement" or "predicate nominative," each of which alone is formidable but when used interchangeably, almost impossible to decipher.

Then there is the matter of multiple meanings of words. The following excerpt from an entry in Heinle's Online Dictionary readily proves the point that we have to be ever-cognizant of this issue with not only English Language Learners but with all students.

Pitch

(1) /pt/ v. pitches 1 [T] to throw or toss: She pitched her bags into the trunk of the car.||They pitched hay onto the wagon. 2 [I;T] (in baseball) to throw the ball to the batter: My father taught me how to pitch when I was young. 3 [I] (in baseball) to play the role of pitcher: Who is going to pitch in tonight's game? 4 [T] to set up, (syn.) to erect: They pitched their tent near the river. 5 [I] (of a ship) to roll back and forth in the waves: Our boat pitched heavily during the storm. 6 [I;T] to fall or be thrown suddenly and forcefully: He hit a bump and was pitched from his bicycle. 7 [T] to set a piece of music on a particular scale: This song has been pitched too high for the men in the choir. 8 [T] to change the way one writes or speaks in order to communicate to a particular group of people: She pitched her speech to the elderly people in the audience. (And, this entry leaves out the pitch of a roof!)

What to Do

- Have students create a running list of words that have multiple meanings.
- Have students create a list of the various words that designate the same action.
- Have students create a list of words that have unique content-specific meaning beyond their generic use.
- The format could be journal entries, class lists on the computer or a poster, or an ongoing learning center.
- Follow up learning experiences with the words can be designed to match the words listed and the learning goals of the curriculum.

The Frayer Model

Students list as many attributes of the word as they can think of, then cross out those that are not essential. The remaining essential attributes will help define the new word. This model helps students build skills at crafting rich definitions of concepts and vocabulary words.

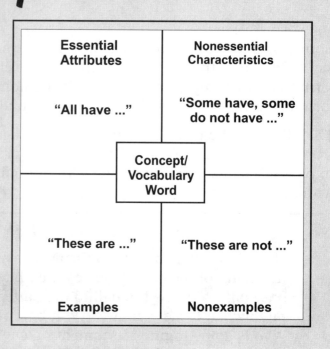

Word Splash

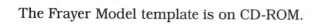

ECOLOGY

cover crops   6.2 billion   spacecraft

three-fourths   chain

mosquitos   soil bank

environment

bows & arrows   dust bowl

cycle   American eagle

home gardens

Words selected from pages 492-498
of *American Civics*, HBJ Publishing

A word splash is a collection of key terms or concepts from a reading. The terms should be familiar to the students. The purpose is to relate the terms to each other and to the new topic of study. It is a particularly powerful strategy when different meanings of some of the words are being introduced. Prior to reading, viewing, or visiting a site, students brainstorm and generate complete sentences to predict the relationships. After the learning experience, they review their predictions and make corrections.

The Frayer Model template is on CD-ROM.

Folded Frayer Model

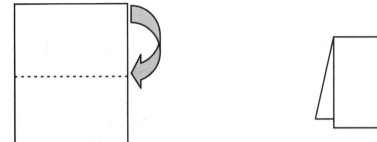

1st   Fold a sheet of 8 ½ x 11 inch paper in half horizontally.

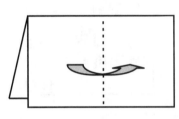

2nd   Fold the paper in half vertically to create 4 sections.

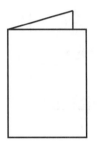

3rd   Fold a right triangle on the corner where all the folds meet. Be sure that the bottom edge of the triangle is parallel to the bottom edge of the paper.

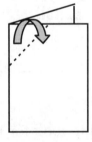 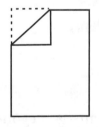

4th   Open the paper flat. Place the vocabulary word or concept to be studied in the diamond-shaped space in the center. Label the four large sections using the terms normally used on the **Frayer Model** or as directed by your teacher.

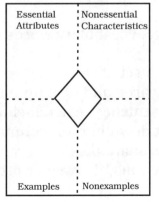

273

Vocabulary Development Strategy
Tic-Tac-Toe

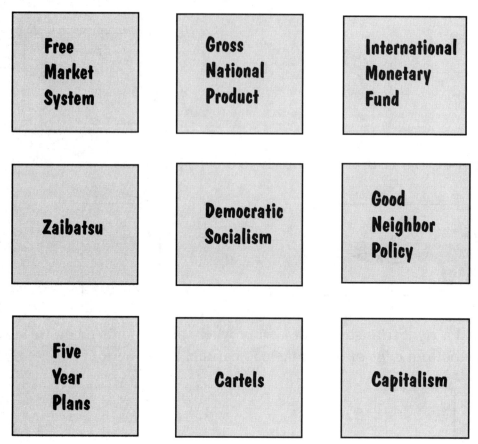

Free Market System	**Gross National Product**	**International Monetary Fund**
Zaibatsu	**Democratic Socialism**	**Good Neighbor Policy**
Five Year Plans	**Cartels**	**Capitalism**

Purposes

- To have students go beyond memorizing definitions and to look for patterns and **connections** embedded in the vocabulary words and concepts being studied
- To promote dialogue and debate

Process

- Place, or have students place, vocabulary words or important concepts on index cards.
- Give each student or group a set of cards.
- Have students shuffle their cards and deal out nine cards in a **3x3 format**.
- Ask students to form eight sentences each, including the three words straight across in each **row**, straight down in each **column**, or on the **diagonals**.
- Have the students or groups share the sentences that capture important **connections**, or "misconnections," between words and concepts being studied.

My Own Vocabulary Deck

Select interesting words from your reading. Write a word in each box. Draw a picture of each word. Cut your cards and add to your **Vocabulary Deck**.

Picture	
Word	**Word**
Word	**Word**
Word	**Word**
Word	**Word**

My Own Vocabulary Deck template is on CD-ROM.

Literacy Across the Curriculum
Text Structure

Almost all expository (informational) texts are written in one or a combination of these five text structures. Teach students to recognize the structure and to use the graphic organizer that is best for organizing the information presented in the text.

Classifications and Taxonomic Listings

Focus on information about different concepts/facts that are classified according to a specific set of criteria. Signal words are "there are several types," and "one subset of this issue is... ." The visual that looks like an organization chart or family tree is a useful graphic organizer for this pattern of text.

Sequential and Chronological Text Structure

Present a series of events in chronological order, or the sequential steps of a process. Information in history texts is often presented chronologically, while information in science is often presented as a sequence of stages. Signal words for this text structure are "first," "next," "then," and "following that." Flow charts are best for capturing the important bits of information in this text structure.

Compare and Contrast Text Structure

Identify items with similarities and/or differences. Signal words for this text structure are "similarly," "likewise," "contrary to," and "unlike." Venn diagrams and matrices are useful graphic organizers with this pattern.

Cause and Effect Text Structure

Use when two events or items are related to each other, with some causing an event and some resulting from the event. Signal words for this pattern include "as a result of...," "consequently," and "therefore." The graphic organizer with the "event" in the middle, with causes flowing into the event and the effects flowing out, is useful with this pattern.

Expository or Descriptive Text Structure

Present a series or list of facts, ideas, or variables that may not immediately seem to be related to one another, or may seem to jump from one point to another. Mind maps or semantic maps and webs are useful in clustering the information.

The graphic organizers displayed on the following page each are designed to represent one of the text structures described above. Help students learn to take notes on texts and other sources of information using the appropriate organizer. There is a template for each of these graphic organizers on the CD-ROM and additional information on graphic organizers can be found on pages 166-169.

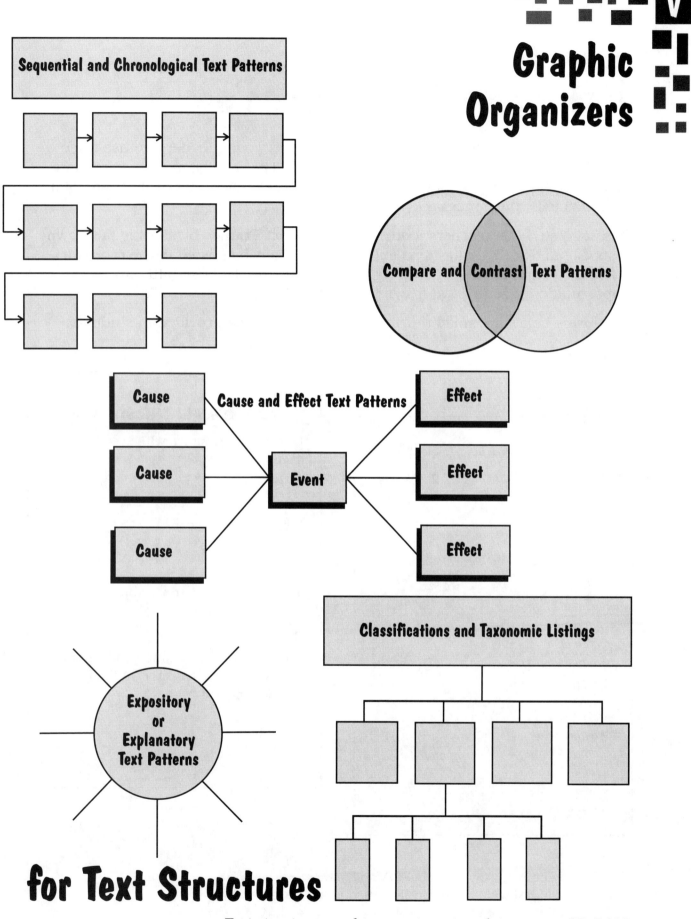

Sequential and Chronological Text Patterns

Compare and Contrast Text Patterns

Cause | Cause and Effect Text Patterns | Effect

Cause | Event | Effect

Cause | | Effect

Expository or Explanatory Text Patterns

Classifications and Taxonomic Listings

for Text Structures

Text structure graphic organizers templates are on CD-ROM.

Literacy Across the Curriculum
Text Frames for Inferencing

Text Frames are scaffolds for students, especially young readers, to use when thinking about deeper levels of meaning in text. They can be used as entries in literature response logs, preparation for literature circles, and as starting points for individual conferences.

It is suggested that teachers model the use of **Text Frames** by sharing their own response to text, that questions for text frames may be posted in the room for reference to guide free response writing, and that students should have opportunities to review text frames for writing ideas.

The forms below are small reprints of the **Text Frames** provided to students.

Text Frame: Inferencing

One section of the text that made me stop and think was

Complete one of the following:
   I think the author is trying to say

   It reminds me of

   I wonder

   It made me feel

   One question I'd like to ask the author is

Text Frame: Questioning

One question I have while reading this section is

I wonder this because

The author leads me to think that

I think that this question will/will not (circle one) be answered in the next section because

Text Frame templates are on CD-ROM.
Ellen Gury, Marsha Hansard, Leslie Kesson, and Jacalyn Colt,
St. Vrain Valley School District, CO

Discuss, Dialogue, Debate, and Present

Literature Circles

Harvey Daniels created **Literature Circles** as a way for students to lead and participate in small group discussions about books of their choice. He suggests that beginning groups use role assignments like Discussion Director, Connector, Passage Master, Illustrator, Vocabulary Enricher, and Summarizer. Assignment of roles is of particular importance for second language learners and other learners who would benefit from more structure to ensure that they prepare for and participate in student-led discussions. These role assignments scaffold the discussion for students.

Visit www.literaturecircles.com for extensive information on organizing student-led discussion groups.

Socratic Seminars

The **Socratic Seminar** is a question and answer method of discussing subjects used by Socrates in his early discussions with Plato. This type of discussion does not revolve around the teacher but around the students who are attempting to discover truths and understanding or new knowledge through analytical discussions with one another.

Students are given a work (literature, article, website, video clip, or song) to read and study. They are to make notes of interesting points and ideas or elements they do not understand. During the seminar the teacher presents a question to start the discussion and then withdraws as students engage with one another. An important component is that seminar participants are expected to "work the text" or other information source; that is, they must support opinions with references from the background material.

All students can benefit from this discussion method, It is particularly useful with gifted and accelerated readers. With modeling, those students should be able to independently lead and participate in **Socratic Seminars** as early as 4th grade.

Access additional information about **Socratic Seminars** at www.studyguide.org. Do a search for **Socratic Seminars**. You will find procedures for setting up seminars, student guidelines for participation, and a rubric for seminar participation.

Literacy Across the Curriculum
Discuss, Dialogue, Debate, and Present

Lectures and Lessons with Discussion Partners

One of the easiest ways to ensure that students are attentive and making meaning of the material being presented is to pause for processing. Since 75% of our learners are extroverted thinkers, partner discussions throughout a lecture make a great deal of good sense. Use the following sequence to promote higher levels of engagement and learning:

- Have students choose partners or assign partners.
- Present for small group discussion a **focus question** or **stem** which provides a set or direction for the lecture to come (4-5 minutes).
  - This discussion can focus learning, surface prior information, or ask for predictions.
  - Focus questions or discussion topics can be on the board, a PowerPoint slide, or an overhead transparency as the students enter the area or room.
  - Process in large groups as you choose. You may want to do that on occasion to ensure accountability; you would not want to use the time to do it after each small group discussion.
- Deliver the first segment of the lecture or lesson. (10-15 minutes).
- Give the small groups the first **processing/discussion topic** (3-4 minutes). Possible processing points might be for students to summarize, react to, elaborate upon, predict, resolve differences, or hypothesize answers to a question posed by the input of new information.
- Deliver the second segment of the lecture or lesson. (10-15 minutes).
- Give the small groups another **processing/discussion topic** (3-4 minutes).
- Continue lecture segments and discussions until the lesson is completed.
- Give the students a **final processing focus** (5-6 minutes). The purpose of this closure discussion is for students to process and make connections between the bits of information presented in the lesson.

This instructional strategy can be scaffolded or extended by the make-up of the partnerships and by the questions you give to various partnerships.

Discuss, Dialogue, Debate, and Present

Collaborative Controversy

To set up this process:
- Assign heterogeneous groups of four as pairs
- Assign each pair a perspective and give students supporting materials to read
- Students present conflicting positions to one another
- Students argue strengths and weaknesses
- Students take the opposite view without reading it
- Students drop assigned roles and work as a team of four to reach consensus

The teacher:
- Presents contrasting viewpoints
- Plays devil's advocate
- Encourages students to probe and push each other for rationale
- Monitors how students process their actions
- Emphasizes rational and spirited discussion/argument
- Restates the question
- Asks for clarification, rationale, example, implications. A key question is "What were the best arguments you heard from the other side?"

Paired Verbal Fluency

This strategy from Saphier and Haley-Speca is a good one to use when you want to ensure equal participation in paired discussions. One student is A and the other is B. When given a discussion point or question, A talks for about one minute while B listens. At the signal, B talks without repeating any ideas shared by A. This can be repeated for two to three rounds with each subsequent round shorter that the previous round. An alternative third round is for both A and B to summarize the key points they heard their discussion partner make.

PAVES

Combes, Walker, et al. use the acronym **PAVES** for Posture, Attitude, Voice, Eye contact, and Smile as a productive way to help students develop expertise at speaking in front of classmates. They also recommend use of a Preparation Self-Assessment Checklist. The main topics of the checklist are:
- Do I know my topic well?
- Have I organized my materials and discussion so that my audience can understand them?
- Am I prepared to answer simple and challenging questions? What questions might the audience ask me?
- Did I answer no to any question above? If so, how can I be better prepared?

Literacy Across the Curriculum
8th Grade Debate

South Carolina Threatens Secession!

You are a United States Senator from the Northern United States. South Carolina has just announced its intentions of seceding from the United States. You and a partner will be debating a team of Senators from the south as to the legality of this action. Your job is to convince them, and the rest of the Senate, that this action is highly illegal.

You will research precedents for this case using the Constitution and the Declaration of Independence. You have four days to come up with research from other sources to sustain your arguments, and refute the opposition's.

Lincoln Elected! Slavery Threatened!

You are a United States Senator from the Southern United States. South Carolina has just announced its intentions of seceding from the United States. You and a partner will be debating a team of Senators from the north as to the legality of this action. Your job is to convince them, and the rest of the Senate, that this action is a perfectly legal and reasonable action.

You will research precedents for this case using the Constitution and the Declaration of Independence. You have four days to come up with research from other sources to sustain your arguments, and refute the opposition's.

Reminders For Good Debating

- As you research for your best points, think about what your weakest ones are; they will probably be your opposition's best arguments.
- As you research your opponent's argument, look for weaknesses; this is where you will want to attack.
- As you formulate your own questions of attack, try to predict what questions your opposition will ask you about your arguments.
- Make sure you know your topic well enough that you can counter any attacks from your opponent.
- Make sure you know your opponent's topic well enough that you can attack them in an area, or in a way that they cannot counter.

Debate Procedures

- Opening remarks from the Southern Senators, then the Northern.
- Counter arguments from the Southern Senators, then the Northern.
- Rebuttal from the Southern Senators, then the Northern.
- Closing arguments from the Southern Senators, then the Northern.

Criteria for Assessment

- Strength of argument: You will be rated on your use of the Constitution and Declaration of Independence, specifically, on how well you apply the sections of state's rights and federalism to your argument. You will also be graded on your use of the Declaration of Independence to strengthen or refute your opponent's argument. Other sources that are brought into the argument will be evaluated according to the skill in use and the appropriateness.

- Ability to rebut: You will be rated on your response to your opponent's argument. You will need to show that you listened carefully to their arguments and counter arguments, and responded to the points that they made. Your rebuttal and counter arguments should show that you have a firm command over your own material as well as your opponent's. Your rebuttal and counter arguments should also show that you can both predict what the opposition might say and adapt for what they actually did.

- Persuasiveness of speech: While delivering your arguments you should make use of the persuasive speaking skills. Your ability to persuade will depend on your voice inflection, your use of hand and body gestures, your ability to dramatize your points, and create empathy for your cause.

To Scaffold This Assignment

- Provide easy access to print and online materials.
- Provide template of debating points.
- Include daily checkpoints.

To Extend This Assignment

- Ask students to identify an issue that divides the United States today. Have them research the root causes and the key points each side is making. Choices might include health care, immigration, global warming, or other topics of interest to them.

- As appropriate have the students follow the debate procedure or present their findings to the class or other audience in a panel discussion.

- Ask culturally diverse students to connect this debate topic to a similar situation in the country in which they previously lived and present that information to the class in a panel discussion.

Give a Great Book Talk!

A book talk is like a commercial for a book. You want to sell the book you read to another student!

General Guidelines
- Start with the title and author of your book.
- Show the book while you talk.
- Include a short description of your book. See suggestions below. This is where you get to be really creative.
- Practice your book talk so that you can speak easily from notes.

Ways to Sell Your Book

There are many ways to present the description of your book in a way that will get your audience interested in your talk. Here are some ideas that can help you to do a great book talk:
- Find a really interesting or exciting passage in your book; it should be something short that will take about 30 seconds to read aloud. Practice reading it with emotion and read it aloud. Before you begin to read, you'll have to tell the audience about the story so they will understand your passage.
- Don't tell the ending of the story – tell the problem the character must solve, but don't tell your audience how the character solves it.
- Think of a question the book raises and pose it to your audience–For example, "What would you do if you were accused of being a witch?" or
"How would you feel if you were stranded in a new land thousands of miles from home?" or
"What would you do if you had to live without any of our modern electrical equipment?"
Then tell us about how this book shows us how the characters in your book solved the problem that your question raises.
- Think about the sort of reader that would like this book and sell the book to that reader. Is your book great for people who like history? Who like mysteries? Who like to know lots of facts? Who like funny stories? Why would your book appeal to that reader?
- Is there a prop you could bring in to create some interest in your book? Perhaps something that people used in Colonial times? If your book has photographs or drawings, are there some really wonderful ones you could show your audience while you talk about particular parts of the book?
- Link your book to another book that you know people have read. For example, is your book like **Sign of the Beaver** or the **Time Warp Trio** books?

Big Idea

A big idea is what you want your audience to remember long after you finish speaking. For example, let's say that you make a presentation on the history of photography. The next semester you see a former classmate from your class. What would you like her to remember about the information you presented?

Directions: Take a look at your research results. Write down what you think are the three most significant aspects of your topic. State each point in a single complete sentence.

Important Aspects

#1

_____

#2

_____

#3

_____

Complete the following sentence, using your topic and three parts. Keep this sentence grammatically correct and as short as possible.

By the end of my presentation, I want my audience to understand that

_____

_____

_____

_____

Big Idea template is on CD-ROM.
Marilyn McQueen, St. Vrain Valley School District, CO

©Just ASK Publications

Reading Reflections

1. What questions did you think about before you started to read this story?

_____

_____

_____

2. What questions did you think about while you were reading this story/book?

_____

_____

_____

3. What questions do you have about this story/book now that you are finished reading it?

_____

_____

_____

4. Does it help you to understand the story/book when you ask questions like you just asked now? How does it help you or why does it not help you?

_____

_____

_____

Reading Reflections template is on CD-ROM.
Sharon Edwards, St. Vrain Valley School District, CO

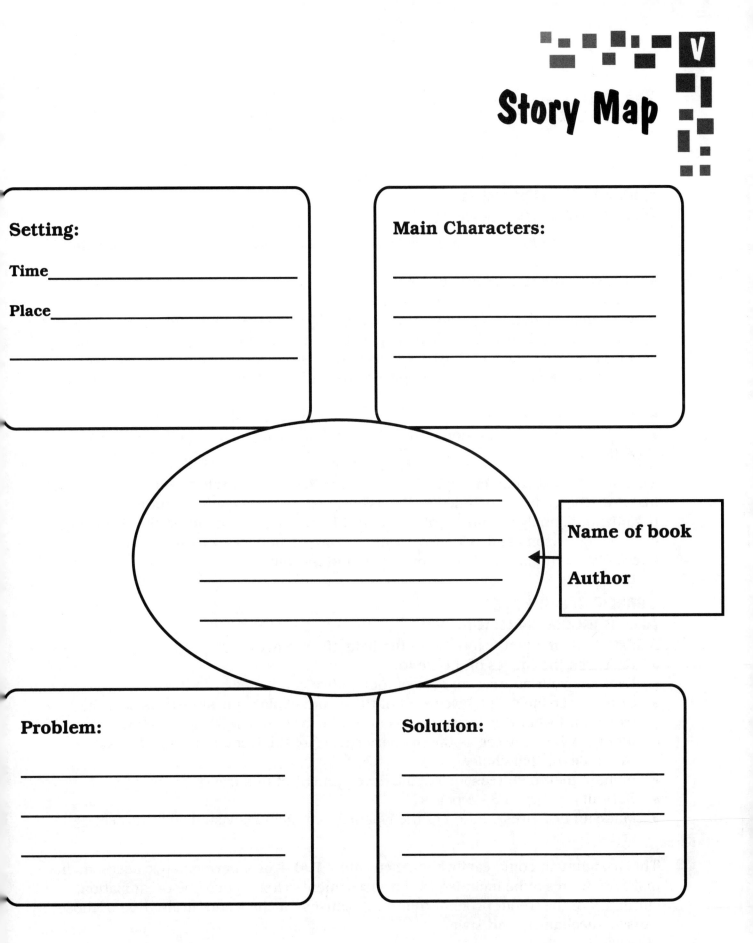

Story Map

V

Setting:

Time_____

Place_____

_____

Main Characters:

_____

_____

_____

_____

_____

_____

_____

Name of book

Author

Problem:

_____

_____

Solution:

_____

_____

_____

Story Map template is on CD-ROM.

Writing Across the Curriculum

Generic Position Paper
(Can be used in any content area)

Ask students to find a question or issue in the field of ... about which reasonable persons disagree. Have them:
- Identify the problem and prove it exists.
- Take a definitive stand on the problem.
- Convince readers to support this position by giving reasons and evidence. Acknowledge likely objections or questions to your solution and refute them. Provide reasons to reject alternative solutions.
- Convince their audience to support a particular policy or to take a specific action.
- Submit a paper that is 3 - 6 pages and uses 5 - 6 credible sources.
- Make an oral presentation of their paper that includes visual or concrete artifacts.

This assignment could easily be turned into a **RAFT** or a performance assessment task. Attributes to be included in the assessment criteria could include organization, analysis and proof of the problem, definitive stand on the problem, convincing reasons and evidence, facing the opposition, reasons to reject alternative solutions, call to action, style, and mechanics.

Generic Trend Paper
(Can be used in any content area)

Ask students to identify a trend in the field of ... . Have them:
- Research the causes of the trend.
- Evaluate your sources and select four to five good ones.
- Summarize the trend, give proof of the trend, explain possible causes of the trend, and what this trend reveals about life at the turn of the century.
- Identify what they see as the primary causes of the trend and explain their rationale for that choice.
- Include their own reasons for the development of this trend.
- Submit a paper of 3 - 4 pages.
- Make an oral presentation of their paper that includes visuals or concrete artifacts.

This assignment could easily be turned into a **RAFT** or a performance assessment task. Attributes to be included in the assessment criteria could be organization, summary of the trend, proof of the trend, causes for the trend, evaluation of those causes, mechanics, and style.

Adapted from Sherida Moore, North Vernon, IN

Author Cards

Introduction

Have you ever noticed there are lots of baseball card clones available now? Baseball cards have led to football cards, basketball cards, magic cards, and Pokeman cards. What if the library had author cards for students to review? What a great idea! Let's create Westview Author Cards!

Task

Create an author card that contains the following:
- Picture of the author
- Biographical information (name, date of birth, hometown, family)
- List of books that the author wrote
- Brief description of your favorite title by that author
- Why you like that particular book or author

Resources

Internet resources include:
- Galenet
- Publisher site
- General search engines

Print sources:
- American Author
- Major Author and Illustrators
- More Authors
- Science, Fiction, Fantasy, and Horror Authors
- The Junior Book of Authors
- Writers of Young Adults
- World Authors

CD-ROM: Available at the circulation desk

Process

Step 1: Read a book by an author on our reading list or prearrange another with your teacher.

Step 2: Research the author. You will need the following information:
- Picture of author
- Biographical information (name, date of birth, hometown, family)
- List of books author wrote
- Interesting facts or information

Step 3: Save the author picture onto a disk as a jpeg or gif file.
- If your picture is on the Internet, right-click on picture, and choose Save Image As. Save it onto your disk
- If your picture is in a book, you can copy with a scanner. Crop the picture to the size you need, then save it to your disk.
- You can also copy, cut, and paste your picture the old-fashioned way with a copy machine.

Step 4: Create your Author Card using Appleworks. See directions posted above each computer.
- The front of your card should include the picture of the author, biographical information, and a list of some of the books that the author wrote.
- Back of the card should include a brief description of your favorite title by that author and why you liked that particular title or author.

Caroline B Cooney

She was born May 10,1947 in New York City, New York.

She has three children: Lousia, Sayre, and Harold.

A few of her books are *Trying Out*, *Saying Yes*, *The Face on the Milk Carton*, *What Happened to Jane*, *What Jane Found*, and *An April Love Story*.

Caroline Cooney likes to write romance novels but she sometime writes mysteries too. She started out writing historical books just for fun because she was bored, but then she decided to try to sell her books. At the beginning, it wasn't a success, but then she started writing mystery and romance novels, and she became a success. She also likes to have teenagers as main characters.

Review of *The Face on the Milk Carton*
It is about a girl named Janie who goes to a normal high school. One day she saw a missing girl and it was her picture! She begin wondering if her parents had kidnapped her when she was young, and she keeps on having something called a "daymare." It is a really good book and I recommend that everyone read it.

ESL Student

Writing Across the Curriculum

American Revolution 2010

To assess students' knowledge and understanding of the American Revolution and their creative writing skills, Greg Nussbaum, as a fourth grade teacher in Fairfax County Public Schools, Virginia, had his students create a story about a fictional school in which events occur that mirror the events of the American Revolution. In their stories, the students were to be the "Revolutionaries" and the teachers and administrators represent the British Crown. He required students to create an event such as the "Homework Act" that matches the Stamp Act and an event that matches the Boston Tea Party. For that he suggested something like the "Burke Lake Test Party." They were also asked to write their own Declaration of Independence. Access more of Greg's creative lesson plan ideas at http://www.mrnussbaum.com.

Research Question

The question I would like to find the answer to is: _____

_____

_____

_____

I will make a presentation to the class to show what I have learned about this question. In my presentation I will:

_____

_____

_____

_____

I will work:
_____ Independently

_____ With a partner. My partner is _____

Some materials I will need are:

_____

_____

_____

Research Questions template is on CD-ROM.

Non-fiction Book Report Template

Book Title _____ **# of Pages**_____

Author_____

The genre is_____. Some characteristics of this genre are

_____

_____

_____

The purpose of this book is _____

_____

Organizational Structure: How is the text organized (chapter, sections, etc)?

_____

_____

_____

Point of View: Which point of view is used and why?

_____

_____

The Main Ideas and Significant Details: Summarize the information in the text, including main ideas, significant details, and the underlying meaning in the text.

_____

_____

_____

_____

_____

_____

_____

_____

_____

_____

_____

_____

_____

_____

_____

_____

_____

_____

Expository Critique: Evaluate the adequacy and appropriateness of the author's information. Is the author biased? Does she have evidence to support arguments? Is there any questionable information that is unsupported with evidence? Give examples of evidence and why/why not you think this is accurate information.

_____
_____
_____
_____
_____
_____
_____
_____
_____
_____
_____
_____
_____
_____
_____
_____

Drawing Inferences and Conclusions: What inference and conclusions can you make based on the information in the text? How might you apply or connect it to other information you know?

_____
_____
_____
_____
_____
_____
_____
_____
_____
_____
_____
_____
_____
_____
_____
_____
_____

Non-fiction Book Report template is on CD-ROM.

Fiction Book Report Template

Book Title _____ # of Pages_____

Author_____

The genre is_____. Some characteristics of this genre are

_____

_____

_____

The purpose of this book is _____

_____

The point of view used in this book is _____

Why do you think the author chose this POV? How does it affect the book?

_____

_____

The Plot: Identify the key events that advance the plot. Be sure to identify the central conflict/problem, the climax, and explain the resolution.

_____

_____

_____

_____

_____

_____

_____

_____

_____

_____

Character Analysis: Analyze the main character considering his/her thoughts, actions, the narrator's description of the character, and other characters' reactions or thoughts about the character. Consider the character's motivation (why she does what she does) and the character's reaction to problems.

_____

_____

_____

_____

_____

_____

_____

Setting: Describe the setting (place and time) and how the setting creates the mood and tone of the text.

_____

_____

_____

_____

_____

_____

_____

Theme: What is the theme (author's message about life and human behavior)? Is this a recurring theme you've seen in any other books? Explain.

_____

_____

_____

_____

_____

_____

_____

Literary Devices: Discuss at least one literary device the author uses (metaphor, imagery, symbolism, irony) and how it affects the story.

_____

_____

_____

_____

_____

_____

_____

Tone and Mood: Discuss the overall tone and mood of the novel, giving examples to justify your interpretation.

_____

_____

_____

_____

_____

_____

_____

_____

_____

_____

_____

Fiction Book Report template is on CD-ROM.

Book Responses
Alternative Book Reactions/Reports

Choose or have students choose from this list of alternative ways for students to respond to the literature they read. These formats can be used in both high school and elementary settings.

Movie Pitch

Write a one page "pitch" to a producer explaining why the story would make a great movie. Who would you cast in the main roles and where would it be set?

An Anthology of Poetry Dedicated to the Novel

Collect a variety of existing poems that you feel best capture the essence of the novel, its plot, conflict, characters, symbols, theme, etc. and organize the poetry in a framework that parallels the novel. Choose three or four of the poems and write about the connections you made.

Monologue

Create two or three monologues for a character(s) from the novel; go beyond the text and add what you think the character is thinking/feeling at that moment and why? Choose scenes that are central to the conflict and that are spread throughout the book (one from the beginning, middle, and end).

CliffsNotes

For a small group of students that might have read the same book, have each student take a chapter and, using the CliffsNotes' format, create their own booklet.

Surf the Net

Prior to, while, or after reading a book, check out the web and its offerings about the book, its author, or its subject, and collect additional information you feel contributes to the experience of this book. Annotate the selections in note form, making connections to the book that you think enhance the reading.

Media Moments

Watch a film inspired by a story (e.g. *Franny and Alexander* is inspired by *Hamlet*) and compare/contrast the works in a one-page piece.

Art-a-Fair

Bring in copies/examples of art related to the book's time or themes; in a one-page paper, compare, describe, and discuss the connections you made.

Book Responses
Alternatives to Book Reports

Movie Preview

Movie previews always offer a quick sequence of the best moments that make us want to watch it; create a storyboard or video and narrate the scenes for your preview.

Adaptations

Adapt the novel for a different audience, medium, or genre, by creating
- a children's book or a book for any different age group than was originally intended
- a drama or screenplay
- a video
- a short story
- an epic poem
- a parody
- a satire

Visual Art

Create a visual representation of one (or more) of the chapters or the entire work in one of the following ways:
- a storyboard that captures the significant events in the novel
- a comic strip of the book's plot (or chosen chapters)
- a drawing of the most important scene in the chapter and explain how its action is central to the plot/conflict
- a drawing or painting that captures the essence of a character, event, symbol or theme in the book
- a video

Collage

Create a collage around the themes, metaphors, imagery, symbols, or characters in the book, and on the back, explain your visual images in a one-page interpretation.

Fictional Friendships

Who of all the characters would you want for a friend? Why?
What would you do or talk about? Create a piece of writing that extends these ideas.

Book Responses
Alternatives to Book Reports

Diversity

Write about or discuss how the story would differ if the characters were something other than they are, of a different race, gender, religion, age or social class.

Poetry Possibilities

Create a series of original poems for one or more of the characters in the novel.
- create a series of sonnets dedicated to a character(s)
- create an epic poem that re-tells the story
- create a parody of a famous poem that inserts elements from this novel
- create a series of poems that best illustrate your poetic style and that make specific connections to the novel

Over Place and Time

What would one character (or set of them) in one story say to another if given the chance to talk or correspond? Write a dialogue, skit, or letter.

Time Warp

What would you do, say, or think if you "traveled" into the story you read? Or, instead of traveling into the book, write a scene or story in which the character(s) travel out of the book into today.

Biography

Write a biography of one of the characters who most interests you. You can take the liberty to begin the biography before the book starts and continue after it ends.

Autobiography

Have the character that most interests you write their autobiography of the time before, during and/or after the story occurs.

Cause and Effect

Talk or write about how it would change the story if a certain character had made a different decision earlier in the story.

Book Responses
Alternatives to Book Reports

Epilogue

After you read the story, write an epilogue in which you explain, using whatever tense and tone the author does, what you think happened to the character(s) after the author finished.

Speculation

At some point before you finish the book, based on everything you know now in the story, what do you think will happen and why do you think that?

Multimedia Connections

Read newspapers, magazines and the Internet to find articles that somehow relate to issues and ideas in the book you are reading; paste them on notebook paper and write your "connections" around the edges.

Interactive Story

Create a digital multimedia, interactive version of the story.

CyberGuides

Search the Net for virtual tours based on the book you read. Write a series of responses to your tours and how they contributed to your understanding of the novel.

The Perfect Gift

You are responsible for choosing a different and appropriate gift for four of the characters from the novel. Create a visual of each gift, name the character who will receive it, and write an explanation of why the gift is perfect for that character. The gifts can be concrete or abstract.

Letters

Write a letter from one character in the novel to a character in another novel to establish a connection between them.

Daily Edition

Using the novel as the basis for your stories, columns, and editorials, create a newspaper or magazine based on or inspired by the book you are reading. Use a desktop publishing program to give it an "official" look.

Book Responses
Alternatives to Book Reports

Performance Art

Create a performance piece that you feel captures the essence of a character, event, or theme. You may chose one of the following mediums:

- an original musical composition
- choreograph an original dance
- choose a piece of music and/or song lyric and write a one page interpretation or a 3 - 5 minute speech to explain your rationale for your choice.
- write a song/ballad about the story, a character, or an event in the novel

Adapted with permission from the Greece Central School District, NY website:
http://greece.k12.ny.us/instruction/ela/Index.htm

Integrating Literacy Instruction
How Am I Doing?

Mark each item: W for Working Well, G for Goal for the Month, or N for Not Yet

____ I create a text-rich environment by collecting, displaying, and using a wide variety of subject-related books, magazines, posters, etc., in the classroom.

____ I provide opportunities for students to locate, organize, and use information from various sources to answer questions, solve problems, and communicate ideas.

____ I use diverse fiction and non-fiction sources to include many authors and perspectives, as well as children's and young adult literature.

____ I teach reading as a process of constructing meaning through the interaction of the reader's prior knowledge and experiences, the information presented in the text, and the context/purpose of the reading.

____ I teach affixes, prefixes, and common roots used frequently in the content area.

____ I identify independent, instructional, and frustration reading levels of groups and individuals and plan assignments accordingly.

____ I provide a balanced literacy program that includes reading to students, reading with students, independent reading by students, writing for and with students, and writing by students.

____ I analyze and evaluate instructional materials by considering readability, content, length, format, cultural orientation, and illustrations/visuals.

____ I use a reading approach aligned with No Child Left Behind to include phonemic awareness, phonics, vocabulary development, reading fluency, oral reading skills, and reading comprehension strategies.

____ I model my thinking aloud while reading so that students hear what good readers do when they are tackling text.

____ I know the habits/behavior patterns held by unsuccessful readers and develop a repertoire of strategies to help students change those habits.

____ Students frequently refer to the Word Walls and use the vocabulary in their writing and discussions.

I provide opportunities for students to

____ Speak for a variety of purposes and audiences.

____ Listen in a variety of situations to information from a variety of sources.

____ Write in clear, concise, organized language that varies in content and form for different audiences and purposes.

____ Read various materials and texts with comprehension and critical analysis.

____ View, understand, and use nontextual visual information.

____ Build a repertoire of strategies and learn when to use which.

____ Do technical reading such as manuals, charts, surveys, and graphs.

Integrating Literacy Instruction Self-Assessment template is on CD-ROM.

Resources and References

Acrey, Cynthia, Christopher Johnstone, and Caroln Milligan. "Using Universal Design to Unlock the Potential for Academic Achievement of At-Risk Learners." *Teaching Exceptional Children*. November/December 2005, pp 22 - 31.

Anstrom, Kris. "Preparing Secondary Education Teachers to Work with English Language Learners: Mathematics." National Clearinghouse for English Language Acquisition, 1999. Available at www.ncela.gwu.edu

_____ "Preparing Secondary Education Teachers to Work with English Language Learners: Science." National Clearinghouse for English Language Acquisition, 1999. Available at www.ncela.gwu.edu

_____ "Preparing Secondary Education Teachers to Work with English Language Learners: Social Studies." National Clearinghouse for English Language Acquisition, 1999. Available at www.ncela.gwu.edu

Archer, Anita. *Dynamic Vocabulary Instruction in Secondary Classrooms PowerPoint Presentation*. Available at www.ode.state.or.us/teachlearn/.../dynamicvocabsecclass-archer.ppt

Armstrong, Thomas. *Multiple Intelligences in the Classroom, 3rd Edition*. Alexandria, VA: ASCD, 2009.

_____ *Awakening Genius in the Classroom*. Alexandria, VA: ASCD, 1998.

Arnold, Ellen. *Brilliant Brain Becomes Brainy!* Rochester, NY: Arncraft, 1997.

Aronson, Elliot and Shelley Patnoe. *The Jigsaw Classroom: Building Cooperation in the Classroom, 2nd Edition*. New York: Addison Wesley-Longman, 1997.

Asher, James. *Learning Another Language through Actions, 6th Edition*. Los Gatos, CA: Sky Oaks Productions, Inc, 2003.

Asher, James, JoAnne Kusudo, and Rita de la Torre. "Learning a Second Language Through Commands: The Second Field Test." *Modern Language Journal*. No. 58, 1974, pp 24-32.

Association of Illinois Middle Schools (AIMS). *Looking at Student and Teacher Work to Improve Students' Learning*. Westerville, OH: National Middle School Association, 2005.

Barone, Diane and Todd Wright. "Literacy Instruction with Digital and Media Technologies". Available at www.readingrockets.org/articles/29126

Resources and References

Bauer, Anne and Stephen Kroeger. *Inclusive Classrooms: Video Cases on CD-ROM Activity and Learning Guide*. Upper Saddle River, NJ: Pearson, 2004.

Beck, Isabel, Margaret McKeown, and Linda Kucan. *Bringing Words to Life: Robust Vocabulary Instruction*. New York: The Guilford Press, 2002.

Beers, Kylene. *When Kids Can't Read - What Teachers Can Do*. Portsmouth, NH: Heinemann, 2002.

Bender, William. *Differentiating Instruction for Students with Learning Disabilities: Best Teaching Practices for General and Special Educators*. Thousand Oaks, CA: Corwin Press and Council for Exceptional Children, 2002.

Bergsma, Barb. "The Importance of Metacognition to the Field of Learning Disabilities." *LDAY News: Quest for Knowledge*. Learning Disabilities Association of Yukon Territory, June 1999.

Bermer, Christine, Sharon Vaughn, Ann Clapper, and Ae-Hwa Kim. "Collaborative Strategic Reading (CSR): Improving Secondary. Students' Reading Comprehension Skills." *Research to Practice Brief*. National Center on Secondary Education and Transition, July 2002. Available at www.ncset/org/publlications/viewdesc.asp?ld+424

Billmeyer, Rachel and Mary Lee Barton. *Teaching Reading in the Content Areas: If Not Me, Then Who? Teacher's Manual, 2nd Edition*. Aurora, CO: McREL, 1998.

Blachowicz, Camile, Peter Fisher, and Susan Watts-Taffe. *Integrated Vocabulary Instruction: Meeting the Needs of Diverse Learners in Grades K-5*. Naperville, IL: Learning Point Associates, 2005. Available at http://www.learningpt.org/pdfs/literacy/vocabulary.pdf

Blachowicz, Camile, Peter Fisher, Donna Ogle, and Susan Watts-Taffe. "Vocabulary: Questions from the Classroom." *Reading Research Quarterly*. October, November, December 2006, pp 524-539.

Briggs, Connie and Sally Forbes. "Orientation to a New Book: More Than a Picture Walk." *The Reading Teacher*. May 2009, pp 706-709.

Bright, Anita. "Working with English Language Learners in the Math Classroom." *WATESOL NEWS*. November/December 2006.

Brophy, Jere. "Failure Syndrome Students." Champaign, IL: Eric Clearinghouse on Elementary & Early Childhood Education. Available at www.vtaide.com/png/ERIC/Failure-Syndrome.html

Resources and References

Bruner, Jerome. *The Process of Education*. Cambridge, MA: Harvard University Press, 1977.

Caine, Geoffrey and Renate Nummela Caine. *Education on the Edge of Possibility*. Alexandria, VA: ASCD, 1997.

_____ *Making Connections: Teaching and the Human Brain, Revised Edition*. Alexandria, VA: ASCD, 1994.

Campbell, Bruce and Linda Campbell. *Multiple Intelligences and Student Achievement: Success Stories from Six Schools*. Alexandria, VA: ASCD, 1999.

Canter, Lee and Marlene Canter. *Assertive Discipline, 3rd Edition*. Bloomington, IN: Solution Tree, 2001.

Cary, Stephen: *Working with Second Language Learners: Answers to Teachers' Top Ten Questions*. Portsmouth, NH: Heinemann, 2000.

Causton-Theoharis, Julie. "The Golden Rule of Providing Support in Inclusive Classrooms: Support Others as You Would Wish to be Supported." *Teaching Exceptional Children*. November/December 2009, pp 36-43.

Centennial BOCES SBE Design Team. *Standards-Based Classroom Operator's Manual*. Alexandria, VA: Just ASK Publications, 2002.

Chamot, Anna Uhl and Michael O'Malley. *The Calla Handbook: Implementing the Cognitive Academic Language Learning Approach*. Reading, MA: Addison-Wesley Publishing Company, 1994.

Claggett, Fran, Louann Reid, and Ruth Vinz. *Daybook of Critical Reading and Writing, 8th Edition*. Wilmington, MA: Great Source Education Group, Inc., 2009.

Clapper, Ann, Christine Bremer, and Mera Kachgal. "Never Too Late: Approaches to Reading Instruction for Secondary Students with Disabilities." *Tool Kit on Teaching and Assessing Students with Disabilities*, 2006. Available at www.osepideasthatwork.org/toolkit

Cohen, Judy. *Disability Etiquette: Tips on Interacting with People with Disabilities*. Jackson Heights, NY: Eastern Paralyzed Veterans Association, 2003.

Cole, Robert, Editor. *Educating Everybody's Children: Diverse Teaching Strategies for Diverse Learners*. Alexandria, VA: ASCD, 1995.

Resources and References

Cole, Sandi, Barbara Horwath, Carrie Chapman, Cathy Deschenes, David Ebeling, and Jeffrey Sprague. *Adapting Curriculum & Instruction in Inclusive Classrooms: Staff Development Kit Second Edition*. Center on Education and Lifelong Learning, Indiana Institute on Disability and Community, Indiana University, Bloomington, IN. 2000.

Combes, Bertina, Michelle Walker, Pamela Harrell, and Tandra Tyler-Wood. "PAVES: A Presentation Strategy for Beginning Presenters in Inclusive Environments." *Teaching Exceptional Children*. September/October 2008, pp 42-47.

Cooper-Kahn, Joyce and Laurie Dietzel. "Helping Children with Executive Functioning Problems Turn in Their Homework." LDOnLine, 2008. Available at www.ldonline.org/article/Helping_Children_with_Executive_Functioning_Problems _Turn_In_Their_Homework

Costa, Arthur, Editor. *Developing Minds: A Resource Book for Teaching Thinking, 3rd Edition*. Alexandria, VA: ASCD, 2001.

Costa, Art and Bena Kallick. *Assessment Strategies for Self-Directed Learning*. Thousand Oaks, CA: Corwin Press, 2004.

Cowan, Gregory and Elizabeth Cowan. *Writing*. New York: John Wiley, 1980.

Cummins, Jim, Colin Baker, and Nancy Hornberger. *An Introductory Reader to the Writings of Jim Cummins*. Bristol, UK: Multilingual Matters Ltd, 2001.

Daniels, Harvey. *Literature Circles: Voice and Choice in the Student-Centered Classroom, 2nd Edition*. York, ME: Stenhouse Publishers, 2001.

De Bono, Edward. *Six Thinking Hats, 2nd Edition*. Boston, MA: Bay Back Books, 1999.

Deshler, Donald, Edwin Ellis, and Keith Lenz. *Teaching Adolescents with Learning Disabilities: Strategies and Methods*. Denver, CO: Lover Publishing, 1996.

Díaz-Lefebvre, René. *Coloring Outside the Lines: Applying Multiple Intelligences and Creativity In Learning*. New York: John Wiley & Sons, Inc., 1999.

Dieker, Lisa. "An Introduction to Cooperative Teaching." *Special Connections*. University of Kansas. Available at www.specialconnections.ku.edu/cgi-bin/cgiwrap/specconn/main.php?cat=collaboration&section=coteaching/main

Resources and References

Doyle, Mary Beth and Michael Giangreco. "Making Presentation Software Accessible to High School Students with Intellectual Disabilities." ***Teaching Exceptional Children***. January/February 2009, pp 24-31.

Dunbar, Folwell. "21 Ideas for Incorporating Music Throughout the Curriculum." ***Middle Ground***. February 2009, pp 15-17.

Duquette, Cheryll, Emma Stodel, Stephanie Fullarton, and Karras Hagglund. "Teaching Students with Developmental Disabilities." ***Teaching Exceptional Children***. November/December 2006, pp 28-31.

Ebbinghaus, Hermann. ***Memory: A Contribution to Experimental Psychology***. Ann Arbor, MI: University of Michigan, 2009 (Originally published, 1885).

Echevarria, Jane, Mary Ellen Vogt, and Deborah Short. ***Making Content Comprehensible for English Language Learners: The SIOP model, 3rd Edition***. Boston, MA: Allyn and Bacon, 2007.

Erickson, Lynn. ***Concept-Based Curriculum and Instruction***. Thousand Oaks, CA: Corwin Press, 2002.

Fathman, Ann, Mary Ellen Quinn, and Carolyn Kessler. "Teaching Science to English Learners, Grades 4-8." ***NCBE Program Information Guide Series***, Number 11, Summer 1992.

Fern, Veronica, Kris Anstrom, and Barbara Silcox. "Active Learning and the Limited English Proficient Student." ***Directions in Language and Education***. National Clearinghouse for Bilingual Education, Vol. 1 No. 2, September 4, 2008.

Fisher, Douglas. ***Theory into Practice: Inclusive Schooling Practices: From Why to How***. Mahwah, NJ: Lawrence Erlbaum Associates, Inc., 2006.

Fisher, Douglas and Nancy Frey. ***Checking for Understanding***. Alexandria, VA: ASCD, 2007.

Frayer, Dorothy, Wayne Frederick, and Herbert Klausmeier. ***A Schema for Testing the Level of Cognitive Mastery: Technical Report Paper No. 16***. Madison, WI: Wisconsin Research and Development Center, 1969.

Friedman, Thomas. ***The World is Flat 3.0: A Brief History of the Twenty-first Century***. New York: Picador, 2007.

Gallagher, Kelly. ***Readicide***. Portland ME: Stenhouse Publishers, 2009.

Resources and References

Gardner, Howard. *Frames of Mind: The Theory of Multiple Intelligences*. New York: Basic Books, 1993.

Gately, Susan. "Facilitating Reading Comprehension for Students on the Autism Spectrum." *Teaching Exceptional Children*. January/February, 2008, pp 40 - 45.

Gelb, Michael. *How to Think Like Leonardo da Vinci: Seven Steps to Genius Every Day*. New York City, NY: Dell Publishing, 2000.

"Getting to "Why" to Solve for "How": Kids in Poverty Now on Our Radar." *Northwest Education: On the Road to Accountability*. Northwest Regional Educational Laboratory, Summer 2005. Access at www.nwrel.org/nwedu/10-04/beegle/

Gibbons, Pauline. *Scaffolding Language Scaffolding Learning: Teaching Second Language Learners in the Mainstream Classroom*. Portsmouth, NH: Heinemann, 2002.

Gordon, Raymond, Editor. *Ethnologue: Languages of the World, 15th Edition*. Dallas, TX.: SIL International, 2005. Online version: http://www.ethnologue.com

Gore, Mildred. *Successful Inclusion Strategies for Secondary and Middle School Teachers*. Thousand Oaks, CA: Corwin Press, 2003.

Gorski, Paul. "The Myth of the 'Culture of Poverty'." *Educational Leadership*. April 2008, pp 32-36.

Graves, Michael and Wayne Slater. *Content Area Reading and Learning*. Philadelphia, PA: Taylor and Francis, 2007.

Grimes, Kimberly and Dannelle Stevens. "Glass, Bug, Mud." *Phi Delta Kappan*. May 2009, pp 677-680.

Gregory, Gayle and Carolyn Chapman. *Differentiated Instructional Strategies: One Size Doesn't Fit All*. Thousand Oaks, CA: Corwin Press, 2003.

Gregory, Gayle and Lin Kuzmich. *Data-Driven Differentiation in the Standards-Based-Classroom*. Thousand Oaks, CA: Corwin Press, 2004.

Guild, Pat Burke and Stephen Garger. *Marching to Different Drummers*. Alexandria, VA: ASCD, 1985.

Gwynne, Fred. *A Chocolate Moose for Dinner*. New York: Simon and Schuster, 1976.

Resources and References

Halsted, Judith Wynn. *Some of My Best Friends Are Books: Guiding Gifted Readers from Preschool to High School*. Scottsdale AZ: Great Potential Press, 2009.

Hammond, Dorsey. "Word Splash." Available at www.mainesupportnetwork.org/handouts/pdf/word%20splash%20directions.pdf

Harry, Beth and Janette Klinger. "Discarding the Deficit Model." *Educational Leadership*. February 2007, pp 16-21.

Help! They Don't Speak English: Starter Kit for Primary Teachers. Oneonta, NY: Eastern Stream Center on Resources and Training (ESCORT), 1998. Available at http://escort.org/files/entireelem.pdf

The Help! Kit A Resource Guide for Secondary Teachers of Migrant English Language Learners. Oneonta, NY: Eastern Stream Center on Resources and Training (ESCORT), 2001. Available at http://escort.org/files/HSc1c12.pdf

Herber, Harold and Joan Herber. *Teaching in the Content Areas with Reading, Writing, and Reasoning*. Boston, MA: Allyn and Bacon, 1992.

Heacox, Diane. *Differentiating Instruction in the Regular Classroom: How to Reach and Teach All Learners, Grades 3-12*. Minneapolis, MN: Free Sprit Publishing, 2002.

Hill, Jane and Kathleen Flynn. *Classroom Instruction That Works with English Language Learners*. Alexandria, VA: ASCD, 2006.

Hogan, Kathleen and Michael Pressley, Editors. *Scaffolding Student Learning: Instructional Approaches and Issues*. Cambridge, MA: Brookline Books, 1997.

Howe, Michael. *I.Q. In Question: The Truth about Intelligence*. Thousand Oaks, CA: Sage Publications, 1997.

Hunter, Madeline. *Mastery Teaching, Revised Edition*. Thousand Oaks, CA: Corwin Press, 2004.

"I Teach Science...Not Literacy!" A presentation of the BSCS Center for Professional Development at the NSTA National Conference, Anaheim, CA, April 2006.

Jameson, Judith. *Enriching Content Classes for Secondary ESOL Students: Study Guide*. Center for Applied Linguistics, 2003.

Resources and References

Jarrett, Denise. "The Inclusive Classroom: Teaching Mathematics and Science for Students with Learning Disabilities." Mathematics and Science Education Center, Northwest Regional Educational Laboratory, September 1999. Available at www.nwrel.org/msec/images/resources/justgood/09.99.pdf

_____ "The Inclusive Classroom: Teaching Mathematics and Science to English-Language Learners." Mathematics and Science Education Center, Northwest Regional Educational Laboratory, November 1999. Available at www.nwrel.org/msec/images/resources/justgood/11.99.pdf

Jeffries, William C. *True to Type: Answers to the Most Commonly Asked Questions About Interpreting the Myers-Briggs Type Indicator*. Norfolk, VA: Hampton Roads Publishing Company, Inc., 1991.

Joyce, Bruce, Marsha Weils, and Emily Calhoun. *Models of Teaching, 8th Edition*. Boston, MA: Allyn and Bacon, 2008.

Kafele, Baruti. *Motivating Black Males to Achieve in School and in Life*. Alexandria, VA: ASCD, 2009.

Kagan, Spencer. *Cooperative Learning Resources for Teachers*. San Juan Capistrano, CA: Kagan Cooperative Learning, 1997.

Kamil, Michael, Peter Mosenthal, P. David Pearson, and Rebecca Barr, Editors. *Handbook of Reading Research, Volume III*. Mahwah, NJ: Lawrence Erlbaum Associates, 2000.

Kapusnick, Regina and Christine Hauslein. "The 'Silver Cup' of Differentiated Instruction". *Kappa Delta Pi Record*, Summer 2001.

Kaznowski, Kimberly. "Slow Learners: Are Educators Leaving Them Behind?" *NASSP Bulletin*. December 2004, pp 31-43.

Kelker, Katherine. *Family Guide to Assistive Technology*. Brookline, MA: Brookline Books/Lumen Editions, 2000.

Klingner, Janette K. and Sharon Vaughn. "Using Collaborative Strategic Reading." *Teaching Exceptional Children*. July/August, 1998.

Kohn, Alfie. *Beyond Discipline: From Compliance to Community, 10th Edition*. Alexandria, VA: ASCD, 2006.

Kolb, Sharon and Shannon Stuart. "Active Problem Solving: A Model for Empowerment." *Teaching Exceptional Children*. November/December 2005, pp 14-19.

Resources and References

Kozal, Jonathan. **Savage Inequalities: Children in American Schools**. New York: Harper-Collins, 1992.

Krashen, Stephen D. "Bilingual education: A focus on Current Research." Washington, DC: National Clearinghouse for Bilingual Education, 1991. Available at ncela.gwu.edu/ncbepubs/focus/focus.3htm.

Lapp, Diane, James Flood, and Nancy Farnan. **Content Area Reading and Learning Instructional Strategies**. Boston, MA: Allyn and Bacon, 1996.

Larkin, Martha. "Using Scaffolding Instruction to Optimize Learning." ERIC Clearinghouse on Disabilities and Gifted Education, 2002. Available at www.vtaide.com/png/ERIC/Scaffolding.htm.

_____ "Providing Support for Student Independence Through Scaffolded Instruction." **Teaching Exceptional Children**. Vol. 34, No. 1, 2001, pp 30-34.

_____ "Using Scaffold Instruction to Optimize Learning." **CEC News and Issues**, December 2002. Available at www.cec.sped.org

Larson, Lotta. "Reader Response Meets new Literacies: Empowering Readers in Online Learning Communities." **The Reading Teacher**. May 2009, pp 638-648.

Lee, Jackson and Wayne Pruitt. "Homework Assignments: Classroom Games or Teaching Tools." **Clearing House**. Vol. 53, 1979, pp 31-35.

Lenz, Keith and Jean Schumaker. **Adapting Language Arts, Social Studies, and Science Materials for the Inclusive Classroom Volume 3: Grades Six Through Eight**. Reston, VA: The Council for Exceptional Children, 1999.

Lenz, Keith, Edwin Ellis, and David Scnlon. **Teaching Learning Strategies to Adolescents and Adults with Learning Disabilities**. Austin, TX: Pro-ed, 1996.

Lochhead, John and Whimbey, Arthur. "Teaching Analytical Reasoning through Thinking Aloud Pair Problem Solving" In Stice, James (Ed.), **Developing Critical Thinking and Problem-Solving Abilities, New Directions for Teaching and Learning, No. 30**. San Francisco, CA: Jossey-Bass, 1987.

Mamchur, Carolyn. "But, the Curriculum," **Phi Delta Kappan**. April 1990, pp 634-637.

Manzo, Anthony and Ula Manzo. **Content Area Literacy**. Upper Saddle River, NJ: Merrill, 1997.

Resources and References

Marzano, Robert and Debra Pickering. **Building Academic Vocabulary: Teacher's Manual**. Alexandria, VA: ASCD, 2005.

Marzano, Robert, Debra Pickering, and Jane Pollack. **Classroom Instruction That Works**. Alexandria, VA: ASCD, 2001.

McAuliffe, Jane and Laura Stoskin. **What Color is Saturday? Using Analogies to Enhance Creative Thinking in the Classroom**. Tucson, AZ: Zephyr Press, 1994.

Menkart, Deborah. "Multicultural Education Strategies for Linguistically Diverse Schools and Classrooms." **National Clearinghouse for Bilingual Education (NCBE) Program Information Guide Series**. Washington, DC. Number 16, Fall 1993.

Murawski Wendy and Lisa Dieker. "Tips and Strategies for Co-Teaching at the Secondary Level." **Teaching Exceptional Children**. May/June 2004, pp 52-58.

Myers, Isabel Briggs and Peter B. Myers. **Gifts Differing**. Mountain View, CA: Davies-Black Publishing, 1995.

Myles, Brenda Smith. **Children and Youth with Asperger Syndrome**. Thousand Oaks, CA: Corwin Press, 2005.

O'Connor, Ken. **A Repair Kit for Grading: 15 Fixes for Broken Grades**. Portland, OR: Educational Testing Services, 2007.

Ogle, Donna. "Critical Issue: Rethinking Learning for Students at Risk." North Central Regional Educational Laboratory (NCREL), 1997. Available at www.ncrel.org/sdrs/areas/issues/students/atrisk/at700.htm

Oliver, Bruce. **Just for the ASKing! e-newsletters**. Archives of all issues available at www.justaskpublications.com/jfta.htm

Ortiz, Alba. "English Language Learners with Special Needs: Effective Instructional Strategies." **LD OnLine**. 2001. Available at ldonline.org.article/English_Language_Learners_with_Special_Needs

Palinesar, Annemarie Sullivan and Anne Brown. "Reciprocal Teaching of Comprehension-Fostering and Comprehension-Montioring Activities." **Cognition and Instruction**. No. 2, 1984, pp 117-175.

Pearson, P. David and Margaret Gallagher. "The Instruction of Reading Comprehension." **Contemporary Educational Psychology** Vol 8. 1983, pp 317-344.

Resources and References

Pellino, Karen. "The Effects of Poverty on Teaching and Learning." Available at www.teach-nology.com/tutorials/teaching/poverty/print.htm

Pink, Daniel. *A Whole New Mind: Why Right-Brainers Will Rule the Future*. New York: Riverhead, 2006.

Pitler, Howard, Elizabeth Hubbell, Matt Kuhn, and Kim Malenoski. *Using Technology with Classroom Instruction That Works*. Alexandria, VA: ASCD, 2007.

Prensky, Marc. "Listen to the Natives." *Educational Leadership*. December 2005/January 2006, pp 8-13. Raphael, Taffy. "Teaching Question Answer Relationships, Revisited." *The Reading Teacher*. February 1986, pp 516-522.

"Reading and Writing in the Academic Content Areas" *Issue Brief*. Washington, DC: Alliance for Excellent Education, June 2006. Available at www.all4ed.org/files/ReadingWritingAcadContent.pdf

Renzulli, Joseph. *The Enrichment Triad Model: A Guide for Developing Defensible Programs for the Gifted and Talented*. Mansfield Center, CT: Creative Learning Press, 1977.

Renzulli, Joseph. "What Makes Giftedness? Reexamining a Definition." *Phi Delta Kappan*. November 1978, pp 180-184, 261.

Renzulli, Joseph and Sally Reis. *The School Wide Enrichment Model: A Comprehensive Plan for Educational Excellence*. Mansfield Center, CT: Creative Learning Press, 1985.

_____ *Enriching Curriculum for All Students*. Thousand Oaks, CA: Corwin Press, 2008.

_____ "Curriculum Compacting: A Systematic Procedure for Modifying the Curriculum for Above Average Ability Students." The National Research Center on the Gifted and Talented, University of Connecticut. Available at www.gifted.uconn.edu/sem/semart08.html.

Rief, Sandra. *How to Reach and Teach Children with ADD/ADHD*. San Francisco, CA: Jossey-Bass Inc., 2005.

Rief, Sandra and Julie Heimburge. *How to Reach and Teach All Students in the Inclusive Classroom*. San Francisco, CA: Jossey-Bass Inc., 1996.

Ross, Donna and Nancy Frey. "Real-Time Teaching." *Journal of Adolescent and Adult Literacy*. September 2009, pp 74-78.

Resources and References

Rothstein-Fisch, Carrie and Elise Trumbull. ***Managing Diverse Classrooms: How to Build on Students' Cultural Strengths***. Alexandria, VA: ASCD, 2008.

Rutherford, Paula. "Academic Versus Non-academic Reinforcers." Unpublished paper. The University of North Florida, 1974.

_____ ***Instruction for All Students, 2nd Edition***. Alexandria, VA: Just ASK Publications, 2008.

_____ ***Why Didn't I Learn This in College?, 2nd Edition***. Alexandria, VA: Just ASK Publications, 2009.

Santos, Rosa Milagros and Debbie Reese. "Selecting Culturally and Linguistically Appropriate Materials: Suggestions for Service Providers." ***ERIC DIGEST***. June 1999.

Saphier, Jon, Mary Ann Haley-Speca, and Robert Gower. The Skillful Teacher. Acton, MA: Research for Better Teaching, Inc., 2008.

Schumm, Jeanne Shay. ***Adapting Reading and Math Materials for the Inclusive Classroom Volume 2: Kindergarten Through Grade Five***. Reston, VA: The Council for Exceptional Children, 1999.

Shoebottom, Paul. ***A Guide to Learning English***. Available at http://esl.fis.edu/index.htm

Shalaway, Linda. ***Learning to Teach***. New York: Scholastic, 2005.

Short, Deborah and Shannon Fitzsimmons. ***Double the Work: Challenges and solutions to acquiring Language and Academic Literacy for Adolescent English Language Learners - A Report to Carnegie Corporation of New York***. Washington, DC: Alliance for Excellent Education, 2007. Available at www.all4ed.org and www.carnegie.org/literacy.

Smith, Jean Louise, Hannk Fien, and Stan Paine. "When Mobility Disrupts Learning." ***Educational Leadership***. April 2008, pp 59-63.

Smutny, Joan Franklin and Sarah von Fremd, Editors. ***Differentiating for the Young Child: Teaching Strategies Across the Content Areas (Pre-K-3).*** Thousand Oaks, CA: Corwin Press, 2004.

Sollman, Carolyn, Barbara Emmons, and Judith Paolini. ***Through the Cracks***. Worcester, MA: Davis Publications, 1994.

Sox, Amanda and Eliane Rubinstein-Avita. "WebQuests for English Language Learners: Essential Elements for Design." *Journal of Adolescent and Adult Literacy*. September 2009, pp 38-48.

Stepanek, Jennifer. "Meeting the Needs of Gifted Students: Differentiating Mathematics and Science Instruction." Mathematics and Science Education Center, Northwest Regional Educational Laboratory, December 1999. Available at www.nwrel.org/msec/images/resources/justgood/12.99.pdf

Stone, Randi. *Best Teaching Practices for Reaching All Learners*. Thousand Oaks, CA: Corwin Press, 2004.

Sylwester, Robert. *A Celebration of Neurons: An Educator's Guide to the Human Brain*. Alexandria, VA: ASCD, 1995.

Taba, Hilda, Mary Durkin, Jack Fraenkel, and Anthony McNaughton. *A Teacher's Handbook to Elementary Social Studies: An Inductive Approach*. Reading, MA: Addison-Wesley, 1971.

Tomlinson, Carol Ann. *The Differentiated Classroom: Responding to the Needs of All Learners*. Aexandria, VA: ASCD, 2004.

_____ "Reconcilable Differences? Standards-Based Teaching and Differentiation." *Educational Leadership*. September 2000, pp 6-11.

_____ *How to Differentiate Instruction in the Mixed-Ability Classroom*. Alexandria, VA: ASCD, 2004.

_____ "Deciding to Teaching Them All." *Educational Leadership*. October 2003, pp 6-11.

_____ "Differentiating Instruction for Advanced Learners in the Mixed-Ability Middle School Classroom." The ERIC Clearinghouse on Disabilities and Gifted Education, October 1995.

_____ "Independent Study: A Flexible Tool for Encouraging Academic and Personal Growth." *Middle School Journal*. September 1993, pp 157-161.

_____ and Caroline Eidson. *Differentiation in Practice: A Resource Guide for Differentiating Curriulum*. Alexandria, VA: ASCD, 2003.

Tovani, Chris: *I Read It, But I Don't Get It*. Portland, ME: Stenhouse Publishers, 2000.

©Just ASK Publications

Resources and References

_____ **Do I Really Have to Teach Reading?** Portland, ME: Stenhouse Publishers, 2004.

2e - Twice exceptional. Subscriptions are available at www.2eNewsletter.com

Understanding and Challenging the Gifted: An Introduction for Teachers. Pennsylvania Association for Gifted Education and Pennsylvania State Education Association. Available at http://www.penngifted.org/page-psea-booklet.pdf

VanTassel-Baska, Joyce. "Standards of Learning and Gifted Education: Goodness of Fit." Available at www.lessonsense.com/articles/gifted-education.html

Vaughn, Sharon, Candace Bos, and Jeanne Schumm. **Teaching Mainstreamed, Diverse, and At-Risk Students in the General Education Classroom**. Boston, MA: Allyn and Bacon, 1997.

Villa, Richard and Jacqueline Thousand, Editors. **Creating an Inclusive School**. Alexandria, VA: ASCD, 1995.

Vygotsky, Lev. **L.S. Vygoysky, Collected Works**. New York: Plenum, 1987.

Weathers, Lawrence. **ADHD: A Path to Success**. Spokane WA: Ponderosa Press, 1998.

Weiner, Bernard. **Human Motivations: Metaphors, Theories, and Research, 2nd Edition**. Thousand Oaks, CA: Sage Publications, 1996.

Wheeler, Rebecca. "Becoming Adept at Code - Switching." **Educational Leadership**. April 2008, pp 54-58.

Williams, Robin. **The Non-Designer's Design Book**. Berkeley, CA: Peachpit Press, 2003.

Winebrenner, Susan: **Teaching Gifted Kids in the Regular Classroom**. Minneapolis, MN: Free Sprit Publishing, 2009.

_____ **Teaching Kids with Learning Difficulties in the Regular Classroom**. Minneapolis, MN: Free Spirit Publishing, 1996.

Wiggins, Grant. "Feedback: How Learning Occurs." A Presentation at the 1997 AAHE Conference on Assessment & Quality. Pennington, NJ: The Center on Learning, Assessment, and School Structure, 1997.

Resources and References

Wiggins, Grant and Jay McTighe. ***Understanding by Design, 2nd Edition***. Alexandria, VA: ASCD, 2005.

Wilhelm, Jeffrey. ***Improving Comprehension with Think-Alouds: Modeling What Good Readers Do***. New York: Scholastic, 2001.

Wood, Judy. ***Adapting Instruction for Mainstreamed and At-Risk Students***. Upper Saddle River, NJ: Merrill, 1992.

Wormeli, Rick. ***Fair Isn't Always Equal***. Portland, MI: Stenhouse Publishers, 2000.

Wright, Karen. "20 Classroom Modifications for Students with Autism." ***Autism/Asperger's Digest***. November/December 2001. Available at www.kdp.org/teachingresources/pdf/podcast/20_classrm_modifications_for_stude nts_with_autism.pdf

Zawilinski, Lisa. "HOT Blogging: A Framework for Blogging to Promote Higher Order Thinking." ***The Reading Teacher***. May 2009, pp 650-661.

Zike, Dinah. ***Big Book of Social Studies: Elementary K-6***. San Antonio, TX: Dinah-Might Adventures, LP., 2000.

_____ ***Big Book of United States History***. San Antonio, TX: Dinah-Might Adventures, LP., 2004.

Zimmerman, Susan and Chryse Hutchins. ***7 Keys to Comprehension: How to Help Your Kids Read It and Get It***. New York, NY: Random House, 2003.

Zimmerman, Susan and Ellin Oliver Keene. ***Mosaic of Thought: Teaching Comprehension in a Reader's Workshop***. Portsmouth, NH: Heinemann, 1997.

Index

Index

Index

Index

Index

Index

Index

Index

Index

Index

Index

Index

Index

CD-ROM Index

Templates are listed by chapter order in the CD-ROM Table of Contents

Template Name, Chapter Folder-Template Number

CD-ROM Index

CD-ROM Index

About the Author

Paula Rutherford is the author of multiple books including: ***Instruction for All Students***, ***Leading the Learning: A Field Guide for Supervision and Evaluation***, ***Meeting the Needs of Diverse Learners***, ***Why Didn't I Learn This in College?*** and ***The 21st Century Mentor's Handbook***. She writes an e-newsletter titled: ***Mentoring in the 21st Century®***.

Paula is president of Just ASK Publications & Professional Development, established in 1989 and based in Alexandria, Virginia. She works extensively with districts as they engage in long-term systemic work to align processes such as hiring, induction, professional development, school improvement plans, and supervision and evaluation. She also leads **Mentoring in the 21st Century® Institutes** across the country and has developed a comprehensive **Mentoring in the 21st Century® Resource Kit** so that districts can replicate the Just ASK institutes and provide extensive follow-up support for mentors. Paula, committed to building in-house capacity, has also developed a **New Teacher Professional Development Kit** that provides over 30 hours of support for new teachers and Certified Local Trainer (CLT) programs based on ***Instruction for All Students***, ***Leading the Learning***, and ***Why Didn't I Learn This in College?***

In addition to her extensive work as a consultant and trainer, Paula's professional experience includes work in regular education K-12 as a teacher of high school history and social sciences, physical education, Spanish, and kindergarten, as well as a special education teacher, coordinator of special education programs, administrator at the middle school and high school levels, and as a central office staff development specialist.

She can be reached at paula@justaskpublications.com.

On-Site Consulting and Workshops

Consulting services and professional development opportunities include on-site workshops and institutes on:

- Standards-Based Education
- Instruction for All Students
- Assessment
- Active Learning
- Meeting the Needs of Diverse Learners
- Mentoring and Induction
- Mentoring in the 21st Century
- New Teacher Induction
- Instructional Leadership
- Leading the Learning
- Creating a Culture for Learning
- Supervision and Evaluation
- Data-Driven Decisions
- Walk-Throughs
- Training for Results
- Results-Based Professional Development

Plus
- Coaching new principals
- Coaching new professional developers
- Building in-house capacity
- Certified Local Trainers (CLT) program

Instruction for All Students
This six-day series is an in-depth study of instruction, assessment, and learning in a standards-based environment. The goals of the workshop series are for participants to become more skillful with the standards-based planning process and to build repertoires of ways to engage students in meaningful, active learning.

Leading the Learning
This six-day workshop series for school leaders is designed to support educators in the supervision and evaluation process. It is based on the belief that instructional leaders can make a difference in teacher practice and student learning through the supervision and evaluation process by keeping a clear focus on teaching and learning. Workshop exercises are designed to provide educators with an expanded repertoire of skills for supervising and evaluating staff in ways that promote professional growth and student learning.

The 21st Century Standards-Based Classroom
ASK Group consultants can work with you and your school district to design and deliver workshops that focus on subsets of the standards work. Topics include assessment, active learning, taking it to the next level (refresher or advanced work), and working with diverse learners.

Meeting the Needs of Diverse Learners
This multiple-day workshop series is designed for teachers who teach in districts with clearly articulated student learning standards, who have mastered their content and developed an extensive repertoire of instructional strategies, and are ready to focus on the diverse needs of their learners. During this series teachers explore ways to provide multiple pathways to learning so that advanced learners are challenged and ways to scaffold instruction for struggling learners, divergent learners, and second language learners.

On-Site Consulting and Workshops

Why Didn't I Learn This in College?®

This multiple-day workshop series is designed for educators with 0-3 years of experience. Based on the construct that a strong instructional program is the best management program, this series helps new teachers create learning-centered environments, use the standards-based planning process, build a repertoire of active learning strategies, and develop organizational skills.

Creating a Culture for Learning

This workshop series, presented in one to three-day formats, revisits the constructs of school culture and collegial collaboration and focuses on how data-driven discussions based on student work and achievement data can enhance our work. A variety of job-embedded professional development formats, including Professional Learning Communities (PLCs), are explored.

Mentoring in the 21st Century®

Educators are entering our profession through different pathways and at different points in their careers. These variables create a need to rethink how novice educators, second-career educators, alternatively certified educators, and even new-to-the-district educators are inducted into our profession. Add to this the incredibly high attrition rate of novice teachers and it is no wonder that we are seeking ways to develop support systems to ensure that we have a fully qualified and fully satisfied teacher in each classroom. This multiple-day workshop series is designed to assist mentors with this important initiative.

ASK Group Consultants are available for keynote and conference presentations. Contact us for more information.

Books

Meeting the Needs of Diverse Learners
by Paula Rutherford

Meeting the Needs of Diverse Learners is designed to help teachers build skillfulness in recognizing, respecting, and responding to the needs of the wide range of students in today's classrooms. This book provides an array of strategies for use with English Language Learners, students with special needs, accelerated learners, and proposes that those strategies are, in fact, productive strategies for all students. A CD-ROM of templates is included.

$34.95   ISBN 978-0-9797280-4-4   325 pages   Order #11033 eBook available

Meeting the Needs of Diverse Learners Facilitator's Handbook
by Paula Rutherford

This 150-page facilitator's handbook is the perfect tool for principals, professional developers, and teacher leaders to use in planning a comprehensive year-long professional development program. It can also be used to plan focused data-driven discussions around specific challenging issues that teachers are facing on a daily basis. Each of the 30 to 60 minute exercises include the purpose, the time needed, the materials to use, the process to follow, and suggestions for follow-up professional practice in the classroom. All handouts are included in hard copy and on a CD-ROM.

$74.95   ISBN 978-0-9797280-9-9   150 pages   Order #11056

Instruction for All Students
by Paula Rutherford

This text provides strategies and resources for actively engaging students and multiple approaches to lesson and unit design. It also includes information on technology integration, formative assessment, 21st century thinking skills that promote rigor and relevance, and formats for job-embedded learning. A CD-ROM of templates is included.

$34.95   ISBN 978-0-9777796-8-0   298 pages   Order #11027 eBook available

Instruction for All Students Facilitator's Handbook
by Paula Rutherford

This 160-page facilitator's handbook is designed to help educators structure their reading and use of the strategies presented in the book *Instruction for All Students*. It can be used for book clubs, study groups, and in team, department, and faculty meetings. The learning experiences are interactive and action-oriented. The handbook is written with the expectation that group participants will use what they study, and come to the next session ready to share and discuss how they used what they learned. All handouts are included in hard copy and on a CD-ROM.

$59.95   ISBN 978-0-9797280-2-0   160 pages   Order # 11043

Why Didn't I Learn This in College?
by Paula Rutherford

Over 500,000 copies of this book are in the hands of new teachers and their mentors worldwide. This new edition includes updated tools and procedures for teaching and learning in the 21st century. Even veteran teachers say that they find the ideas and strategies here invaluable. It is based on the construct that the best management program is a good instructional program. If student learning is our goal, we want to shift our focus from control and compliance to creating positive learning-centered environments. A CD-ROM of templates is included.

$29.95   ISBN 978-0-9797280-1-3   330 pages   Order #11002   eBook available

Leading the Learning
A Field Guide for Supervision & Evaluation
by Paula Rutherford

This text, which is philosophically aligned with the ISSLC Standards for Educational Leaders, explores the collaborative contexts in which educational leaders work to ensure that student learning is the central focus of all stakeholders. It provides in-depth information about best practices to note, suggestions to make, and reflective questions to ask around six commonly used standards for teacher performance. Strategies for gathering and analyzing data from multiple sources are accompanied by clearly explained feedback options. A CD-ROM of templates is included.

$34.95   ISBN 978-0-9797280-7-5   300 pages   Order # 11057   eBook available

The 21st Century Mentor's Handbook
by Paula Rutherford

The 21st Century Mentor's Handbook is cross-referenced to *Why Didn't I Learn This in College?* and *Instruction for All Students*. Mentors find it an indispensable tool in planning their interactions with new teachers. This handbook provides a multitude of resources including a mentoring calendar, needs assessments, tools for goal setting and reflection, instructional design templates, guidelines for observation and coaching, and field tested ways to deal with the potential problems of novice teachers. A CD-ROM of templates is included.

$34.95   ISBN 978-0-9663336-6-4   380 pages   Order # 11003   eBook available

Strategies in Action
Volume I: A Collection of Classroom Applications
Volume II: Applications in Today's Diverse Classrooms

These two collections of strategies in action provide glimpses into the classrooms of PreK-12 teachers across the spectrum of content areas as they implement the strategies found in *Meeting the Needs of Diverse Learners*, *Instruction for All Students*, and *Why Didn't I Learn This in College?* Volume I emphasizes how teachers used instructional, assessment, and organizational systems. Volume II focuses on the ways teachers have scaffolded instruction for students with special needs, engaged resistant and reluctant learners, sheltered instruction for English Language Learners, and extended the learning of accelerated learners.

$19.95   ISBN 978-0-9797280-3-7   134 pages   Order #11049
$19.95   ISBN 978-0-9797280-8-2   152 pages   Order #11054

Meeting the Needs of Diverse Learners PLC Pack

If your collaborative team members have identified the need to expand and refine their repertoires of strategies for working with diverse learners as a priority or you, as a teacher leader or administrator, need to orchestrate focus discussions on this topic, then the **Meeting the Needs of Diverse Learners PLC Pack** is just what you need.

The Meeting the Needs of Diverse Learners PLC Pack includes:
- A copy of *Meeting the Needs of Diverse Learners* for each staff member (The **Meeting the Needs of Diverse Learners PLC Pack** includes 25 copies of *Meeting the Needs of Diverse Learners.*)
- A copy of the *Facilitator's Handbook for Meeting the Needs of Diverse Learners*
- A copy of *Strategies in Action: Applications in Today's Diverse Classrooms Volume II*
- Over 40 full-color **Visual Tools** on a CD-ROM with JPEG and PDF files that can be used in PowerPoint and Keynote presentations and to make overhead transparencies and posters
- Six sets of **Meeting the Needs of Diverse Learners Cards**

Purchase the standard **Meeting the Needs of Diverse Learners PLC Pack** for $799 and save at least 20% off the list price when items are purchased separately.

Order #11052
List Price $799.00

Ordering Information

Books

	Order #	Price
Creating a Culture for Learning	11055	$ 34.95
Instruction for All Students	11027	$ 34.95
Instruction for All Students Facilitator's Handbook	11043	$ 59.95
Leading the Learning Second Edition	11057	$ 34.95
Meeting the Needs of Diverse Learners	11033	$ 34.95
Meeting the Needs of Diverse Learners Facilitator's Handbook	11056	$ 74.95
Results-Based Professional Development Models	11058	$ 24.95
Standards-Based Classroom Operator's Manual	11012	$ 24.95
Strategies in Action: A Collection of Classroom Applications - Volume I	11049	$ 19.95
Strategies in Action: Applications in Today's Diverse Classrooms - Volume II	11054	$ 19.95
The 21st Century Mentor's Handbook	11003	$ 34.95
Why Didn't I Learn This in College? Second Edition	11002	$ 29.95
Why Didn't I Learn This in College? and *The 21st Century Mentor's Handbook* Save 20%	11029	$ 50.00

DVDs

	Order #	Price
Collegial Conversations	11031	$ 195.00
Helping New Teachers Succeed	11021	$ 60.00
Lesson Collection: Biology Visual Learning Tools (ASCD)	11026	$ 95.00
Lesson Collection: HS Geometry Surface Area and Volume (ASCD)	11034	$ 95.00
Lesson Collection: HS Reciprocal Teaching (ASCD)	11035	$ 95.00
Lesson Collection: Primary Math (ASCD)	11025	$ 95.00
Points to Ponder	11016	$ 29.95
Principles in Action	11019	$ 19.95
Success Factors in a Standards-Based Classroom	11017	$ 75.00
Teaching and Learning in the 21st Century: 2nd Grade Writer's Workshop	11053	$ 95.00
Teaching and Learning in the 21st Century: 3rd Grade Science	11047	$ 95.00
Teaching and Learning in the 21st Century: 4th/5th Grade Writer's Workshop	11048	$ 95.00

Other Products

	Order #	Price
Mentoring in the 21st Century® Resource Kit	11028	$ 985.00
New Teacher Professional Development Kit	11046	$ 795.00
Instruction for All Students PLC Pack	11051	$ 799.00
Meeting the Needs of Diverse Learners PLC Pack	11052	$ 799.00
Poster Pack	11006	$ 16.95
Visual Tools: The Complete Collection CD-ROM	11041	$ 375.00
Visual Tools: Meeting the Needs of Diverse Learners™ CD-ROM	11040	$ 100.00
Visual Tools: Instruction for All Students™ CD-ROM	11036	$ 100.00
Visual Tools: Leading the Learning™ CD-ROM	11039	$ 100.00
Visual Tools: The 21st Century Mentor's Handbook™ CD-ROM	11038	$ 100.00
Visual Tools: Why Didn't I Learn This in College?® CD-ROM	11037	$ 100.00
What Do You Do When... Cards: Mentoring and Supervision Scenarios	11032	$ 49.95
What Do You Do When... Cards: New Teacher Challenges and Concerns	11050	$ 49.95
Scavenger Hunt Cards: *Instruction for All Students*™	11044	$ 10.00
Scavenger Hunt Cards: *Why Didn't I Learn This in College?*®	11045	$ 10.00

To Order

Call
800-940-5434

Online
www.justaskpublications.com

Prices subject to
change without notice

Fax
703-535-8502

Mail
2214 King Street, Alexandria, VA 22301

Order Form

Just ASK Publications & Professional Development

<table>
<tr><td colspan="2">Ship To</td><td colspan="2">Bill To (If different)</td></tr>
<tr><td colspan="2">Name _____</td><td colspan="2">Name _____</td></tr>
<tr><td colspan="2">Title _____</td><td colspan="2">Title _____</td></tr>
<tr><td colspan="2">School/District _____</td><td colspan="2">School/District _____</td></tr>
<tr><td colspan="2">Address _____</td><td colspan="2">Address _____</td></tr>
<tr><td colspan="2">City_____ State____ ZIP____</td><td colspan="2">City_____ State____ ZIP____</td></tr>
<tr><td colspan="2">Email _____</td><td colspan="2">Email _____</td></tr>
<tr><td colspan="2">Telephone _____</td><td colspan="2">Telephone _____</td></tr>
<tr><td colspan="2">Fax _____</td><td colspan="2">Fax _____</td></tr>
</table>

Order #	Title	Quantity	Unit Price	Total Price

Please attach a sheet of paper for additional products ordered

Subtotal	
Shipping and Handling	
TOTAL	

Contact us for quantity discounts and special offers
Call 800-940-5434

Shipping and Handling
$6 S&H minimum per order
15% on orders under 10 units, 10% on orders 10 units or more
$49 S&H for each resource kit

Payment Method (Select One)

☐ Check (Please make checks or purchase orders payable to Just ASK Publications)

☐ Purchase Order   Purchase Order Number_____

☐ Credit Card   ☐Visa   ☐MasterCard   ☐AMEX

Name as it appears on the card _____

Credit Card # _____

Expiration Date ☐☐ / ☐☐
              Month   Year

Mail or Fax to:
Just ASK Publications
2214 King Street
Alexandria, VA 22301
Fax: 703-535-8502

☐ Check here to receive information about Just ASK workshops, institutes, and train-the-trainer opportunities.

Meeting the Needs of Diverse Learners